Winner of the 2015 Queensland Premier's Award for a Work of State Significance

'From day one of the white invasion of our sacred homelands, soldiers and patriots of the Aboriginal nations fought an heroic war of resistance. To this day too many of the stories of these magnificent warriors have gone untold. This book is one further step in reclaiming those stories and honouring the courage and sacrifice of those magnificent men and women who fell to the guns and poisons of the invader. I salute Libby Connors and I thank her for her work. This book shall now live on as an enduring record of one of our greatest heroes.' – **Sam Watson, activist and writer**

'This is history told with flair, and the general reader will find a lot to like . . .' – **Rohan Wilson,** *The Weekend Australian*

'. . . a *tour de force*. We now have much better understanding of the first thirty years of the European occupation of the Brisbane region . . . Connors sums up Brisbane's frontier as one of the longest in Australia's history.' – **Associate Professor Ross Johnston,** *Australian Journal of Politics and History*

'. . . a largely forgotten story of a man who could be considered a war hero—just one who fought against the colonists.' – *The Daily Telegraph*

'Libby Connors . . . has worked hard to untangle fact from myth about Dundalli. He was a legendary leader and his dramatic life and brutal execution in Brisbane tells us much about the colonial frontier.' – *The Sydney Morning Herald*

'The latter years of south-east Queensland's convict era are brought to life by Libby Connors in astounding detail through the biography of Dundalli.' – *The Queensland Times*

'We have a convincing picture of a man, remarkable in both appearance and intellect, a natural born leader who deserves to be better remembered.' – **Dr Brian Stevenson,** *Queensland History Journal*

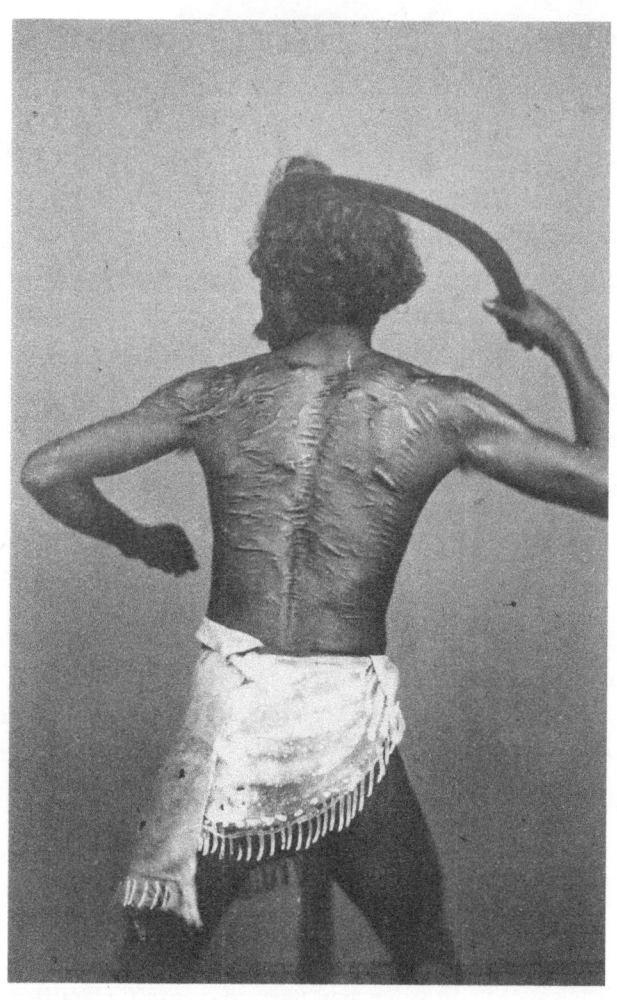

Above

Daniel Marquis, *Studio portrait of an Aboriginal man from the back holding boomerang*, ca 1865, Albumen silver carte-de-visite photograph. National Gallery of Australia, Canberra, Purchased 2005

Front cover, bottom image

Conrad Martens, *Brisbane*, 1855, Watercolour, 29.8 × 42.9 cm. Purchased 1999. The Queensland Government's special Centenary Fund. Collection: Queensland Art Gallery

WARRIOR

A LEGENDARY LEADER'S DRAMATIC LIFE AND VIOLENT DEATH ON THE COLONIAL FRONTIER

LIBBY CONNORS

ALLEN & UNWIN
SYDNEY · MELBOURNE · AUCKLAND · LONDON

First published in 2015

Copyright © Libby Connors 2015

All rights reserved. No part of this book may be reproduced or transmitted in any form or by any means, electronic or mechanical, including photocopying, recording or by any information storage and retrieval system, without prior permission in writing from the publisher. The Australian *Copyright Act 1968* (the Act) allows a maximum of one chapter or 10 per cent of this book, whichever is the greater, to be photocopied by any educational institution for its educational purposes provided that the educational institution (or body that administers it) has given a remuneration notice to the Copyright Agency (Australia) under the Act.

Australian Government

This project has been assisted by the Australian Government through the Australia Council for the Arts, its arts funding and advisory body.

Allen & Unwin
83 Alexander Street
Crows Nest NSW 2065
Australia
Phone: (61 2) 8425 0100
Email: info@allenandunwin.com
Web: www.allenandunwin.com

Cataloguing-in-Publication details are available
from the National Library of Australia
www.trove.nla.gov.au

ISBN 978 1 76011 048 2

Map by Darian Causby
Index by Libby Connors
Set in 12/17 pt Minion by Midland Typesetters, Australia
Printed and bound in Australia by Griffin Press

20 19 18 17 16 15 14 13 12 11 10

The paper in this book is FSC® certified. FSC® promotes environmentally responsible, socially beneficial and economically viable management of the world's forests.

Contents

Preface vi
Prologue: The public hanging x
1 Growing up in the Blackall Range 1
2 The young negotiator: Trade and diplomacy to
  March 1842 27
3 The Great Toors of 1842–43: The Bora men change
  strategy 57
4 The attack on Gregor's station 89
5 White politics and black politics 108
6 Attempts at conciliation 150
7 The feud continues: Capture, trial, aftermath 182
Epilogue: Remembering Dundalli 212
Acknowledgements 215
Bibliography 217
Notes 228
Index 261

Preface

The much loved colonial artist Conrad Martens spent several months in Brisbane and the Darling Downs in 1851–52. Like his patrons he came north to make money, in his case by painting their homes and stations as a record of their accomplishments over the previous decade. He lovingly captured the light, the open spaces and the dense foliage of the subtropics. In the painting on the cover of this book—looking across Kangaroo Point from New Farm to Petrie Bight and the small township of Brisbane—Martens conveys a sense of peace and prosperity, although his skyline hints at the potential drama of the hot and humid climate.

Martens painted this landscape in 1855, a year of considerable drama in what were then the northern districts of New South Wales. Dundalli, one of the great warriors of the Dalla people who owned parts of these northern lands, had been executed by order of the sheriff of New South Wales in January of that year and the local newspaper nervously reported the movements of his followers.

The young man whose photograph overlays Martens' landscape could have been one of the fighting men of 1855. His tribal scars indicate that he is a Dalla man. The Dalla's lands included the mountainous country of the D'Aguilar Range north to what is today the Sunshine Coast hinterland. Other scars are possibly a result of combat, an interpretation enhanced by his aggressive pose. His hair has been cut, however, rather than fashioned into the dreadlocks that Indigenous men in southern Queensland typically wore. For ceremonies and fights they styled these tresses into a knot which was secured on the head by feathers and beeswax. He also has body hair whereas in Dundalli's time the fighting men removed all their body hair by singeing or with beeswax; they then accentuated their impressive tribal markings with body oils so that both their muscles and their group identity were accentuated. This man was photographed by Daniel Marquis in a studio in about 1867, yet there seems little doubt that Marquis wished to record the martial skill of the men who dispensed Aboriginal law to European and Aboriginal offenders alike. Dundalli and his allies became part of Brisbane legend, with old-timers still recalling the great warrior's fearsome deeds almost seventy years after his death.[1]

Only one artist tried to capture Dundalli's image in his day. In November 1854 Silvester Diggles, an amateur scientist, musician and artist on his way by steamer to Brisbane to make his fortune, met Sydney legal officials who were also travelling north for sittings of the supreme court on circuit. Through them Diggles learnt of Dundalli's reputation and decided to attend his trial. He was no sympathiser; his unflattering pen and ink portrait of Dundalli in European prison garb does no justice to the great warrior.[2] Diggles probably made some money by selling a copy to the *Illustrated Sydney News*, which published a crude engraving alongside an equally hostile report of his trial.[3]

Biased sources, both visual and written, make the telling of Dundalli's story difficult—but not impossible. Notable colonial figures such as Archibald Meston and Thomas Welsby admired Dundalli and wrote about him, but neither man actually knew him;

Meston's family arrived in Australia in only 1859, and Welsby was born in 1858. They drew on Aboriginal informants, some of whom had been Dundalli's political opponents, thus contributing further to his bloodthirsty legend. Only Tom Petrie, who spent his youth with Aboriginal friends, learning their language and being invited to their meetings and ceremonies, provides any counterbalance.

Dundalli was born into a world governed by customary law and traditional authority. This is what Aboriginal people mean when they refer to sovereignty—the everyday informal and formal rules that governed traditional society and enabled a system of law and order to govern the smallest family group or large regional associations of several thousand people. Court records, newspaper reports and some settler memoirs contain frequent references to Aboriginal assemblies and to the preponderance of their constructed meeting places of cleared and flattened grounds, with earthen walls at least 30 centimetres high or surrounded by wooden fences. Sometimes they also planted avenues of trees or erected rows of wooden carvings along the pathways leading to these meeting grounds.

During the 1840s and '50s, when Dundalli was an adult, internal Aboriginal politics grew increasingly rancorous as the tribal peoples disagreed over how to respond to European violations of their lands and laws. During this period a fascinating and tragic political dynamic developed among the traditional owner groups of Moreton Bay, consuming their interests as much as elected legislative councils and manhood suffrage preoccupied the European community. Yet individual and class rivalries between European men have been celebrated as the stuff of founding democracies, while the tensions and disagreements among the traditional owners have been portrayed as betrayal and innate treachery.

The European community struggled to maintain law and order in this period, initially enforcing it with the use of floggings, the military and gruesome public hangings in the main street of Brisbane.

Similarly, the Indigenous community sought to maintain order and uphold its laws through its ancient system of hand-to-hand contests, with death reserved for only the most serious infringements. The former was regarded as the expression of civilisation, the latter as savagery and barbarity.

This book is an attempt to go beyond this one-dimensional view, to tell a little of this story through the life of one man. Two political and legal systems operated in the Brisbane region in the 1840s and '50s but on both sides the same human story was unfolding—of ill-fated courtships, political alliances, spiritual idealism and concern to protect the security of the next generation. Dundalli's successful ejection of Europeans from Aboriginal lands and his commitment to exacting Aboriginal justice, as well as his unswerving loyalty to both his people and his culture, made him a hero to the Indigenous tribes and a feared enemy of European settlers.

Author's note

Traditional owners and their families and supporters do not always agree on language and land boundaries, and sometimes dispute claims of descent from many of the people who feature in this history. This work does not claim authority on any specific native title claim or language boundary, as the contours of Dundalli's life are its central purpose.

Prologue

THE PUBLIC HANGING

A short man whose blond hair was streaked with grey was adjusting ropes on the timber platform he had constructed before the 3-metre tall wooden doorway to Brisbane Gaol. It was hard to tell whether his blue eyes were bleary from alcohol or mental deterioration, which had already set in despite being only fifty-two years of age. The scar left across his face from an axe-wielding convict twenty-five years earlier—he had just hanged the convict's mate—added to the sense of depravity that surrounded Alexander Green, the hangman for the colony of New South Wales.[1]

It was not yet nine o'clock on the morning of Friday, 5 January 1855, but this dismal figure was already drawing a crowd. The town constables arrived first, anxious that the condemned man who had eluded them for more than eleven years might even at this late hour effect an escape or be rescued by his countrymen. Such was the anxiety of the Brisbane officials that the police magistrate had asked that a detachment of mounted Native Police, in town for an inquiry, also turn out on duty under their white officer. Police Magistrate Wickham himself was absent—he was boarding the steamer to Sydney, but had left strict instructions with his servant to take the dog cart straight home to Newstead as Aborigines were likely to attack the town.²

The residents of the Brisbane township were making their way past the gardens and scrub which ran the 250 or so metres from where their businesses and dwellings stopped to the northern end of Queen Street and the gates of the gaol. Queen Street was a dirt road and the old gaol was on a slight rise in the middle of bush. Today it is the location of Brisbane's GPO. The white men, women and children gathered in their hundreds. Last August they had come to view the public hanging of Davy, a Wakka Wakka man, but not in these numbers.³ Davy had been accused of killing white men up near the Burnett but this man, Dundalli, had assaulted and killed Europeans in and near Brisbane for more than a decade. His name was enough to fill them with dread, and tales of his daring and ferocity had circulated about the town for years.

Aboriginal people were gathering too. Dundalli was not just a great warrior renowned for his size and strength—Judge Therry, who had presided at his trial, described him in his memoirs as the biggest man he had ever laid eyes upon—he was also a key figure in south-east Queensland Aboriginal politics. He was a lawman for people who lived to the north of the town and whose control of Bunya gatherings gave them power and influence across the region. These regional Aboriginal summits contributed to competition and rivalry with the Quandamooka people and their allies to the south. Even more than this, he represented one side in the Aboriginal debate about how to respond to the invasion of their lands by white men.

So Dundalli's friends and enemies gathered too, but they sheltered in the bush opposite the gaol, beyond the reach of the Native Police rifles, on elevated ground that overlooked the gallows. Today it is the site of Brisbane's Central railway station, which opens onto Ann Street and is linked to the GPO by the open space of Post Office and Anzac squares. Ironically this event, which was so central to frontier conflict around the state's capital, is not remembered as part of the war memorial in Anzac Square or in any public space.

The settlers also knew that Dundalli represented an Aboriginal view of how to respond to Europeans; it was why they feared him so much and why this hanging gripped the town with tension.

To understand how Dundalli came to be in this situation we have to start at the beginning: with the love and security that bound him to his people; at his elders' instructions to him to build relations with the white people in 1841 and how those hopes were dashed by killings of the innocent in early 1842; at the internal debates about how to deal with colonisers and his precise and moderate responses according to Aboriginal law. The settlers thought that they were executing a murderer. The evidence points the other way: they were executing an Aboriginal lawman, and his death would simply take the south-east Queensland frontier into a new phase when young men without Dundalli's finesse would hold up the settlement of Brisbane's northern suburbs and outskirts for many years.

1

GROWING UP IN THE BLACKALL RANGE

The mountain air of Dundalli's country is crisp and refreshing, especially on summer days when down on the coast the air is humid and thick with haze. The Blackall Range lies roughly parallel to what is now called the Sunshine Coast, ending in a valley of the Stanley River, an upper tributary of the Brisbane. On the other side of the valley it continues south as the D'Aguilar Range, which reaches all the way into the western suburbs of Brisbane. The eastern escarpment looks out over the coastal plain. In the south are Moreton Bay and its many islands, from Stradbroke to Moreton; before them the isolated volcanic peaks of the Glass House Mountains rise spectacularly from the green plain. The backdrop to all this beauty is the blue of the Pacific Ocean, the vista from the northern escarpment reaching all the way to the Cooloola Coast north of Noosa.

In 1820, before whites had ventured this far north, this coastal hinterland was at the centre of a rich regional economy. The range itself is lush and fertile; waterfalls plunge over deeply cut gorges; and several clear mountain springs become tributaries of the Mary River, which flows due north before turning east to empty into Wide Bay behind Fraser Island. The streams draining the southern part of the range seep into wetlands and lagoons that form the Brisbane River's most north-easterly catchments, which then flow south-west.

These uplands of the Glass House Mountains and the D'Aguilar, Conondale and Jimna ranges were the homelands of a group of tribal families. They spoke the Dalla language, which could be understood by peoples as far apart as the South Burnett and the Logan, and the southern Moreton Bay islands. It was closely related to the Gubbi Gubbi language, which is the broader identity that many descendants prefer to use today.

Dundalli's lands were rich in food sources throughout the year: bush game of kangaroos, possums, bandicoots and echidnas, as well as carpet snakes and goannas, scrub turkeys and rainforest birds, whose eggs were also good for eating. The rivers and streams supplied delicacies of freshwater turtles, cod, eels, mussels and crayfish. Women made cakes from native seeds and nuts, and daily bread from pounded and roasted fern roots: they roasted, crushed and soaked river chestnuts, which they mixed with honey to make a sweet cake; they soaked cunjevoi seeds for three weeks to release toxins and then crushed and baked them into cakes to accompany the roasted game meats; and they gathered the roots of a particular waterlily, which taste like artichoke, as well as pencil orchid roots and wild yams, among other vegetables. The forests produced a variety of fruits such as wild passionfruit, oranges and limes, and quandong berries, which the Dalla buried in sand for four days until they turned sweet. People liked to coat the tops of young cabbage tree palms in honey as a sweet treat.[1]

Honey was a frequent indulgence. As well as being eaten on the spot as soon as it was found, it was also used to make teas and cordials. It was soaked up by the sponge-like gympie bark and mixed with water to make an important refreshment kept to hand by the head man should his address to the camp go too long into the night.[2] Another cordial was made from the honeysuckle flower.

Fig. 1.1: Aboriginal country and pastoral stations in south-east Queensland in the 1840s

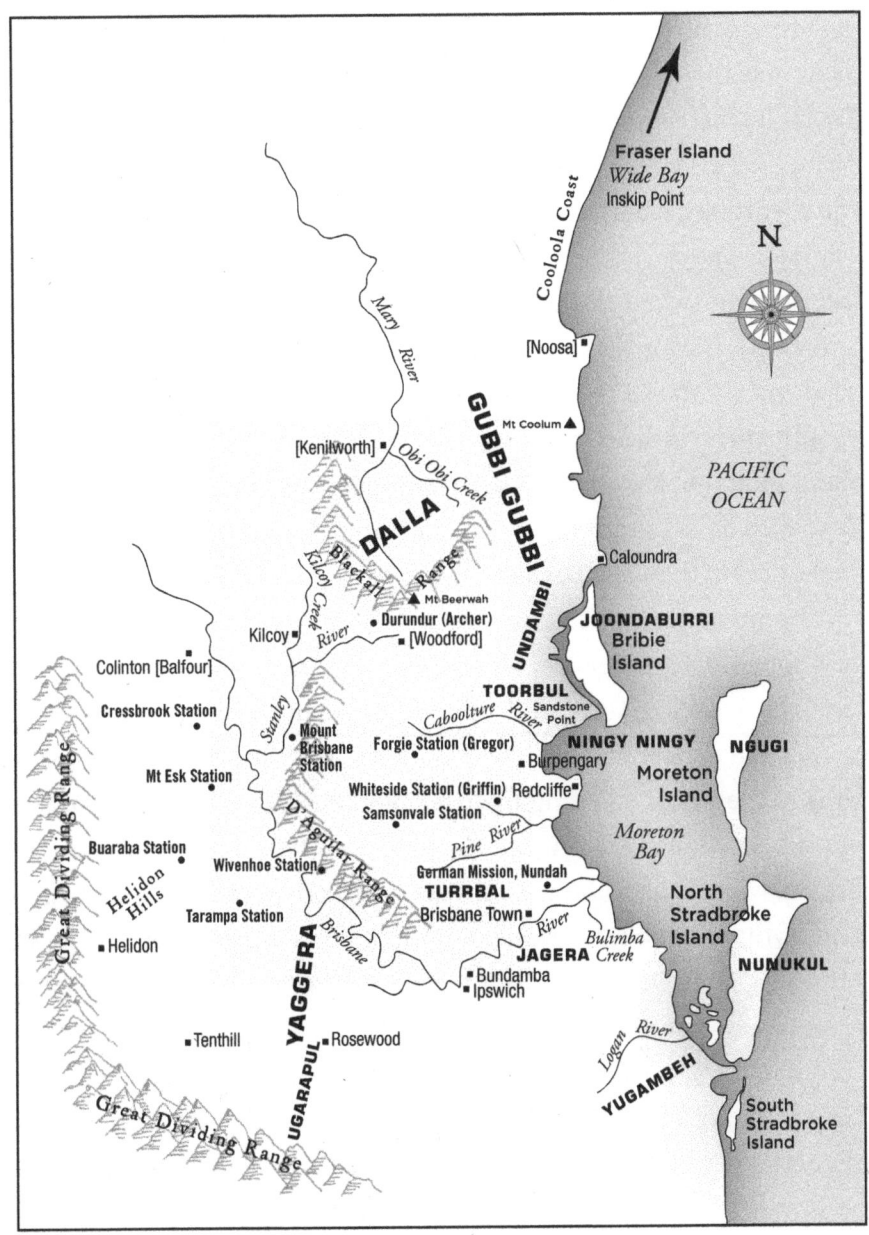

The most prized delicacy of the region, however, was the bunya nut. The harvest of these nuts was the basis of important trade and social gatherings. In the 1820s the trees grew all over the Blackall Range, as well as the uplands that branch off to the north-west to form the South Burnett and the region now known as the Bunya Mountains National Park: the traditional lands of the Wakka Wakka. Here in the east though, the trees were the property of the Dalla. Each year Dundalli and his family would wait till the sugar gums and white gums began to lose their bark so that their trunks gleamed clean and white; this meant that the bunya nuts were ripening—it was time to send invitations to friends and relatives from neighbouring regions to join them in feasting. They met at Baroon Pocket, a clearing in the mountains that a German missionary, Reverend Karl Schmidt, described as a 'paradise'.[3] It now lies partially dead, drowned under the waters of the Lake Baroon Dam.

The invitation to feast was usually returned annually by coastal neighbours—for instance, when Blue Mountain lorikeets appeared near the Brisbane River, indicating to Brisbane people that migrating mullet had arrived in their river and bay. Now the Dalla could spend time at the beach enjoying their hospitality. There, Dundalli's father and uncles would catch more fish than one tribe could eat—mullet, bream, whiting and flounder. Everyone gathered shellfish and oysters and, if they were lucky, a dugong might come in close enough to be hunted. When Dundalli was a teenager Moreton Bay was so rich in oyster beds that the commandant of the penal station, Foster Fyans, recorded how on North Stradbroke Island near Amity Point 'the banks ... are covered with good oysters, taken in tons, brought to the Settlement, and burned for lime, eighteen to twenty tons at a time'.[4]

The region was so economically rich that it hosted two separate Bunya feasts—one in Wakka Wakka and the other in Dalla country—and these, in combination with the coastal mullet migration, meant that Dundalli's people were part of a far-ranging economic, social and cultural network. The abundance of food made trade possible across a wide region encompassing southern Queensland, from the coast west to Goondiwindi and from Rockhampton to the New England Tableland and further south-west in New South Wales.

The Dalla's neighbours to the west were the Wakka Wakka; along the Mary River were Gubbi Gubbi people, whose lands met those of the Badtjala of Fraser Island; to their east were the 'Mwoirnewar' or 'Saltwater people'—a colloquialism the Dalla used to refer to the Undambi, including their communities of Ningy Ningy on Brisbane's bayside and Joondaburri at Bribie Island. Lying between the Dalla and the Saltwater were the lands of the Pine River people; following the Brisbane River downstream, their neighbours were members of the Yaggera language group, whose lands are broadly identified as the right bank of the Brisbane River, from the Brisbane River Valley to the present South Bank and almost to Moreton Bay. The Aboriginal name for what is now the Brisbane CBD is Mianjin; in Dundalli's childhood the Mianjin elder was well-known to the penal station officials who called him the 'Duke of York', believed to be a corruption of Daki Yakka. The south-east mainland of Moreton Bay was Quandamooka land. This group included the Ngugi, traditional owners of Moreton Island, and the Nunukul and Goenpul of Stradbroke Island and the islands in the southern parts of the bay.[5]

When Dundalli was ready to enter the world, sometime around 1820, his mother erected a hut for herself and four older women, about 400 metres from his father's camp. She moved into the hut about a week before his expected delivery. During the past months she had sewn a new possum-skin rug to carry him in and it now kept her warm through those final few nights. His father and siblings shared a fur rug big enough for four adults back at his hut. When the baby arrived, one of the older women assisting at the birth cut his cord with a sharp mussel-shell knife. They wiped him clean with possum fur and softened gympie bark and placed him in a cradle of softened ground before his mother's hearth, insulated with a cushioning of cut grass and covered by a blanket of kangaroo skin.

His mother remained at this birthing hut for a week after delivery, before moving into a new hut 100 metres nearer the main camp. Here she and the baby stayed another seven days. His father sent her food but otherwise had no contact with her.

After seven days she and the baby moved again into a third hut a further 100 metres nearer the camp, where they were rubbed all over with ashes from an ironbark tree. Now his father could see his mother and their new baby. Dundalli would again be rubbed with black ironbark ashes every second day until they were both finally allowed to join the camp at the end of that week. Until her haemorrhaging stopped his mother wore a girdle of possum skin coated with an absorbent powder made from gympie bark. She breastfed Dundalli until he was about four years old, when the arrival of his brother supplanted him at her breast and forced him to look to the wider group for affection and attention.[6] As a toddler he learnt to drink from a 'gunduar', a small water carrier fashioned from bark or the small knobs that form on gum trees. He was taught that he must not drink from his father's cup or that of his paternal uncles or tribal sisters.[7]

His mother's father and her brothers were his 'natja'—his mentors and sponsors, who would prepare him for entry into the full adult life of the community. Until then the whole camp nurtured him, his siblings, cousins and 'tribal' brothers and sisters—for those who shared his 'moiety' or 'skin group' were also regarded as kin and called brother or sister. Among the peoples of south-east Queensland there were two moieties that were further divided into four sections, and the bond of sharing 'skin', not just blood relationship, shaped an individual's identity and loyalties. Children inherited their mother's moiety which, under Aboriginal law, was of the opposed class to their father's. Both friendly tournaments and legal disputes decided by combat were fought by groups who were related by 'skin'. At big inter-tribal meetings where strangers gathered, often knowledge about a person's skin was powerful information that only the elders knew.

Dundalli's mother named him within a week of his birth. This name related to his totem, inherited from his mother along with her moiety. His moiety determined whom he could marry and his totem gave him responsibilities towards the care and sustenance of that animal, including a ban on hunting or eating that species.[8] Totems among the Dalla included honey bees, mammals, birds and reptiles. There were three totems associated in three groups, and each group included a bird. This totem system was just as complicated as the moiety system, and it was not only linked to moiety but also crossed it. For example, a honey bee Dalla man could not marry a woman who had a related totem such as possum or emu.

This first name given by Dundalli's mother was a pet name that would last only for his childhood. He was given a new name once he was made a 'kipper'—an adolescent undergoing initiation—and a final name when he had passed all tests and was recognised as a grown man and fully initiated member of his community. This naming system applied across the region and included the Gubbi Gubbi, the Dalla's close neighbours to the north. Since Dundalli does not appear in written records until he was a young man, we only know his final name as a fully initiated man. 'Dundalli' is the wonga pigeon, a ground bird that inhabits rainforests and wet eucalypt forests with thick undergrowth in much of eastern Australia—consistent with his birthplace. The name of his brother, Oumulli, means 'breast', possibly referring to the striking white V on the breast of the wonga pigeon.[9]

During Dundalli's childhood, while the adults were out each day on the hunt, his grandparents and any older siblings too young to join in food collection watched over him. They told him fairytales, or 'ninangura', stories about feats beyond the power of ordinary men and women, until he was old enough to be taught about Ben:ewa, the all-powerful spirit. It was Ben:ewa whom hunters quietly invoked each morning before heading off.

Fear of angering Ben:ewa, who provided them with the catch and aided them in times of trouble, formed the basis of order within the camp.[10] It is unlikely that Dundalli's father ever physically chastised him but his mother might have used the flat of her hand to control him. If she ever felt he was beyond her control, she called upon Dundalli's natja to assist her. The very worst childhood punishment was the threat of 'smoking' by the tribal council, which all children feared and sought to avoid. The Dalla believed that difficult children were provoked by an evil spirit, and only the elders standing the child in the smoke of a fire could drive the bad spirit away.[11] Parents called upon the 'imarbara' to sing unsettled babies to sleep. Among the Dalla this was a special role for which only the most gentle of young men and women were selected. Dundalli grew up knowing great affection and very little physical punishment. An early European observer noted, 'they are remarkably fond of their children ... the idea of whipping a child ... appears monstrous to the natives, as does ... the practice of Europeans'.[12]

It's important to note the warmth and happiness of the Dalla childhood for it was obviously an important grounding for the challenges of the warrior culture that awaited Dundalli in adulthood. The missionaries recorded cases of men shedding tears over wives and children—the reverse side of the toughness and aggression expected of men in their public roles.[13]

When Charles Archer, whose brother David took up the first pastoral lease on Dalla country, decided to write to his much younger brother and nephew back home in Norway in 1844, it was the children of the Dalla whom he chose as his subject:

> We have several little black boys staying with us and you would be astonished to see a child not more than four years old climbing up a high tree which I am sure I couldn't ascend looking for

honey; they can also even at this age throw small spears with much certainty ... they throw sticks at each other with great force but they jump about so quickly and are so active that they seldom hit each other.[14]

Like children everywhere they played at being grown ups, and that meant imitating adult practices of hunting and fighting in organised battles. At the age of ten, both boys and girls moved away from their parents' hearth into shared boys-only and girls-only accommodation.[15] At this age children were expected to help contribute to food gathering, but also had plenty of time to play team games and sports. One game involved getting a 'buroinjin', a kangaroo-skin ball stuffed with grass, to a pole without being touched by the other team. They also had fun with a game called 'Turtles', played in a lagoon between opposing sides who tried to catch the elusive 'turtle', whose aim was not to be caught; in the Brisbane River and its creeks children played 'Marutchi' or 'Black Swan', which had the same aim but they searched for the 'swan' from a canoe. Boys competed in throwing and bouncing small war clubs, known as waddies, boomerangs and semi-discs fashioned from the fig-leaf box tree. In their pretend fights they used shorter spears with blunted ends to avoid injuries.[16] At the end of the day the head man, or 'komaron', called the children home using his small bull-roarer, the 'gungarbi'.[17]

Play was preparation for real life competition at beach and Bunya gatherings. Women generally, although not necessarily, went to live with their husband's people, so Dundalli had family living all over south-east Queensland. Everybody looked forward to these gatherings to catch up with childhood friends. Perhaps as Dundalli's mother eagerly prepared for one of these visits she covered his hair and body in carpet snake fat to repel water if rain was approaching or, if they were on their way to the mangrove fringes of Moreton Bay, sweet-smelling beeswax as a protection against insect bites.

On these trips Dundalli met his wider family, skin brothers and sisters from other communities, other boys with whom he might one day go through the 'Bora'—a prolonged series of ceremonies, tests and trials lasting about four months. The experience of sharing these rigours of initiation bonded young people, adding another layer of 'tribal' brotherhood. Like other young people, Dundalli made friendships and developed personal loyalties that extended beyond family, 'skin', totem and tribe. He also met complete strangers, and was taught the etiquette that governed such encounters. He learnt of the tensions and personality conflicts that bigger groups engendered. One of the major lessons was the importance of settling a quarrel or disagreement as soon as possible so that it did not fester and become a longstanding grudge that could embroil innocent parties.[18]

His people were very generous and hospitable. When some German missionaries undertook an expedition into the mountains they noted the importance for the Dalla of sharing a meal before any major business or conversations were carried out.[19] The value of sharing was impressed upon the missionaries wherever they travelled in south-east Queensland. Gift giving and sharing valued possessions was essential to cement relationships. 'The worst character they are able to give of a man,' Reverend Christopher Eipper noted, 'is that he does bail give it' meaning 'he will not share'.[20]

Many a summer night the children fell asleep listening to the admonishments of the komaron addressing the camp assembly or village. At a big gathering Dundalli learnt that his local komaron was only one of many 'big men' who formed a 'tribal' council, who in turn deferred to the men of the Bora council, who appointed them. The Bora council comprised between ten and twelve men, and its task was the promotion and enforcement of ancient law; they held the power of life and death over those who infringed the laws of the ancestors.[21] When he was a small boy their political intrigues escaped him, but here he learnt the lessons of personal authority and tribal governance that would later infuse his dedication to the strict observance of ancestral law.

For a small boy nothing was as thrilling as seeing young Dalla men, including his own father, 'brothers' and uncles, vie for glory in physical competition with their neighbours. If the adults headed towards the Jimna Range then there was the anticipation that perhaps they were going to Manumbar for the annual competitive wrestling; here, and at another site at Tingalpa near Brisbane, the strongest young men from each of the participating groups faced each other in teams of six to tussle for the prize of a highly decorated spear. When the Dalla won they would proudly secure this trophy at Mount Archer until they met again for another bout the following year, when it would be claimed by the next victors.[22] Wherever people met, there were likely to be team sports in which men competed to see who could return boomerangs most accurately, throw a spear the farthest, bounce a waddy or ngoi ngoi stick—a version of a waddy made for this game—with the most force and land a buroinjin nearest the goal post. Dundalli and his generation learnt anew the exhilaration of victory, the camaraderie of group struggle and the joy of physical prowess.

Hero-worship was not confined to the great sportsmen; there was also special admiration for songmakers and dancers, and evenings were crowned by the performance of a new dance by a visiting group. Everyone spruced up to impress friends and rivals on these social occasions. Both men and women removed body hair, either by singeing or waxing with beeswax. Group identity was easily established by the body scars on shoulders, chests and backs, which were beautifully highlighted after rubbing with echidna or snake oil. The explorer Ludwig Leichhardt, who stayed several months in Dalla country, wrote appreciatively of their appearance:

> They are a fine race of men, tall and well made, and their bodies, individually, as well as the groups which they formed, would

have delighted the eye of an artist. Is it fancy? But I am far more pleased in seeing the naked body of the black-fellow than that of the white man ... When I was in Paris, I was often in the public baths in the Seine, and how few well made men did I see! There is little fat in the black-fellow, but his muscles are equally developed and their play appears on every part of the body, particularly on the back, when you are walking behind him and he is carrying something on his head.[23]

Women adorned themselves with necklaces and flowers, men with shells and plaited headbands, and both styled their hair with bird feathers, attached using beeswax. Then, at the meeting place as the sun began to set, the songmakers would begin styling their people with body paint, strikingly applied in thick bold colours of red, yellow and white to identify group membership. The entertainment began—men's and women's corroborees alternately, or performances by the different visitors, but among the Dalla the evening usually ended with the Married Men's dance, the 'Nupar nuri', 'in which the men alternated with the women in the line, and young fellows with their sweethearts were also allowed to join'.[24]

Oratory too was a valued skill and an essential part of the gatherings. There was news to be exchanged and concerns affecting the whole group to be discussed. The tribal council comprised the senior men of each of their regional groups, generally ten men. The komarons of the different peoples were recognisable by their special headbands of dingo fur and tail. Among the Dalla high status was also denoted by the 'duling', a pendant crafted from nautilus shell in the shape of a half moon, which was worn on formal occasions only by the chief singer, the leader of the corroboree, the head of the Bora council and the komaron.[25] It was the responsibility of the head man to know what was happening in his area so that he could report to the council, which met every three or four months.[26] The son of a Brisbane settler,

Tom Petrie, who attended the Bunya summit in about 1845, likened the experience to a Salvation Army congregation:

> all would return to camp, where they settled down to a sort of meeting somewhat after the style of a Salvation Army gathering. One man would stand up and start a story or lecture of what had happened in his part of the country, speaking in a loud tone of voice, so that all could hear. When he had finished, another man from a different tribe stood forth and gave his descriptions, and so on till all the tribes had been represented. Then perhaps a man of one tribe would accuse one from another of being the cause of the death of a friend, and this would lead to a challenge and fight.[27]

Personal, family and inter-group disputes were brought for adjudication, so conflict was inevitable.[28] The Dalla were at an advantage at the Bunya gatherings, for the komaron of the hosting people always spoke last. Some German missionaries attended comparable assemblies at Toorbul and described similar scenes: at the end of the evening meal, if there were no dances planned, an angry accusation would ring out across the camp and everyone would fall silent, waiting to hear the response. If the accused—or one of their 'brothers'—was a good talker or they had a valid explanation, conflict could sometimes be avoided. But if they had flagrantly hunted outside their own territory, stolen property or perhaps behaved improperly with someone's spouse or betrothed, then they may have to confront the aggrieved party in combat.[29] The preparation for such showdowns was verbal jousting; the blood had to be heated with an outpouring of grievance and contempt for one's accuser before resorting to weapons.

This form of dispute resolution was a cultural shock to the German missionaries and on some of their early trips to 'pullen pullen'—the local term for these meetings—they spent much of their evenings verbally intervening in showdowns. They noted that the participants did not always object. The missionaries' criticism of the fights that did eventuate puzzled the Dalla and their Saltwater neighbours: 'we took occasion to warn them against their many fights and quarrels', reported Peter Niqué and William Hartenstein, two of the lay missionaries, but 'they were surprised that we should despise such fine play as the fights were'.[30] They had been invited to participate in a regional summit numbering two thousand people where some of the best warriors were performing.[31]

Women too had their fights for both sport and justice. The missionaries offended the older women when they interrupted a group dispute that had arisen over a 'love affair':

> What a scene did we behold! the whole of the women were engaged in a regular battle; it was quite overwhelming ... no contest of men could be fiercer ... each had her antagonist, who parried her blow by holding her stick between her fingers over her head ... unable to look at it any longer, we rushed betwixt them, and at last succeeded in separating them at the peril of getting a few blows ... Some old women, however, were very much displeased, and pointed their spears at [us] ... one threw it at Mr E.[32]

The missionaries had not been present for the start of the fight and so were unaware that the senior women were responsible for its conduct. Women had their own Bora councils to uphold correct female behaviour.[33] Men's fights were also managed by a head man of each side who decided the rules of combat, ensured that they had equal numbers of warriors per side and that they were matched in terms of opposing moiety, the 'skin' groups into which all peoples of southern Queensland were born. The number of men called upon by the senior men usually depended on whether the offence had been against an individual, a family or the whole language group. The fights usually began around 10 a.m. and would be fought to a conclusion. If there was no clear outcome the head men would decide when enough was enough and call a halt to proceedings. Fighting always stopped if anyone was killed, but despite the level of vitriol, the war cries and the capabilities of the weapons, such deaths were not frequent. Charles Archer was invited by the Dalla to witness one of these gatherings, which he described to his father as having

> more of the nature of a tournament than a battle. The weapons used are certainly deadly enough, but their expertness in avoiding the spear and boomerang is so great that a life is seldom lost on either side . . . At the only bullanbullan I witnessed they did not get angry enough to use the spear but decided the quarrel . . . with the Waddie (club) and telaman (shield). A series of single combats took place between the most celebrated warriors of either tribe. After a great deal of altercation, one steps forward from each of the parties; a circle is formed round them and they batter away at each other . . . at a most fearful rate . . . A good deal of science is displayed in these encounters; the great object appears to be to get as close upon an adversary after he has delivered his blow and before he has recovered himself.[34]

In 1823 three Sydney castaways, Thomas Pamphlett, Richard Parsons and John Finnegan, had the good fortune to be rescued by the Ngugi, Nunukul and Goenpul in Moreton Bay, and lived with them for about seven months. They described fighting grounds on the south side of the Brisbane River, which were circular pits about 90 centimetres deep and between 7 and 12 metres in diameter, surrounded by a palisade.[35] In these arenas young warriors engaged in hand-to-hand combat. The fights were overseen by the head man of each contestant, who was ready to call a halt to proceedings before serious injury was inflicted.

Here Dundalli learnt a sense of justice, and that a fair fight required rules of honour: that it was dishonourable to cut a man on the upper body in a way that might disfigure his tribal scars, the scars that proved his identity and his manliness; dishonourable to spear a man who had fallen; dishonourable to hide weapons or strike before or after the komaron had signalled to begin or end; dishonourable to challenge or insult an imarbara, as they were forbidden to pick up, let alone possess, weapons of any kind.[36] Such behaviour would not be tolerated by respectable people. Finnegan described the grave response to a breach of the rules at a fight in 1823. His friends were preparing the corpse of a man who had been killed while another one-on-one combat continued in the ring,

> when it appeared, from a tremendous shout, that some unlooked-for event had happened in the pit. I afterwards learned that the spectators judged that foul play had taken place between the combatants. The crowd upon this drew away from the pit; and our party, accompanied by those tribes that were friendly to them, formed themselves in a line, while their adversaries did the same opposite to them. The battle then became general. Several from each side would advance, and having thrown their spears, again retire to the line, in the manner of light infantry.[37]

Nor would an upright man ignore the killing of a friend or brother, but he must seek to avenge his untimely death. While the Moreton Bay peoples'[38] famous 'Cry for the Dead' was a song of mourning and remembrance, it also reminded the men of their grievances to shore up group anger and courage. Tom Petrie recalled how:

> the daybreak cry for the dead . . . would start perhaps by one old man wailing out, and then in another direction some one would answer, then another would take up the cry, and so on, till the

different crying and chanting of all the different tribes rose on the air, with the loud 'swears' and threats of what they would do when the enemy was caught, relieving the wailing.[39]

A talent for verbal aggression and contempt for one's enemies and rivals was an important personal gift which helped to strengthen the group and was part of the game of intimidation and bluff of one's opponents.

When Dundalli was a boy, a big fight was held on a plain in what would become Brisbane's western suburbs, possibly on what is today the J.C. Slaughter Falls picnic area at the base of Mount Coot-tha. The group fight was initiated by Eulopé, a fighting chief of the Quandamooka group from Stradbroke Island, in an alliance with Daki Yakka, the elder from the area of what is now Brisbane's CBD; Bribé, an elder of the Joondaburri; and Mulrobbin, an elder whose lands covered the south side of what is now inner Brisbane. Their five hundred warriors were pitted against seven hundred warriors under Moppy (sometimes spelt 'Moppé') and Gorowamba, described as the chieftains of the Gatton-Tenthill and Peak Mountain peoples, respectively—the latter probably the area we today call Peak Crossing.[40] On one of those famously clear sunny days of winter–spring that are a delight of Brisbane's climate, with air 'redolent of perfume from the aromatic shrubs' which skirted the plain, Eulopé appeared, dressed by his men for battle. He was described by a resident of the convict settlement as

> lubricated with emu oil and pounded charcoal, a rush . . . thrust through the cartilage of his nose, his long hair was carefully tied up in a knot, into which a bunch of yellow feathers of the white cockatoo was inserted . . . as he stood before me with his contan (shield) on his left arm, his war spears in his right hand, nulla nulla and boomerang in his belt, [he] was strikingly grand

and imposing. On the slightest motion, his great muscular power was fully developed; he trod the ground with the air of a conqueror, and was the observed of all observers. I felt that the fate of the battle rested on him.

When all was ready, Eulopé

> formed [his men] into line two deep, and they marched into the centre of the plain, shouting their war cry . . . they sat down with their legs crossed under them, silent and motionless, watching the movements of the Mountaineers. The kippers followed in the rear . . . In a few minutes [the opposing chieftains] marshalled their men in a similar manner, and advanced . . . shouting the war cry . . . when about fifty yards from them they sat down in the same silent and motionless manner. The death like silence that followed the[ir] terrific shouts . . . had a singularly depressing effect—not a whisper could be heard on either side—the gins and children being equally silent as the warriors.

After remaining motionless for some time, Eulopé broke the tension by throwing his boomerang

> with such force at a gigantic Mountaineer that it split his shield, and wounded him so severely in the head that he fell senseless to earth. A shower of spears and boomerangs followed, which was kept up for some time without any apparent advantage on either side. Eulopé . . . rushed into the thickest of his foes dealing death and destruction around him; and he was so ably seconded by the brave old Duke of York, Molrooben and Bribé, that [his opponents] gave way, notwithstanding the desperate efforts of Moppé and Gorowamba, the chief of the Peak Mountain tribe, whose daring courage and noble bearing astonished me . . . the

havoc made by Moppé and Gorowamba soon inspired them,—they rallied round their leaders, and fought with such skill and determination that the Settlement tribes began to retreat.

The tide turned when in the midst of battle Eulopé challenged Moppy over an insult prior to the start of the battle. Those around them ceased fighting to allow these two men to conclude proceedings, 'confident in the skill and prowess of their respective chieftains'. The two battle leaders

> were evidently suffering from their great exertions during the battle. Yet when they stood opposed to each other, and saw around them, spectators of the combat, the best and bravest of the Coast and Mountain tribes, it had an instantaneous effect on both, and their prostration and exhaustion vanished, with the hope of adding to the fame they had acquired by the defeat of their renowned adversary.

Moppy was described as a man of gigantic proportions and immense strength despite being about forty years old. On this occasion, however, it was Eulopé who triumphed and sent the inland men, and their families, into disarray and retreat.[41]

Dundalli's childhood was filled with such heroic scenes. A colonial newspaper published a dramatic report of what took place in the late 1820s, when Mulrobbin, whose daughter had been 'stolen' by a man from the Pine Rivers, issued a challenge to him before a gathering that included tribal people from Bribie Island and the 'Bunyas'. Dundalli's people were often described by settlers as 'bonyi', bunya or bunya bunya people. They and the Bribie Islanders gave support to the Pine River tribe. Again some of the leading men of Dundalli's childhood were involved. Mulrobbin's 'warlike feats' were 'celebrated by every bard, from Huon Munday's to Moppee's' (from Noosa in the north to

Gatton in the west). He commenced hostilities late one afternoon when he approached the huts of his opponents and sang a war song at them for thirty minutes while they stared at the ground, in silence. Mulrobbin made as if to return to his people, only to suddenly throw a boomerang at his enemies, who rose as one. Women raced to get children out of the line of fire, young kippers to get torches for the men to fight by, and the Pine River warriors to seize their weapons. It fell to one of the visitors, a Dalla man who had been slightly wounded by the boomerang, to respond to Mulrobbin's challenge. He 'was upwards of six feet high' and muscular, determined to defend the Pine River man's winning of Mulrobbin's daughter. 'The attitude of the men was singularly beautiful as they stood before each other, covering their bodies with their contars or shields, warding off the blows with great skill.' It must have been an impressive sight as the young kippers encircled them on this moonlit but cloudy evening with thirty tea tree torches illuminating the scene. Woorgan from Bribie Island also took issue with a young warrior from Stradbroke Island who supported Mulrobbin, so two sets of men fought in hand-to-hand combat until Woorgan and the Dalla man were overwhelmed. Then a man from among the Pine River warriors stepped forward to fight Mulrobbin. Astonishingly, this chieftain withstood this second bout of hand-to-hand combat. Mulrobbin was victorious and his daughter finally returned to him. Their reconciliation was greeted with celebration by his people, the South Brisbane Jagera.[42]

Dundalli's immediate family comprised five hundred or so relatives, with an extended family that was even larger again.[43] So even if Dundalli was not at these particular fights, there is no doubt that stories of these elders and warriors were part of his childhood world.

A loss in battle was usually met by a demand for a further fight to redress the imbalance. Tom Petrie witnessed one of these group fights, which concluded with personal combat between an Ipswich man and a Bribie Island man, who fought with knives. The culmination was

Table 1.1 Names of some leading men of south-east Queensland during Dundalli's childhood ca 1830

Name	Language group	People	Place
Moppy (often spelt as Moppé). Born ca 1787; died 1842 or 1843. Father of three sons, one of whom was Multuggerah (also known as Jem Campbell, Cambell and Cambela)	Yaggera	Ugarapul	Gatton–Tenthill area west of Ipswich
Gorowamba	Yaggera	Ugarapul	Peak Crossing, south of Ipswich
Mulrobbin (various spellings include Molroober, Molrooben, Malrobbin and Mullrobin). Died June 1852	Yaggera	Jagera	South Brisbane–Coorparoo–Lytton
King Billy. Father of Mulrobbin and Delackey	Yaggera	Jagera	South Brisbane
Duke of York (Rod Fisher gives his Aboriginal name as Daki Yakka)[44]	Referred to as Turrbal by Petrie; disputed by others	Mianjin	Brisbane CBD, which the Turrbal called 'Mianjin'
Bribé Woorgan was another fighting man from Bribie Island. His name was often spelt as Worgan or Wogan By 1841 Naimany was the senior elder on the island	Gubbi Gubbi	Joondaburri	Bribie Island (Aboriginal name is Yarun)
Eulopé Papooniya, a young fighting man from Stradbroke Island—probably Petrie's Parpunyi in *Reminiscences*, p. 224	Quandamooka	Nunukul or Goenpul	Stradbroke Island

Table 1.1 Names of some leading men of south-east Queensland during Dundalli's childhood ca 1830 *continued*

Name	Language group	People	Place
Yunmonday (various spellings of his name include Ewan Mundy, Huon Munday, Yanmonday and Eumundi)	Gubbi Gubbi	Undambi	Sunshine Coast coastal plain, south of Noosa Heads
Ubie Ubie (various spellings of his name include Obi Obi and Ubi Ubi). Died end of December 1843. Son: Jacky; brother: Burumballi	Dalla/Gubbi Gubbi	Dallambara	Upper Mary River west to Kilcoy

astonishing to Petrie, for eventually 'the pair were separated by those looking on. It was found that the Ipswich black had less wounds than the other, so the former had to stand and allow his enemy's friends to cut him to make things more equal. This as I have already stated, was always done'.[45] Aboriginal justice was built on a foundation that both blessings and hardships should be borne equally by all. For peace and social order to be restored, an injury to one group must be offset by similar pain to another. This sense of justice and fairness impelled Dundalli throughout his life.

As well as providing justice, one of the main purposes of these shows of physical strength was to give security against the exploitation of people and resources and back up negotiations over trade, which was an important function of the gatherings. So, as much as physical prowess was valued, equally important were skills of diplomacy and amiability for skilful trade negotiations. The Dalla prized the beautiful pearl shells that were only available on the coast; they crafted them into duling, which signified high status. They also depended on mussel shells for fine cutting knives and found that the coastal streams produced the best white clay for body paint for performances.

The Wakka Wakka and peoples further west had the hardest stone for axes and tomahawks. The Badtjala lands produced the best timber for spears, and the Jagera, that for nulla nulla clubs. The tasty bauple nuts, now internationally famous as macadamias, grew only on Gubbi Gubbi lands, and there were other unique goods and services to trade. On the coast the possum rugs deteriorated rapidly in the heat and humidity whereas mountain possum furs were thick and resilient; the mountain timbers also made fine boomerangs and the lightest and strongest 'telemons' or shields; the feathers of the mountain eaglehawk were valued for the treatment of wounds, and those of the inland cockatoos, for adornment. For the Dalla, while the ochre mined on the Stanley River on their lands was the brightest red in the district, their ace in these exchanges was the bunya harvest.[46]

The young people looked forward to the time when they could draw the admiration of their family and friends at these public occasions, and their first step on this path was to earn the tribal cuts on their bodies. At the age of twelve or thereabouts, Dundalli's tribal uncle first prepared him for the cuts by removing all his body hair with warm beeswax. Then, using a sharp mussel-shell knife, he made fine nicks on his chest, shoulders and all the way along his spine. These were then rubbed with charcoal so that when they healed they were raised; when shiny with animal fat, they were quite beautiful in their symmetry.[47]

When Dundalli was almost sixteen, his komaron sent messengers to neighbouring peoples known to have a cohort of boys about the same age so that they could be prepared for initiation. The date was set by the stars: when the sky rings—two dark circles visible in the southern skies—were in their north–south position and the Bora sites, the sacred places for male initiation, mirrored the eternal celestial rings 'where the spirits of the dead performed their ceremonies', then the Bora council called the ceremony.

One of Dundalli's mother's brothers was responsible for instructing him and preparing him for the Bora. In these tests Dundalli had to prove his understanding and command of all the laws and customs, including those governing totems, country and moieties. Tom Petrie had the rare honour of being allowed to accompany his young Undambi and Toorbul friends through the Bora ceremonies. There were trials of silence, of restricted vision, of isolation and of fasting. They were instructed in secret songs and sacred knowledge that were never to be divulged to the uninitiated. No women were allowed near them during this time, until the Bora ended with a ceremonial battle by the young kippers, as they were now called, in full dress; they wore a special head band made of snake skin, and belts of possum hair criss-crossed their chests and backs. Lastly they were presented with their first ever dilly, a woven bag made especially for the occasion by their sister or mother.[48]

Great mystery surrounded these secret ceremonies, and breaches could be punished by death. The women greeted their young sons and brothers with relief that they had passed these ordeals. But the anxiety was not over yet. The next phase took the kipper away from home for up to a year. Four young tribal uncles and a member of the Bora council led Dundalli on a journey to give him further instruction about his duties in daily camp life and to harden him for adult life ahead. Among his obligations were the protection of his totem and its breeding sites: places referred to as 'mimburi'. His older companions were each selected for their skills so that Dundalli was taught how to fish, to hunt and to climb. The last skill he acquired was how to craft weapons, for he was not allowed to own them until he had completed his initiation. Additionally, one of Dundalli's tribal brothers accompanied the group as messenger under the instructions of the Bora men and would return to the camp at each new moon to give a progress report to his parents and friends.

At the age of seventeen Dundalli returned to his parents and worked for them for another two years or so. The opening test of adult life would be his first group combat among the Dalla. For the first time in his life he was obliged to fight in battle on the opposite side to his father, for in any dispute among his own people he must line up with those of his moiety; his mother's moiety by definition was an opposite class to his father's. His primary duty must be to his brothers and to his mother's brothers and the other men of his skin group. Such were the complex and demanding loyalties and duties of adulthood as a warrior. It was a strong inducement to minimise conflict within the group.

His special skills having been identified by the men of the Bora, he was assigned his role in the community. Everyone had a vital role to play: hunter; fisherman; songmaker; toolmaker; even a 'gundir', the esteemed medicine men and women who could channel both good and evil spirits. Once his training was completed his final name was granted and he was deemed ready to marry.[49]

We have no written record of Dundalli's bride's name but we know she was important to him. As we shall see, in the brief moments he had to address his people before he died, he directed his words to her.

Courtship was one of the special times when the songmaker's role in Dalla life was crucial. Once Dundalli's romantic interest in a young woman was certain he approached the songmaker with a request to compose a song that was his marriage proposal. This was a risky business for the songmaker, for if the marriage was not allowable—that is, if the two young people were not of the correct moieties, or if the young woman was betrothed to someone else—he could find himself the cause of a longstanding feud between families. Dundalli prepared well so that there were no barriers to the union, the songmaker composed the words and song and then approached the young woman to sing the proposal. The union could only proceed if she, her parents and Dundalli's all agreed. The marriage formalities comprised three ceremonies: the first was a corroboree held by the bride's people for her, which Dundalli was not permitted to attend, but a few days later they held a second corroboree for him. Her mother was not allowed to attend the second because she and her brothers became 'jalu' to Dundalli upon marriage; under ancient law any relations between the son-in-law and mother-in-law were forbidden. His mother-in-law and her brothers would become invisible to him and they were not permitted to talk to one another. The day after the corroboree, the komaron or muningburum, the men of the Bora council in formal dress, and Dundalli's family came to her camp for the last of the formalities. The bride's uncle put a white cockatoo feather firstly in Dundalli's hand, then he placed the same feather in his niece's hair; the women of her village fixed it in place with string made from possum hair while her uncle addressed the gathering. Dundalli's family stood up while he spoke and at the end of the speech each village gave their war cries. When the day's events were over, his bride removed the feather and it was given to her mother to keep.

When Dundalli and his fellow Dalla man, Anbaybury, met the German missionaries at a gathering at Toorbul in August 1841, he was a married man and already of some status, secure amid the warmth and prosperity of his people and country. While they were at Toorbul, the sheep stations of Colinton in Wakka Wakka country, Kilcoy on the western boundary of Dalla lands and Durundur in their heart were being stocked by squatters.[50] Nothing would ever be the same again. The discipline and endurance of his Bora training were tested to the limit in the years ahead.

2

THE YOUNG NEGOTIATOR: TRADE AND DIPLOMACY TO MARCH 1842

Even as a young man Dundalli was highly regarded by his people. In 1841 he was called upon to speak on the Dalla's behalf to representatives of the German mission. The Dalla had received word that the small mission based at Nundah since 1838 was planning to move deeper into Aboriginal country and two men, Anbaybury and Dundalli, were given the task of persuading the young German evangelicals to settle on Dalla country. To understand this extraordinary assignment one has to appreciate how the founding of Moreton Bay Penal Establishment affected the local politics of southeast Queensland, and why it was that a group of eleven young German men accompanied by eight wives were being urged to move *onto* Aboriginal lands. It is a story that highlights the idealism and good will as well as the divisions of Aboriginal and European societies in the 1830s and 1840s.

The Aboriginal peoples most affected by the blight of a penal settlement on their country were Daki Yakka's people—whose traditional lands included the present site of the Brisbane CBD known as

Mianjin—and the Nunukul and Goenpul of Stradbroke Island. Daki Yakka was the man colonial authorities dubbed the Duke of York[1] and he appears frequently in colonial literature. Conflict with Aboriginal people at Redcliffe, the site originally selected for the penal settlement, had been one of the factors driving the removal of the penal station up river to the present site of the city of Brisbane in 1825, and the Mianjin too were hostile initially. While Dundalli was enjoying a carefree childhood among the mountain peoples, at least three Mianjin men and three Europeans lost their lives and many others were injured in clashes over the settlement to the south. A regimental guard of one hundred men was required to defend the British settlement, which the Mianjin were forced to bypass on their way to their main camps at York's Hollow and Breakfast Creek. (In today's terms their main campsite stretched from the Normanby Fiveways past the Exhibition Grounds to the suburb of Albion.) From as early as 1826, though, the Mianjin had captured and returned convict runaways and in exchange the commandants had given them 'a little sugar and water, blankets and tomahawks'.[2] This relationship had developed to a point where the Quaker missionaries James Backhouse and George Walker, who visited the penal station in 1836, noted Aboriginal people moving freely through the settlement: 'We visited the prisoners in the Penitentiary, in the morning and those in the Barracks in the afternoon. A few Blacks came into the Barracks, and seemed desirous to understand what was going forward; but no one could interpret into their language on religious subjects.'[3]

In another passage Backhouse noted the extent of the Mianjin's accommodation of the British—they enjoyed the new foods the Europeans brought with them but had no time for their other cultural preoccupations:

> Sixteen Blacks came to the Settlement, and we presented them with some cotton handkerchiefs, with which they seemed much

pleased, and not less so, with some Bananas, given them by the Commandant. The Blacks here show less value for articles of European manufacture, than those of some other parts of the Colony; and though less contaminated by intercourse with white people, they are evidently less civilized; they, however, find Sweet-potatoes, Maize, and other food, such as they obtain from the military and officers, so much superior to the roots they generally feed upon, in their native haunts, that some of the males visit the settlement daily, to obtain them.[4]

The British had of course only acquired their own love of potatoes and corn as a result of the European conquest of Central and South America, so it was hardly surprising that other peoples would enjoy these new foods with equal relish. Commandant Fyans recalled this same incident between the Quakers and the Mianjin. He had ordered that twenty hands of bananas be made available to them. Daki Yakka and his son immediately took a hand each and the rest of the group took the remainder back to the camp for their families, promptly discarding the gift of handkerchiefs.[5]

The availability of this extra food and other goods would have given the Mianjin a number of advantages over their neighbours. It gave the men more time to work on making their weapons, tools and songs; gifts of tomahawks, blankets and clothes provided interesting new items to trade; and most importantly, the presence of glass and metal enabled them to enhance their weapons and tools, especially axes, spearheads and knives. The Mianjin tolerated the penal settlement as long as it elevated their political power where it most mattered: among the Aboriginal nations who governed south-east Queensland.

Exclusive access to European goods provoked regional political tensions. A deputation of seven Undambi men regularly visited the settlement, to the annoyance of the Mianjin. According to Fyans these men 'from the north', whose presence was opposed by the local people, came to visit their friend, the runaway convict John Graham, who had lived with them for many years but was now serving out his sentence. 'Twice or thrice during my reign, these natives paid their visit, leaving us on good terms with a supply of maize corn, and a blanket to each, never failing to take a store of broken glass for their spears, an article much prized by them.'[6]

The Ngugi of Moreton Island and the Nunukul and Goenpul of Stradbroke Island similarly began to incorporate European goods and accommodate the people by 1836, but only after a period of severe interracial violence. A pilot station had been established at Amity on North Stradbroke Isand in 1827 to assist vessels into the bay and the Brisbane River; later a store and gardens were built at Dunwich, also on Stradbroke, so that vessels could offload and resume their journey rather than have to wait for the right weather conditions. In July 1831 a soldier and a convict were killed; the British response was the cruel entrapment and beheading of a Nunukul elder—most likely Eulopé, whose bravery and physical strength were known far beyond his island home. From there the violence escalated, with a number of military sorties on both islands up to December 1832, no doubt contributing to the decision to close down the Dunwich stores.[7] Despite this brutality, by 1836 a reluctant understanding had been reached by the survivors.

By the time Dundalli was commencing the long learning and rituals required for adult initiation, a number of Stradbroke Island's Quandamooka were more or less permanently camped by the pilot station. In 1847 when the pilot station was removed to Bulwer on Moreton Island, a group of Quandamooka—probably the de facto Aboriginal wives of the white crewmen and their children and relatives—moved with the staff. At about the same time, a group of Ngugi, from Moreton Island, moved to Moongalba, a favourite meeting place on Stradbroke. Both groups nevertheless retained their respective group identities and historical connections to their former places.⁸ By 1837 Major Cotton, the commandant at Moreton Bay, was writing confidently:

> The tribes which occupy the lands immediately adjacent to Brisbane Town, after an acquaintance of several years, come amongst us in confidence, a good understanding prevails between them and us, both within and without the limits of the Settlement; amongst these are the tribes which live near Amity Point, and on the banks of the 'Brisbane' beyond the Settlement.⁹

So by 1838, the Quandamooka, weakened by the loss of their warrior-chief and many fighting men, were often allies of Daki Yakka and the Mianjin people. Both sought to use their relations with the Brisbane penal station and its outposts to their advantage in the Aboriginal politics of south-east Queensland.

Between March and June of that year, however, a new group of white men arrived. They had been inspired by Reverend John Dunmore Lang, a leading Presbyterian minister and personality of colonial New South Wales, to set up a mission to the Aborigines. Lang was concerned that, since there was already talk of closing the penal station and opening the northern district to settlement, it was essential that missionaries make contact with Aboriginal people before they were polluted by the evil influences of ticket-of-leave men,[10] emancipist convicts and the ruthless pastoralists who employed them. Major Cotton allocated the missionaries 640 acres of land at what is now known as Nundah, because he did not want them too far from the reach of government authority. 'Zion's Hill', as the missionaries named their station, was 11 kilometres from the main settlement and 3 kilometres north of the government's Eagle Farm, where the convict women had been moved.

It was a location fraught with problems. Sir George Gipps, governor of New South Wales, complained that they were too close to the settlement and that they should have set up in the Bunya Mountains—meaning Dundalli's country in the Blackall Range—since that was the great regional meeting place for traditional owners. In 1838, however, even Nundah was isolated, for the mission had no horses and no means of communication with the settlement other than to walk there. A 50-mile [80-kilometre] exclusion zone officially prevented anyone from entering the settlement without the permission of the commandant, so their only neighbours were the Aboriginal locals.

Fortunately the site also possessed advantages for missionary aims. It was partly open country and well watered by a stream, which the missionaries named Kedron Brook. Indigenous pathways also criss-crossed the region and Cotton, presumably by accident, had placed the missionaries on the major route to the north. As Reverend Christopher Eipper, one of the two ordained ministers who made up the group, reported in 1841, their station

> is, from its situation, peculiarly adapted for missionary exertions, as it lies at the great thoroughfare of the Aborigines, when proceeding either from the north or south along the sea-coast, [or] . . . from the interior; and it may safely be said, that nowhere are there so many natives met with together as at Moreton Bay.[11]

After March 1842, when the penal station was formally closed and settlers no longer required government permission to enter Brisbane, they too used this north–south pathway, which eventually became Sandgate Road.

We know little about how the traditional owners of this part of Brisbane received the missionaries because few of the mission papers prior to November 1839 have survived. Perhaps their location at what was a site used by all the tribal groups of the south-east meant they were initially tolerated. By the end of 1839 it was clear that they had a special relationship with a Ningy Ningy elder whose name they spelt as 'Deciby' and whom they variously described as 'the king of the Toorbal' or 'the king of the Ningi Ningi'. Their relationship enabled a truly remarkable experiment in trying to overcome cultural barriers, with good will and idealism evident on both sides.

The mission had its beginning in the sectarian disputes of the early nineteenth century. While Lang was in London in 1837 he was introduced to a group of German and Swiss dissenters. They were young, pious and idealistic. One of the group, Christopher Eipper, had connections with the Church Missionary Society but his refusal to take vows of obedience to a bishop prevented his ordination as an Anglican priest and any appointment through the Church of England.[12] The other ordained minister of the group and the lay missionaries had been trained by the Reverend Gossner in Berlin. Gossner had converted from Catholicism but in 1836 he quarrelled with the Berlin Missionary Society and subsequently established his own missionary society.[13] All of the party had personal experience of religious conflict and the depth of feeling that accompanies personal and group contention, so community politics was something they had in common with their potential Aboriginal flock.

The missionaries sought to convince Aboriginal people to settle permanently in one place and pursue Western work practices, believing that it was essential for conversion. This notion was part of a broader debate taking place between Christian evangelicals and secular imperialists about whether Christianity should precede civilisation of non-Western peoples, or the other way around. The impracticalities of this goal were soon apparent to the missionaries at Moreton Bay. Although they never gave up the attempt to teach agricultural skills and retain Aboriginal people at their station, they soon realised that if the traditional owners would not linger then the only solution was to accompany them on their travels. The result was a number of expeditions with Aboriginal people through their country between 1839 and 1843, which were occasions for rich cultural interaction.

The mission undertook no less than sixteen expeditions between November 1839 and April 1843, in which they slept in Indigenous camps, attended their fights and journeyed with them on foot and by canoe.

The records of these expeditions are fragmentary and the problem of omissions is compounded by questions of interpretation and translation from German, for only the ordained clergy had English language skills. The lay missionaries were learning English formally at the mission, and Moreton Bay pidgin English as well as Yaggera and Gubbi Gubbi as they travelled. Eipper diligently collected words in his journal throughout 1841–42, only to have his papers accidentally destroyed in a camp fire in July 1842.[14] The clergymen conscientiously forwarded the mission diaries and expedition journals to Dr Lang in Sydney, and some of these were edited and published in Lang's newspaper, the *Colonial Observer*, presumably in an attempt to maintain the public's interest in and financial support for the mission. In these articles, Aboriginal voices were generally rendered into the formal English prose to which the supporters of colonial missions were more receptive.[15]

The arrival of the missionaries must have caused some consternation to the Ningy Ningy. Their reception was probably helped by the fact that the main penal establishment was being wound down, so initially there was no sense that they were part of a coming influx.[16] The eldest of the 'brethren', as they referred to one another, had not turned thirty when they commenced—they were all born between 1809 and 1816 and began the mission with an average age of just twenty-five.[17] The presence of so many fit young men in company no doubt made outright attack seem like an unwise option for the Ningy Ningy, although once the missionaries' crops were established they made frequent night raids. This food source seems to have convinced the Ningy Ningy, or 'Toorbal' as the missionaries also sometimes referred to them, to shift from being hostile to the European presence to being accommodating. Here was an opportunity to match their Quandamooka and Mianjin rivals in terms of European goods and technological adaptations.

This turning point in Ningy Ningy attitudes was evident on the first missionary expedition to Redcliffe in November 1839. The missionaries had spent the past seventeen months building eleven cottages, clearing the land for cultivation and constructing stockyards, all with minimal tools and only the most basic materials. In the evenings, when they had sufficient oil for lighting, there was instruction in English and regular prayer meetings. As the mission diarist noted in his still-awkward English:

> Although we are almost continually overwhelmed with work, yet we trust, the object of our Mission has never been lost sight of. We found that there could be not expected any great decrease of work, though hard labour might cease for a time and that it was our duty, to try every means, to come into closer contact with the Blacks, chiefly also for the sake of their language in which we are still very poor. With this view had in November last four of the brethren made an attempt of travelling with them in the bush and accommodating themselves to their mode of living; and as it was just the season for planting maize, potatoes, melons and pumpkins, they took a quantity of seed and vines with them . . .

The Ningy Ningy were happy to host some of the men of this rather sorry little group who seemed to know so little of good culture and the ways of the Australian bush; they commenced the journey in high spirits, the diarist noted, until at 'Umpie Bong', the Aboriginal name for Redcliffe, the mood turned: 'when the brethren . . . would begin to plant, they would scarcely permit it, because they apprehended, this was only a scheme of ours, that now we began planting and by and by we should come and build houses, as we have [at Zion's Hill] and they should be made to work'. After persuading the owners of the land that the crops were for their use, not the missionaries, they were finally allowed to proceed. The Ningy Ningy hosts of the missionaries on this journey subsequently declared that the potatoes and maize belonged to them 'and would not allow any other to come near'.[18]

We do not have a record of the first formal meeting between local peoples and the missionaries but it must have occurred sometime just before this November 1839 meeting which ended so positively. We do know that the Ningy Ningy sought to formalise relations with the young men of the mission through 'name exchange' because the existing records often identify senior Aboriginal men as 'brother' to each of the missionaries. The local peoples' adoption of individual Europeans as a brother was a means of maintaining law and order and incorporating these strangers into their society. By making someone a brother they had a place in the group and in their politics; it became clear to whom they were obligated and who in turn must aid and support them. Becoming a brother also gave one a 'skin' or moiety. Without a skin, marriage in the group was problematic, but once given a skin, unlawful intercourse could be punished with death; thus the authority of the Bora could be upheld and social order maintained. The pastoralist Henry Stuart Russell explained the process that occurred in a friendly meeting with the Gubbi Gubbi near present-day Inskip Point in May 1842.

> As a token of brotherhood the greatest compliment we could pay them, we were aware, was an exchange of names: such ceremonial accordingly, we politely requested them to participate in; which they showed themselves so ready to do . . . I then found that I was of the exalted caste of 'Terwine,' next in grade being the 'Barang' and 'Poonta'.[19]

Russell goes on to explain that he was now obliged to share some of his belongings with his brother, Boralee. Boralee had explained to him his moiety and skin group, which Russell incorrectly called a 'caste'. The Reverend Lang better captured the duty, although perhaps not the honour, that went with this ceremony; he noted that Aboriginal men 'conceive that they have not only peculiar claims upon the adopted brother, but that the latter is bound to take up the quarrels and to avenge the wrongs of his supposed relative, as if he were a real one'.[20]

Not all of the name exchanges with the missionary brothers necessarily happened at the one time and men from different tribal groups initiated relations. One of these men, a mountain man called Gavanmary, became well known by his 'brother's' name, 'Nicker' (a rendition of Niqué), and his popularity outlasted the mission by many decades.[21] Dundalli was not among these men; perhaps he was still too young in 1838 or 1839 to bestow this honour on outsiders.[22]

By July 1841 local relations were so good that an Aboriginal garden had been established on the opposite side of Kedron Brook, in the area now known as Toombul, and given the Indigenous name 'Girkum'. The missionaries had also built three huts of similar construction to their own which belonged to local men Parry, Biralli and Wogan. Huts would soon be added for Wunkermany and Deciby, who also frequently stayed at Girkum with his family. Wunkermany, whose name is spelt with several variations in the mission records, appears to be the Jagera man whom the British referred to as Uncle Marney or Uncle Mainey. Both he and Wogan feature frequently in the newspaper records of the late 1840s as difficult elders presumed to be antithetical to colonial interests,[23] yet here in mid-1841 they were working cooperatively with the mission. Each side seemed to believe that they were evangelising and culturally educating the other. Even the public hanging of two Yugambeh men at the penal station's Windmill in July did not disrupt this relationship.[24] Aboriginal people used the houses and gardens according to their customs and in turn invited the missionaries to their most exciting meetings. In August three Ningy Ningy men died at the Girkum mission camp, causing the rest of the Ningy Ningy to avoid the place; they explained to the missionaries that only when the bones of the dead had dried sufficiently to be placed in a dilly would the devil have no power over them and it would be safe for them to return to the place of the deaths.[25] After twenty-two months of growing interactions, each side of the cultural frontier was slowly but surely sharing more information.

Table 2.1 Aboriginal name exchanges with the German mission

Aboriginal name	Main name in colonial records	Probable people according to colonial records	Missionary 'brother'	Other European 'brothers'
Anbaybury		Dalla	Gottfried Wagner	
Bianco		Pine River	Reverend Schmidt	
Dabianco/ Dabianionne		Ningy Ningy	August Rodé	
Deciby	King of Toorbal; King of Ninge Ninge	Ningy Ningy	William Hartenstein	
Dunkely	Dunkly	Mianjin	Reverend Christopher Eipper	
Not known	Franz		Charles Franz	
Gavanmary	Nicker (Anglicisation of Niqué)	Dalla	Peter Niqué	
Wogan		Joondaburri	Johan (John) Hausmann	William Kent, Brisbane[26] (chemist)

The Ningy Ningy's embrace of the missionaries in November 1839 appears to have alerted their northern neighbours, such as the Joondaburri of Bribie Island and the Dalla or 'Bonyi' people, to the benefits of a containable European presence. By August 1841 word had spread among the peoples of the north that the missionaries were considering moving their station to another location. In that month a large Aboriginal council met at Sandstone Point for several weeks. It was an auspicious occasion. It served as a means of not only settling internal matters but also of competing for the interest of the missionaries, or rather for their plans for planting crops. Reverend Eipper recorded how

> The natives of Toorbal had all along expressed a desire that we should cultivate ground at their own places of abode, and especially Naimany, the Lord of Yarun, [the elder of Bribie Island] wished us to do so on his island, but we found the soil very sandy, so that we could [not] think of acceding to his wishes ... When the Toorbal and Bonyer natives heard that we had not found the soil of Yarun eligible for cultivation, they seemed to rejoice in it, and invited us to inspect their own ground to-morrow.[27]

The lay missionary Gottfried Wagner bravely headed into Bonyi country to inspect the soil, guided by his brother Anbaybury and other Dalla. He was unarmed and unaccompanied by any Europeans. As he explained on his return to Zion's Hill, after they had crossed a creek that marked the start of Dalla country, he had inspected the soil for its potential and found it highly suitable for cultivation.

> At this the natives evinced great joy, saying, if we would bring hoes and axes with us their women would work, and they should hunt for us, and when the crops were ripe, they would

not sleep but watch over them. But it was necessary to have fire-arms, lest strange natives should rob them. They quite exhausted themselves in making promises of good behaviour and industry; but their joy was not quite pure, for we had before observed the whole of them moved by jealousy which tribe should have the benefit of cultivation amongst them.[28]

The Dalla were enthusiastically making it clear that they were not only hankering for the benefits of cultivation but also for firearms to maintain their ascendancy over their tribal rivals.

Traditional owners were still enthusiastic in their welcome of the missionaries when the brethren Peter Niqué and William Hartenstein ventured to Sandstone Point the following week, on 20 August 1841. More than two thousand people were still gathered for the council and tournament, and the new invitees noted the presence of families from Brisbane, the Toorbal locals, 'Eumundi' peoples of the Undambi— whose elder the missionaries called Yanmonday—and the Dalla. The benefit of the missionary presence was being fiercely contested. Negotiations over the right to host cultivation on their lands were intense as the missionaries and each of the participating owner groups sought to gain the upper hand. The result was that the missionaries were completely overwhelmed by the seriousness of this test of local political power and its level of violence.

It was fortuitous that it was William Hartenstein's turn 'to itinerate with the natives', for he was the brother of Deciby, the 'King of Toorbal', and so their hospitality towards him was assured and generous.

> The natives were much pleased at seeing us, especially the King ... and Gavan Mary, Mr N.'s brother, each of them wished to receive his brother into his house, they also offered us some Kangaroo flesh ... In general we found the people very friendly.

They embraced Mr N., and every one brought his family as if they wanted to ask for a blessing upon them ... Early in the morning we were requested to see the King of Yanmonday; he was introduced by the King of Toorbal; he appeared very shy.

Three days later, while Hartenstein held school classes for children, Deciby again arranged for Niqué to speak to Yanmonday:

In the afternoon [Mr Niqué] went to the Yanmonday tribe to give the king a few potatoes and bread; the potatoes were very much to his taste, and he was pleased when the King of Toorbal told him that we should teach them to plant potatoes. He then showed Mr N. all his people, and our natives told them that we had come to do them good, and to make known to them the God of Heaven who seeth and knoweth all things.

Deciby was keen to win the favour of the missionaries for any future plantings and seemed to want the Eumundi's support in any such venture; for at the same meeting the Dalla had renewed their claims upon the missionaries. This time Anbaybury brought Dundalli along to act as Dalla ambassador and negotiator. On 21 August, Anbaybury and Dundalli said to them, 'Now we see you are Missionaries, and no liars: you have come as you promised. How many hoes have you brought with you? Have you also corn for seed with you? Our women shall labour, and we shall hunt for you, that you may have something to eat.' They then offered the missionaries 'a large piece of Kangaroo flesh'. As Niqué in turn 'promised to consult Mr Hartenstein', Anbaybury and Dundalli 'requested him to speak very strongly' so 'that he might accede to their wishes'.

Despite the fact that they were in the midst of a competitive fight of two thousand people, Niqué and Hartenstein aggravated the internal tensions with their attempts to exact a commitment of work as well as suitable land from the locals—they were trying to make the tribal groups outbid one another in promises for the reward of hosting a new mission. The missionaries soon took the news of the Dalla's offer to the Ningy Ningy.

> We certainly found [Dundalli and Anbaybury] ... very willing to receive us, but resolved to speak once more to the natives of Toorbal, in order to excite their jealousy, threatening that if they would not work with us we should go farther to the Bonya natives. The Toorbal natives, however, replied 'the Bonya natives were only liars, and if we went to them they kill us.' We told them, we were by no means afraid of the Bonya natives, nor did we fear death, for then we should go to the great Father in heaven, at which they marvelled, and said they would begin to-morrow.

In fact there was no digging of any gardens or preparation of any land the next day, for the morning was taken up with dressing and preparing for that day's battle. When it commenced it was fierce. The missionaries were taken aback by the level of fury—one of the Eumundi 'fell down apparently dead, another was hit in the face, a third had a spear run through his body'. Fortunately for them, the Ningy Ningy prevailed, although the visitors did not see it through to the end but went 'in great emotion back to our hut'. The contests continued for another week, relieved at nights by singing and dancing and by days set aside for hunting and collecting food.

The missionaries soon became an annoying distraction at this tournament; they completely failed to appreciate the spectacle and importance of this testing of regional strengths, were miserly in their sharing of food and kept harping on about working on a garden. On the Thursday the locals 'laughed and mocked at us when at worship; we prayed for them. Afterwards we asked them to work with the hoe; some went, but threw up a deep trench to annoy us. We planted some corn, melons, and pumpkins, but they trod the ground fast with their feet.'

Even if the Ningy Ningy were the festival hosts, a gathering of foes was not a good time to expect them to plant: as Anbaybury and Dundalli had explained, digging for food was women's work; the men were there to show their fighting prowess to their rivals. Not making much progress and unable to cope with the tournaments, Niqué and Hartenstein left when the meeting still had a week to go. The negotiations over a new mission site were left unresolved, although Deciby extracted a promise that members of the mission would return to Toorbul if Deciby sent some of his people to collect them.[29]

If Anbaybury and Dundalli were disappointed at their failure to secure a new mission on their lands, it was shortlived. Events in the hinterland in August 1841 rapidly overtook this concern. While the Toorbul council was underway, pastoral leaseholders, Sir Evan Mackenzie and three Archer brothers, arrived in the northern Brisbane Valley with sheep and cattle, which potentially offered just as great a reward to the Dalla.

The Archer brothers established Durundur on the head of the Stanley River, a tributary of the Brisbane, close to where the town of Woodford now stands; in August they staked their claim and by September they moved stock on to it. They would later sell the station in 1848 to another pastoral family, David and John McConnel, after the brothers took up leases in the Burnett.[30] Luckily for the mountain people, the three eldest brothers were of a similar idealistic outlook as the young Swiss and German missionaries.

The older Archer sons had been born in Scotland, where their father was a wealthy timber merchant. The family business collapsed with the end of the Napoleonic Wars and, on grounds of economy, their father moved his large family to Norway, where the younger siblings were born. Much of the colonial enterprise of the Archer sons—there were nine of them as well as four daughters—was driven by the need to repay their father's debts as well as to make their own way in the world, and they wrote reassuring letters home, through drought and depression, about their economic ventures.

Of the four brothers who founded Durundur, Charles was the oldest but he did not join the station until it was already quite well established, in 1843. He was well-educated and open-minded, with an outlook that had no doubt been broadened by his colonial experience in Tobago in the West Indies. He was there when the British Parliament abolished slavery and when there was an uprising in nearby Demerara.[31] The next brother, Jack (John), was quiet and pious. He helped to claim and stake Durundur and wrote detailed letters home to his father of the forest timbers of the region, but returned to the life of a sea captain after only a couple of years. The third son, David, was the driver of the Durundur enterprise and was its business and moral compass. Like Jack he was devout and reflective, although not as reserved, and unlikely to moralise or send religious homilies home; but also like Jack he was more than a little uneasy about the usurpation of the land from its traditional owners. Tom was the youngest and the least educated, and his letters show a rough hand compared to the refined handwriting of his older brothers; he had been sent out to New South Wales to join his brothers at the age of fourteen and had all of three years' colonial experience when he drove their stock from western New South Wales to Moreton Bay. He was outgoing, young and fit and took to the pastoral life with seeming ease; and perhaps too he was the most impressionable when it came to his fellow squatters, although as he matured he cast a more critical eye to produce some very biting portraits of his Brisbane Valley neighbours for his mother and sisters.

The brothers came north to catch the tail end of the rush for pastoral land commenced by the Leslie brothers on the Darling Downs in 1840. Tom recalled in his memoirs—written late in life for the younger members of the extended family—that they passed over miles and miles of fine unstocked pastoral land which they knew had already been claimed by others. They pressed on to the Brisbane Valley where, with some disappointment, they passed over well-watered grassy plains on the western side of the river because they were within the prohibited 50-mile (80-kilometre) limit of the penal station. The Archers followed the law and pressed on past Evan Mackenzie's claim of Kilcoy to establish Durundur, only to find that other pastoralists, the Bigge brothers, took up the land they had regretfully passed over. Tom recalled that 'when reminded of the prohibition, Mr Bigge's only reply was a sardonic smile. The prohibition was never enforced, and before long country much nearer Brisbane was freely occupied.'[32]

The Archers' respect for the penal settlement's geographical limits was also reflected in their responses to Governor Gipps's land reforms of the mid-1840s, which also set them apart from their pastoralist neighbours. Only the young Tom growled about unfair 'taxation', the radical language of American republicanism that the militant squatters used to oppose Governor Gipps. Charles wrote home of the monetary loss to the brothers but nonetheless told his father that Gipps's changes were equitable, while David acknowledged that they included some useful provisions.[33] Perhaps David's religious sympathies had made him more open to Gipps's land regulations, for the Presbyterian, Congregationalist and emancipist Irish, each in their own camps, were the backbone of democratic forces and they looked askance at the militant language of the pastoralists which was so clearly based in flagrant self-interest.

Certainly David's view of Indigenous land tenure was influenced by the evangelical religious thought of the 1830s and 1840s, as was Jack's. Jack wrote to David in early 1845 advising him about his plans to move to a station in the South Burnett:

> I suppose safety will be out of the question for some time ... I need not tell you that conciliation has proved itself to be the best way of protecting your property even viewed only in the light of

expediency and enforced as it is by our religion. I think there is but few cases in which recourse ought to be had to more stringent measures.[34]

David's concerns about the morality of the colonial enterprise led him to write to his clergyman cousin, Edward Walker, 'as to whether European foreigners and aliens are or are not entitled to intrude upon the Aboriginal population of this soil'. Edward replied confidently that 'the intent of the Almighty [is that] we should cultivate the ground';[35] nonetheless, David's approach at Durundur was that of co-tenure. In contrast to his squatter neighbours he refused to dispossess the traditional owners of the land despite warnings of attacks on property in the region. Jack's view was that these 'depredations' were 'as usual, occasioned by the misconduct of the whites, who seem to imagine the blacks will allow themselves to be ill-used without attempting revenge'.[36]

Tom was much harsher in his racial attitudes although his memoirs, unlike the letters home at the time, were composed at the height of social Darwinism and perhaps some of his reflections on 'the savage nature which lurked . . . not very far below' were enhanced by the passing years and a retired colonist's bravado.[37] Tom never hesitated in his use of terms such as 'savage' but he did acknowledge, almost wistfully, in a letter to his father that the traditional owners 'lead I suppose the most independent life of any people in the world, wandering from place to place as their inclination leads them'.[38]

It was the older brothers who determined the rules for interaction with the Dalla. They did not interfere with their camps and corroborees but they did curtail contact with the hired hands; interaction was to be through Jack, David and Tom at the head station. Any work was paid for in goods such as tobacco, rice, 'damaged flour and any other cheap thing about the place', as Tom admitted in one letter.[39] At the same time, any thefts were met with 'active steps'; on one such occasion in the early weeks of establishing the station, someone took all the clothes and provisions from a camp of two of the shepherds. Jack, 'who was in charge at the time', told Tom 'to see what could be done to find the robbers'. Tom took a broad interpretation of this request and persuaded two local Dalla men to track the perpetrator. With two shepherds and the two local men, Tom then organised a counter raid of the camp of that man's extended family, brandishing one aged and one broken weapon in what must have been a terrifying ordeal:

> 'gins' [women] and 'piccaninnies' [children] were yelling, screaming and tumbling over each other in their efforts to escape, and some did ... but ... we had them huddled up in a confused mass between us ... I advanced into [the camp], seized all the spears and clubs we could lay hands on, and after breaking and burning them, we took possession of the plundered goods, consisting of flour, tea, sugar, some blankets, and sundry garments.

Tom returned home the next day to his very worried and angry older brother.

> It now appeared that [Jack] had wanted me only to go and find out in which direction the culprits had fled: But being young and rash I thought it best to run down the game while the scent was fresh. My brother's wrath was, however, considerably mollified when he heard the result of the adventure, and the raid did a world of good, as it was long ere the natives from that side of the country again committed any open depredation.[40]

Whatever Tom's rationalisation, it is likely that this early aggression was a factor in the brothers' positive relations with the Dalla. Warrior culture respected a show of strength and this pattern of reacting to a menace with a counter display of aggression—showing the capacity to retaliate without necessarily enforcing it—was common in the accounts of two other men who had excellent relations with traditional owners, namely Tom Petrie and James Davis, or Duramboi, the runaway convict.[41] Aboriginal men valued as a potential friend and ally someone who could not be exploited but could match your strength and prove their worth to you in the event of conflict.

By the time Charles arrived at the station in 1843 he could write home confidently:

> Davie considers the Black as the hereditary owner of the soil and that it is an act of injustice to drive him from his hunting grounds—at the same time punishing any case of sheep stealing or petty theft when the culprit can be got hold of. The result has been that the Blacks here appear to have acquired some idea of the rights of property, and this tribe, so far from doing any injury, are of the greatest assistance in procuring bark, breaking up ground with the hoe, carrying rations to the sheep station etc ... While our neighbours the Messrs Mackenzie are frequently annoyed by attacks, both upon their flocks and shepherds, I do not think a single sheep has been stolen from here by the Blacks since I came to the station and I believe for a long time previous.[42]

Relations were not quite as untroubled as Charles believed but they certainly were more peaceable than any of their neighbours.

The Archers benefited from the extended negotiations that Deciby, Yanmonday, Anbaybury and Dundalli had been undertaking with the missionaries. The Dalla men, including Dundalli and Anbaybury, and their wives and families had stayed on at the great Toorbul fight after the departure of the missionaries in late August 1841. By the time the Dalla returned home the Archers and their flocks were in the process of moving to their planned head station. The Indigenous man whom the Archers referred to as the head man, Paddy, appears to be the komaron for the Dungidau, one of the regional groups of the Dalla,[43] and he became the main negotiator with the Archers. Paddy found these young Scottish men far more generous than the impoverished missionaries, for as well as Tom's list of goods provided as payment for labour, other letters reveal that they also paid with beef, sweet potatoes and the Indian corn that was so beloved by the Moreton Bay peoples, as well as clothing, which was less valued.[44] This probably explains the readiness with which Paddy's people took to working for the Archers. Tom returned from collecting a flock of sheep to find the site for the head station cleared, the heavy timber lopped, bark stripped for roofing and the ground hoed for the garden, all within a matter of weeks of their arrival. This could only have been achieved with the willing help of the Dalla.[45] Tom perceptively noted the rivalry that marked the traditional owners in the north, although he failed to appreciate how it was driving support for the Archers' presence:

> If one can get your ear to himself, he will try all in his power to convince you what a fine fellow he is & what rascals all the rest are. At Briallan [on the Castlereagh], it was quite different— if a blackfellow there heard that another had said anything to the detriment of his character he considered himself bound in honor to demand satisfaction and if it was refused a fight was generally the consequence. The blacks here are however not so lazy as those over there . . .[46]

Had the Ningy Ningy and Mianjin not been able to use the benefits of European contact to advance their standing over their traditional rivals, it is doubtful that Paddy and the Dalla would have been so ready to tolerate the presence of the Archers. The brothers had unwittingly settled on some of their most sacred lands. Of the four Bora rings belonging to the Dalla, three of them were on the Archers' run, two of which were close to their head station, and the fourth was on the neighbouring Kilcoy run of Evan Mackenzie. Even more important were the sacred river sites. Again there are four such sites and three of them were on the Archers' lease: Burgarum, a lagoon near the head station; Buruja, a wetland near the foot of Mount Archer; and Burgalba, a lagoon about 8 kilometres from the head station at the head of the Stanley River. These water sites were places of healing, where medicine men and women sourced the sacred stones Mingom and Jinding, which were used in healing. Gairwar, the rainbow snake, dwelt in Burgalba. This lagoon was also 'mimburi'—a sacred fertility site. Specifically, it was an important breeding site for the eaglehawk, whose feathers were used in healing.[47] The Dalla would welcome Europeans who could help them defeat their neighbours in battle or give them an edge in their trade, but loss of land was never part of the negotiations.

Having made the decision to allow the Archers on their land, Paddy and his people seem to have put up with episodes of aggression such as Tom's retaliation. As long as their free movement across their lands and access to the sacred sites were not inhibited, the Dalla would seek to incorporate these strange white people into their world in exchange for their beef, flour and corn. In return the Dalla brought wild vegetables to the head station, which were much appreciated in the early days when stores were low and the gardens not yet productive. They were also generous in their supply of bark for roofing, and Paddy agreed to keep non-local people away from the main station enclosure. David's authority was recognised by the Dalla and his return to the station after an absence was met with a general cry from the camp near the homestead site—an alert for the camp as much as the homestead.[48] The Dalla also sought to bring the brothers into their system of law and culture, and Charles's report of an invitation to one of the ceremonies showed the Archers had some awareness of Dalla protocol:

> They see us approach their camp without alarm, and I have been present at several of their corroborees, or dances, and the

other day at a Bullen-bullen, or fight, without interrupting their proceedings. It is seldom they like to see white men on these occasions, but I had an invitation from one of the chief men of the tribe to come and look on.[49]

Durundur Station was doubly remarkable—for its preparedness to co-exist with the traditional owners and for the maintenance of this policy after the Archers sold it. David and John McConnel bought the station in 1848 and John's son, Arthur McConnel, spent much of his childhood there. Arthur recalled the manager, Mr Butler, killing cattle to provide for the large numbers of people who attended a corroboree on the property in 1864 so that they would not be tempted to kill the stock. The Dalla would work for the station until the time for their traditional meetings would oblige them to leave; they never lost their connection to the land or the animals on it but incorporated the introduced stock into their cultural world. According to Arthur McConnel, when discussing station matters with the manager, the Indigenous stockmen 'in speaking of certain animals would describe it as "that fellow belonging to you & me"'.[50] The Dalla maintained their camps in the area even after the subdivision of the pastoral lease in 1901[51] and there is evidence of ceremonial life being maintained in the region well into the twentieth century.

By October 1841 the balance of power among the tribal nations was beginning to shift. The extent to which the Dalla's relations with the Archers affected the region are not clear. The missionaries felt the disquiet. The absence of any visitors to Girkum for many weeks led Reverend Eipper to go to the Aboriginal camp at Breakfast Creek to see if there were any children interested in instruction. He found that the men, women and children there 'were not at ease on account of a quarrel to be settled that day'. It required them to travel to the mountains and Eipper found it such a distraction for the children that he finally gave up.[52] The Dalla, as the owners of Bunya lands, had many advantages over their southern neighbours, the Mianjin and the Quandamooka, but for nearly two decades Daki Yakka's people had had privileged access to maize, glass and steel, courtesy of their proximity to the penal settlement—how would the balance of power now stand between old friends and foes given that others now had access to European foods and goods?

Deciby's power was also being undercut. In October 1841 young men from Yanmonday's and Naimany's people—from the Sunshine Coast and Bribie Island, respectively—had 'stolen' the daughters of Parry, Dabianco and Gavanmary.[53] Their fathers were keen to rescue them and so a fight had been called in the vicinity of Brisbane.[54] This was an audacious challenge by the young men, for the Ningy Ningy had been dominant in fights in August 1841, and Parry, Dabianco and Gavanmary were senior men and associates of Deciby's. The Sunshine Coast and Bribie Islanders may have been spurred on by the young women concerned; when the elderly Gaiarbau explained Dalla ways to anthropologists in the 1950s he spoke of Indigenous women in active rather than passive terms—'the running away of a woman of one tribe with a man of another'—and noted this as one of three main causes of fights.[55] Petrie also noted of Indigenous marriage protocols that 'in spite of all this arranging, two young people would sometimes make use of their own fancy, and run away together'.[56]

Unfortunately we do not know the outcome of the young men's 'theft' of Parry, Dabianco and Gavanmary's daughters—the missionaries did not record it—but Deciby and his family were back at Girkum on 10 November, when the mission diary also recorded that 'Parry, Biralli and others left for a fight in the mountains'. Mianjin, coastal and mountain people were testing their respective strengths now that the pastoralists had arrived.

In November 1841, the settlement in Brisbane was still officially closed, however, and Deciby's support for the missionaries remained strong in these months. There were two incidents of violent colonial intrusion at Girkum that month which shocked the missionaries by their impudence. An armed convict showed up at Girkum demanding a 'gin' and refusing to leave for some time despite the presence of the missionaries. The next night two convicts were found intimidating the women in the camp, forcing Reverend Eipper to confront them and threaten to report them to the commandant.[57] These incidents took place only a week after Brother Rodé had reprimanded three soldiers he had found at the camp and had reported to their commanding officer, Owen Gorman, the most senior government official in the district and the last commandant of the penal station. As the old penal station wound down, armed convicts thought nothing of holding whole families hostage, suggesting that management of the settlement had become lax in the last months of its operation.[58] It was a forecast of the potential for sexual violence once the district was declared open.

The missionaries undertook a number of journeys and residencies with the traditional owners in the six months between the arrival of the pastoralists and the opening of the settlement. In January 1842 large numbers of people were reported to be passing by the mission on their way to a fight near the river between the 'Toorbal' and 'Moppe's tribe'. A man was fatally wounded in the fight and a large group of people, including his mourning wife, returned to camp near the mission. The missionaries feared that their ripening corn crop would certainly be raided in such circumstances and were delighted when they were not only spared this harassment but also assisted with the harvest by eighteen of the visitors.[59]

The smooth relations were not to last. It was not Dundalli who opposed the European presence in these momentous months. He clearly abided by the decisions of the Bora. A lone operator, Yilbung, known to the whites as 'Millbong Jemmy', waged a personal campaign against the settlement. Yilbung appears to have been one of Dakki Yakka's people although he moved freely among all the peoples of south-east Queensland. He was a memorable character because he had a damaged eye—'Millbong', meaning poor eye, was from the local dialect[60]—and because he had been involved in a number of fracas at the convict station over thefts and the assault of a constable, for which the commandant had sentenced him to twenty-eight days confinement.[61] On 8 March 1842 two of the missionaries, Zillmann and Hausmann, discovered that they had been robbed of two bags of corn, 20 pounds of sugar, a large amount of rice and a nightgown from the clothesline. The Indigenous children at the school informed them that 'Millbong Jemmy' had been taking the supplies over several nights and hosting feasts at the camp. Deciby sought to placate the missionaries by challenging Yilbung to one-on-one combat but the missionaries believed the fight to be a sham for their benefit. Yilbung seems to have had a different view, for he returned later with Wogan for a fierce altercation with Deciby. The description in the diary is interesting in that it shows that the Girkum camp was starting to divide over attitudes to the mission. The two men

> came with shield and waddy to fight the King [Deciby]; but Dabianco rising as champion did Jemmy first the honour to wrestle with him and to throw him down; after which he boroed him—(lifted him up by the genitalia) and then attacked him with the club. This gave the best opportunity to drive him away from our place, as a disturber of the peace and when a few of the Brethren went towards him apparently with a view to catch him, he took to his heels and was followed to the camp to search for the linen in his dilly, but he set off immediately for the Pine River. Some of the Natives well knowing that they had been accessory to the robbery, thought it after this measure no longer safe to continue with us and went off likewise; the rest remained.[62]

On 27 January 1842 the first of a regular steamer service had arrived in Brisbane, just two weeks prior to the public declaration of open settlement to commence in May. The steamer had brought nineteen free servants to work for the Mackenzies and Archers, and the group stayed at the mission on their way to the north. The arrival of more Europeans further accentuated growing division among traditional owners. In 1842 the mission continued to enjoy the protection of Deciby, a point he was forced to stress to 'strange natives' when Niqué and Rodé journeyed to Redcliffe in March. The missionaries' report of this journey was optimistic, for Deciby's people were exceptionally attentive: four Indigenous men carried their provisions; Deciby met them on the road returning south to the mission after retrieving the clothing Yilbung had stolen; a hut was made specially for them at Redcliffe; and when Yilbung joined them from Toorbul he was 'much afraid of us, but we told him, God would punish him'. When during a fight a womeran—possibly a type of local waddie[63]—was thrown over their hut, 'our guides became very angry and one of them taking up his club and shield ran up to the man, who had cast the womeran & beat him saying, did not you see the white men? The other said, that was nothing to him to which he replied, that the white men were under his care, and he did not wish to see us in danger.' Their hospitality was unwavering even after the missionaries, they believed, had jinxed their catch: the Ningy Ningy complained that the missionaries had scared the fish away because they had sliced the mullet they had been given instead of baking them whole, a traditional belief that the missionaries ridiculed.[64]

Niqué and Rodé returned to bad news at the mission. While they had been away 'a great number of Natives ... arrived from the northward ... to fight the Moppe's and Point Danger Blacks'. On leaving Girkum they 'destroyed nearly the whole of Wogan's, Biralli's, Parry's, Wunkermany's potatoe crops. The latter was almost beyond himself and threatening one moment, he would shoot them and the next, that he would ask for a detachment of soldiers at Brisbane Town to send these robbers away.'[65]

The men from the north were probably Gubbi Gubbi men from the Sunshine Coast, growing more confident about their ascendancy over these southern people now that other tribes had access to European food and glass, which the southern tribal peoples had once monopolised, and becoming more forceful in their disagreement over the European presence. The balance of power in south-east Queensland was shifting away from the Mianjin and the older local men led by Deciby. Whether it was intended as a show of contempt for mission practices or disrespect to their native hosts, or both, the destruction of the gardens was a sign of the growing disagreements over attitudes to whites in the region, and the situation was about to get much worse. On 17 February 1842 Evan Mackenzie's draymen had called at the mission and reported the murder of two shepherds by Aborigines on Kilcoy Station 'without any provocation'. Niqué and Rodé, however, were informed by the Ningy Ningy at Redcliffe on 16 March that 'many natives' had died on a squatter's station from 'eating something "ban" (nasty, poison?)'.[66] This was the infamous Kilcoy poisoning at Mackenzie's station. The shock of these deaths was going to take more than Deciby's authority and diplomacy to calm, and Yilbung was going to find more of his people ready to listen to his grievances.

The effects of the deaths of between thirty and sixty people at Kilcoy Station reverberated across the region; the situation required a great deal of consideration and discussion before appropriate action could be taken. A young Dundalli had been keen to act as diplomat and negotiator alongside Anbaybury in August 1841; he had agreed that his people should seek to benefit from contact with the Europeans. But how would the Bora council respond to growing numbers of Europeans and to such underhand tactics? Which tribal groups would be most weakened by these deaths? Could the Europeans be taught the 'proper way' to behave on Aboriginal lands, and who would be commissioned to perform the required payback? No doubt Dundalli was at the April gathering to hear the views of the Bora and of his elder, Ubie Ubie.

3

THE GREAT TOORS OF 1842–43: THE BORA MEN CHANGE STRATEGY

The Bora had identified Dundalli's congenial manner as well as his size and strength as appropriate to handle the diplomacy required for negotiations with the missionaries. Events of 1842 would force them to reassess his role. The Dalla and Yaggera lost several fighting men between August 1841 and June 1842 but it was the loss of two of their greatest warriors, a young man named Commandant and the great Moppy, which caused the greatest grief. While Deciby's and Paddy's arrangements with the mission and the Archers for the most part were respected by the Dalla and the 'Jarbu', as the Dalla called their western tribal members,[1] the Yaggera from Rosewood west to the escarpment of the Great Divide, had no time for European interlopers. From August 1841 the Aboriginal men west of the D'Aguilar Range had decided on campaigns to evict them from their lands. As momentum built in south-east Queensland around the need to oppose the European presence, Dundalli dutifully retrained for fresh challenges.

Much as opinions differed among the various tribal groups over how to deal with the European settlers, a vast gulf divided the Brisbane Valley settlers, too, over relations with the country's traditional owners. Those who settled in the western parts of the river catchment did not share the Archers' good will, so first-contact experiences varied enormously. While Aboriginal peoples near the east coast had been vying for the right to host European settlers on part of their lands, the Dalla and Yaggera to the west had to contend with European trespassers whose initial stance was one of hostility and aggression. That aggression quickly escalated to open violence within six months of the Europeans' arrival.

The Brisbane Valley stations formed a crescent around the spine of Brisbane's D'Aguilar Range. They occupied the river and creek flats of the Brisbane River as it curved west and north of the old penal station, and the pastoral leases reached right into the foothills and scrubs of the mountains that fed the river. These mountains were Dalla heartlands. To the immediate west of the Archers was Kilcoy Station, formed by Evan and Colin Mackenzie, sons of Sir Colin Mackenzie of Kilcoy, Scotland. Moving slightly north-west came Colinton Station, another station formed by Scottish brothers, John and Robert Balfour, whose father was a merchant and colleague of Sir Colin's. Elite colonial and Scottish connections linked almost all the leaseholders of the Brisbane Valley. To the Mackenzies' south was Mount Brisbane Station, taken up by the Bigge brothers, nephews of the judge and commissioner J.T. Bigge. To their west was Cressbrook Station, taken up by David Cannon McConnel as early as July 1841. His Scottish father had made his money from Manchester's cotton industry but David had maintained the Scottish connection by studying at Edinburgh University. South-west of Cressbrook was Eskdale Station leased by business partners Graham and Ivory; the former was the son of an Edinburgh professor and the latter, of Scotland's crown prosecutor, the 'Lord High Advocate of Scotland'. Moving south at Mount Esk Station were more Scottish brothers: the Scotts, who ran cattle, and then another member of a renowned

Scottish family, John Borthwick, who co-owned Buaraba lease with his business partner Oliver.[2]

The Archers assured their parents that their neighbours were gentlemen 'with whom we are on a very friendly footing'.[3] The eighteen-year-old Tom, accustomed to the rough company and isolation of their Castlereagh station, was most impressed by the quality of their dress, of their horses and of their arms.[4] Tom's recall of Francis Bigge's red silk cummerbund is as striking as his image of entering pioneering pastoralist Pemberton Hodgson's slab hut at Eton Vale on the Downs to find 'the Hon Mr. Murray' wearing white kid gloves and reading by the fire.[5]

The fashionable taste of some of these settlers was not matched by sophisticated cross-cultural communication. The open foothills and river flats of the Brisbane Valley leases enabled the hostile factions of the Yaggera and western Dalla to amass there in large numbers. The first to feel their power was John Balfour at Colinton Station. His stock arrived on 19 August 1841 and for the next five weeks he claimed that he enjoyed friendly relations with the Aboriginal owners. They ended abruptly when on 27 September one of his outstations was attacked 'by a large body of blacks from about 3500'. This is an extraordinarily large figure, which was not questioned by Commandant Gorman when he forwarded Balfour's concerns to Sydney, but it is not out of the question given the Aboriginal population of south-east Queensland. We know that Ubie Ubie of the Dalla was a warrior elder of great influence but his lands were said to reach no further south and west than Kilcoy Station. Much further south was renowned fighting chief Moppy of the Yaggera, who was said to be able to call upon 1200 fighting men.[6] Between Moppy and Ubie Ubie were more Dalla mountain people, the Garumngar of the D'Aguilar Range, whose tree-covered uplands enabled the fighting men to obtain cover and refuge from mounted and armed Europeans.

The attack on Colinton was probably a combined assault; it certainly seemed well-coordinated. Balfour claimed 1100 sheep were stolen on this first day, followed by an attack on another of his runs the next day, when he fired 'repeatedly upon them'. On the third day the Dalla set fire to the grass, forced four shepherds to retreat to their hut and stole another 150 sheep. Balfour had to retreat to McConnel's station—his men refused to remain at Colinton. He headed to Brisbane to appeal to the colonial government, but not before first leading a counter-raid on a Dalla camp. His official communication with the colonial government mentioned this only in passing so it is impossible to know who was at the camp, when it took place or what level of violence was applied, but Balfour reported that he succeeded in retrieving more than 900 sheep.[7]

It is likely that lives were lost during Balfour's return of fire on 28 September or during his counter-raid, for interracial violence escalated in October when warriors speared shepherds at Kilcoy and Cressbrook stations. On 26 October Gorman reported that one of these men lay dangerously ill in the Brisbane convict hospital.[8] The Yaggera continued their attacks too, killing two European station workers on their lands to the south in the same month, in retaliation for the Europeans' theft of 400 sheets of roofing materials from one of their villages.[9] The lead up to Christmas Day in December 1841 must have been a tense time for the European pastoral workers.

While all this was going on, back at Girkum the German mission took no time out from their evangelising, spending part of their days giving religious instruction to the children at the Girkum camp. Meanwhile, the Dalla prepared for the bunya season as usual, sending invitations to friends far to the north. The perplexing white newcomers were an added fascination of the 1841 Bunya meeting and large numbers from other tribal groups travelled from as far north as the Burnett River catchment to camp on Ubie Ubie's lands. The northerners must have been intrigued by the contrasting attitudes of their neighbours. While the Yaggera and Dalla had been engaging in raids against the European settlers, the Ningy Ningy had been hosting three of the German brethren—Franz, Zillmann and Hausmann—at Toorbul, Pine River and Redcliffe.[10] Clearly these white people required considerable study.

Tom Archer's account of the long and patient surveillance of the Europeans by the Dalla and their visitors at neighbouring Durundur gives a sense of the anxiety that it provoked among the Europeans: 'When the news of our arrival spread abroad they came down upon us in great numbers to have a look at the "white fellows" ... scores ... would sit round and look at us for hours, and at night withdraw to their camp, a mile or two off, only to repeat the operation next day.'[11] The Archers were so unnerved that Tom claims his brothers ordered additional armaments from Sydney. Their salvation was Paddy of the eastern Dalla who, like Deciby at Toorbul, explained to visitors that these Europeans were under his protection.

On neighbouring Kilcoy Station, convict pastoral workers and inexperienced Scottish labourers were left on their own to deal with this influx of strangers, for the station owner, Evan Mackenzie, was absent in January and February 1842.[12] The shepherds' response was drastic: scores of Aboriginal visitors were poisoned in a mass killing on or about 5 February 1842.[13] Missionaries Niqué and Rodé first received news of the massacre on 16 March 1842 when encamped with the Ningy Ningy at Redcliffe; by the time they returned to the Nundah Mission on 31 March, they found rumours of the tragedy had already reached Brisbane.[14] The mission's close contact with the Dalla and the return of two runaway convicts from the north further confirmed events in the months that followed. The Dalla's version was that the northern peoples had asked the shepherds for flour, sugar and tobacco, about which they had heard such wonderful reports. The shepherds had obliged by sharing flour after mixing it with arsenic. Since it was the women's role to make bread cakes each evening, the first victims of the poisoned flour might well have been their children. The convict escapee James Davis, in the account he provided to officials on his return to Brisbane in May 1842, however, reported that he understood that his Gubbi Gubbi people had been given poisoned mutton and that three of his own brothers were among the dead; while Lang claims that natives told Reverend Schmidt in June 1842 that they had been given 'a large quantity of hominy or maize meal pudding'.[15] It is quite possible all accounts are correct and that the shepherds had put poison in various rations that they distributed. Whatever the precise source, all versions agree that a large number of men, women and children died: two Europeans who had been adopted into traditional culture—the runaway convicts Bracewell[16] and Davis—guessed thirty, and between fifty and sixty, respectively.[17]

The men of the Brisbane River Valley wasted little time in responding. Within days, on 15 or 16 February, three of their best fighting men—Monday, Commandant and King Billy—were said to have been part of a group that launched a sneak attack upon two Kilcoy shepherds, taking them by surprise near 'their usual watering place'.[18] David McConnel described all three warriors as 'very strong men', but it was Commandant who instilled the most dread among the Europeans, for he was 6 foot 3 inches tall and 'strong in proportion'.[19] After killing the pastoral workers the three warriors rifled through their possessions, and a fob watch that had belonged to one of the shepherds was passed from tribe to tribe until it reached the father of three of the victims, Pamby Pamby; he was now, in the eyes of the traditional owners, 'the rightful owner'.[20]

But the grief over deaths on such a scale could not be so easily assuaged. The system of governance that operated across south-east Queensland regarded avenging injury as essential. The system of payback was intrinsic to the balance of power and to the rights of tribal nations. If a man did not avenge a wrong against himself or his brother or people, what was to stop his enemy stealing his wives, his daughters, his game and his lands until he was left without the sustenance of life? Ancestral law and political reality required all unnatural and unforeseen deaths to be repaid in kind, and the peoples of the region had developed elaborate inquest practices to determine guilt in such cases.

The dual Bunya festivals created a shared culture among tribal nations who lived almost 1000 kilometres apart, from the Kamilaroi and Bundjalung in the south to the Darumbal near present-day Rockhampton in the north. There were variations in inquest processes even among neighbours within this area, but there was general agreement on the principle of identifying the culprit by listening to messages from the dead. The Pine River peoples did not hold an inquiry until the body had decomposed and the female relatives had separated and claimed the bones of their dead kin. Then a meeting would be held and the female elder would sit in the middle of the gathering and chant the names of the accused, hitting the bones with a tomahawk as she did so. A simultaneous crack in the bones proved the guilt of the person whose name had been sung.[21] Among their coastal neighbours the dead whispered the name of the guilty party to the gundir as attendants held up the dead person's skin on two spears and carried it around the assembly.[22] These processes are not unlike coronial practices from other parts of Australia[23] and share the underlying belief in the desire of the dead to be avenged and the righteousness of such retaliation, whatever the differences in ritual detail. As Tom Petrie's daughter Constance noted, 'Father has been present on these occasions, and the blacks would always draw his attention to the unquestionableness of the conclusion arrived at. Nothing could persuade them that it was not fair, and should they come across the poor unfortunate singled out his death was a certainty.'[24] There was thus wide agreement about the moral precepts and laws that operated in the case of murder; once guilt had been determined, the victim's male next of kin—usually one's biological brother (or skin brother where there was no biological one), or uncle in the case of young children—must avenge the death.

The law was unequivocal but not rigid. Regional politics and diplomacy meant that the process of enacting punishment could take months or even years. It required group agreement about the guilty party and agreement about what was reasonable retaliation. The most drawn out process was when a killing required a revenge party. In such a case the next of kin needed to build alliances with others who shared the legal obligation or at least the sense of hurt and who could be trusted in such a risky undertaking. They also needed to be sure of community support; too severe a response could trigger a feud and spread discord throughout a region. Traditional law had a number of measures to prevent righteous payback escalating into interminable feuds, one of which was group agreement about who was responsible for avenging a death and how severe a penalty should apply. Commandant, King Billy (a Jagera man and Mulrobbin's father), Monday and others may have exacted two European lives immediately, but fifty or sixty deaths would require much higher payback.

Rather than take unilateral action, Ubie Ubie's first response was to call a meeting of all the Dalla and their coastal neighbours at meeting grounds near Durundur Station. So that the summons could go out to the Dalla at the far flung reaches of their lands, the meeting was called for about eight weeks after the mass poisoning, five weeks after word had reached the Ningy Ningy at Redcliffe. The convict runaways Bracewell and Davis explained this gathering for the commissioner of crown lands: 'The meeting is called a Toor (Ring) by the Blacks from the circumstance of a circular ditch of varying dimensions being dug by the Women for the ceremony. It is summoned by any Tribe, as occasion may require, for the purpose of settling disputes which may arise among them.'[25]

Paddy and his people, who had allowed the Archers onto their lands, approached the meeting with trepidation. Would Ubie Ubie accuse them of being the cause of these deaths? Or were the Jarbu and their allies going to demand retaliation on all whites, including those on whom Paddy had bestowed his favour and protection? Since some of them, like Anbaybury, had become the blood brothers of whites, would they be held accountable for the deaths?

The participants began arriving at Durundur Station on 11 April and the nervousness of the local traditional owner group was immediately apparent. The missionary clergyman Christopher Eipper was visiting Durundur Station at David Archer's invitation and his scant journal notes hint at the growing anxiety of the local people. They repeatedly sought David Archer's intervention as a means of removing their challengers. 'The natives have come in to say that the murderers of Mr McKenzie's two shepherds, whose names they mentioned, are at the camp, and that they would entice them to the station that Mr A. might secure them; but they never came near', he noted. Two days later he recorded that at least five tribes had gathered at the station, but unfortunately does not name them. The following day commenced with verbal jousts which suddenly flared into a full-blown fight and the wounding of a 'Salt Water native'. As he was carried from the field the Durundur people again appealed to David Archer to intervene and arrest the man who they insisted was one of the group who had killed the shepherds at Kilcoy.[26]

So who were these 'Mwoirnewar' (the Dalla name for coastal peoples or 'Saltwater')? They appear to be Yanmonday's people from the Sunshine Coast and perhaps, too, Joondaburri from Bribie Island. Perhaps the confident young men who had stolen Parry, Dabianco and Gavanmary's daughters were now working with King Billy and Commandant's people. Eipper's record is too spare to help resolve these questions but Dundalli must have been among the assembly of Dalla watching this power struggle unfold and the ground shift among the different member groups of the Dalla and their neighbours.

The fight resumed the next morning before the white station workers were even aware. Paddy's Durundur people were beaten on the field and messages were hastily sent to David Archer, who was off working in the woolshed, but by the time he arrived at the Toor the action had swung dramatically again. Ubie Ubie's brother, Burumballi, who had struck the accused Saltwater man on the previous day, was targeted in the morning's fight and now fell on the field, pierced by three spears and with a heavy blow to his head. The battle was over, the coastal people and their allies were victorious and the 'enemy left immediately for the coast and the mountains'. Ubie Ubie, who was also injured, was left to bewail his young brother, 'a fine young man' according to Eipper.[27] He retreated to his mountain homelands. Loyally, Paddy's Durundur people appear to have taken up Ubie Ubie's cause; after a few days' recovery they left to fight the Jarbu who had allied with the Saltwater at the recent fight. They were away from the station from 18 to 25 April, avenging Burumballi's death.[28]

The Gubbi Gubbi and their allies had also suffered at the Kilcoy poisoning, and their large meeting to discuss their response was called for 6 May 1842, twelve weeks later. The news of the disaster had had to travel 220 kilometres to the lands of the Bundaberg hinterland and then messengers had to follow with the call for a regional assembly at present-day Tiaro on the banks of the Mary River, 130 kilometres north of Kilcoy. The main witness for these events is the convict runaway James Davis, who was initiated into traditional society under the name of Duramboi. In his report to the commissioner of crown lands on his return to Brisbane in May 1842, Davis explained that he lived initially with the Gubbi Gubbi on the Mary River for about twelve months in 1829–30 but then travelled 60 miles (100 kilometres) northwards along the coast until he came to a major river; this he followed roughly 60 miles (100 kilometres) into the interior where he joined a traditional owner group estimated as 150 strong. One of the fighting men, Pamby Pamby, believed that this strong young white man was his dead son returned to life, so he was adopted into the tribe with the totem and moiety of Pamby Pamby's son, enabling him to live with them for the next twelve years.[29] Davis's description suggests that his adopted home was the Bundaberg hinterland in the Burnett catchment; the name he gave of 'Ginginburrah' is no longer identifiable but fits with Tindale's description of the lands of the Taribelang.[30] He was just thirty years of age, having escaped from Moreton Bay Penal Establishment at the age of seventeen on 30 March 1829.[31]

When another convict runaway, Bracewell, came upon the Tiaro gathering on 13 May he was taken aback at its size; hundreds were assembled at what he said was the largest tribal congress he had seen in many years—and that didn't even include his adopted people from the Cooloola Coast. Duramboi's people were one of fourteen or fifteen tribes that had met to collect intelligence on the mass poisoning. The survivors gave detailed reports on the effects of consuming the provisions they had received from the white men, and dramatically re-enacted the 'swelling of the head, foaming at the mouth, violent retching ... trembling ... and sudden prostration'. Among the five or so peoples who had gathered at Durundur in April and the fifteen or so tribal nations at Tiaro in May, 'nine or ten tribes', according to Duramboi, had lost family members. Inter-group initiation ceremonies that bound the participating young men as brothers, as well as patterns of inter-marriage across the region, meant that it was unlikely that any of those present did not feel a personal sense of loss as well as some legal obligation to avenge the dead. So the gatherings were not just to inform but also to win allies with the goal of retaliation on behalf of dead friends and family. To this end the Tiaro meeting was successful, for Bracewell and Davis reported back in Brisbane that 'these tribes vowed vengeance and said that they had already had some, but were not yet satisfied'.[32]

The account of this May meeting, like the Durundur one in April, ends abruptly. The main witness, Duramboi, decided to decamp with a party of Europeans led by Tom Petrie's father, Andrew, who had unexpectedly sailed into the riverside gathering. Petrie's expedition had been instigated by Governor Gipps during his week's visit to Brisbane in March 1842. Aware of the importance of the bunya forests to the traditional owners of the region, Gipps had given instructions that pastoral leases were not to be granted there and requested that Petrie, as superintendent of works at Moreton Bay, investigate the extent of the bunya pine's range.[33] Despite Gipps's aim of protecting traditional owners from squatters' incursions into their most important lands, Petrie invited three young men on a quest for fresh pastoral lands to join his government-sponsored expedition. So it was that the pastoralists Henry Russell and Walter Wrottesley, and Captain Joliffe, the agent for John Eales, a large landowner and one of the wealthiest men in New South Wales, were witnesses to the extensive process of law in south-east Queensland. Despite witnessing these remarkable scenes Joliffe would again cross the path of Gubbi Gubbi justice, for on his return to Brisbane he immediately commenced plans for claiming a lease on Eales's behalf on the very lands where the northern Toor had been held, and for transferring 16 000 of Eales's sheep to Moreton Bay en route to Wide Bay.[34]

The 1842 meetings appear to have ended without any firm commitment for joint action for the time being, but the inland peoples continued their campaigns to evict the Europeans while the eastern peoples continued to strive for accommodation of them. Within only a few weeks of the Durundur meeting an out-station worker at the Bigges' Mount Brisbane Station was killed. Henry Mort, the superintendent of Cressbrook, which was only 24 kilometres away, set out with some of the station staff to arrest the men responsible. They captured two men at one of their cattle stations who named Commandant, Monday, King Billy and others as responsible for this new attack. On 27 June 1842, Mort persuaded these three men and a small boy accompanying them to voluntarily come in to Cressbrook Station to assist in the search for the killers.

At this time David McConnel, the owner of Cressbrook, was all of twenty-four years old and his mood readily inflamed by reports of Aboriginal activity anywhere near his station. McConnel had been away when Mort had gone out seeking the men but his presence with eleven other white men at the station's main hut appears to have alerted Commandant, King Billy and Monday to the danger of their position. David's letter to his brother Henry is glib in its passing references to the brutality that followed:

> they became desperate & being very strong men, they all broke loose; so we fired on them; killed one, Commandant, a fellow 6ft 3 high & strong in proportion on the spot, stabbed one twice with a bayonet, put 4 balls into him besides, & 2 balls into the third; the 2 latter got off, but I am sure, could not go far; the boy got out by the chimney at the commencement, no one touching him.[35]

He was wrong, at least about Monday, who was definitely alive and at Redcliffe when the missionaries visited in November 1842.[36] Commandant's death was a terrible loss, however, and McConnel makes no mention of how the station disposed of the body. When the explorer Ludwig Leichhardt visited Cressbrook in November 1843 he found that Commandant had been beheaded and his skull retained by Mort, who embellished the story of his death by claiming that he had killed Commandant in hand-to-hand combat.[37] McConnel's failure to return Commandant's body to his people for the mourning and funeral rites must have accentuated the grief for the warrior's female kin.

The killing was reported to Dr Stephen Simpson, the commissioner of crown lands for the pastoral district of Moreton Bay and the leading government official over this wide area. He indicated to his superiors that an inquiry was to be held, although the depositions never reached the Crown Law Office.[38] 'The next morning', David wrote,

> I removed my sheep & men from the outstations apprehensive of danger & brought them to the headstation. The same day the tribe from which these blacks came, sneaked upon & killed barbarously a hutkeeper a watchman of Balfour's, & came to my outstation but found the place fortunately deserted & broke open the door, & robbed a few small articles lying about.[39]

McConnel might have viewed this killing as 'barbarous' but the warriors were operating according to the ancient laws of the region; McConnel, on the other hand, was disdainful of his own country's legal code and was intent on forceful dispossession. 'When ever they camp on this run, it is our intention, if we can, to drive them off by powder & ball', he explained further in his letter to his brother.

The heroic Commandant had led attacks at the Balfours' Colinton in 1841, enacted payback against the two Kilcoy shepherds immediately after the mass poisoning and killed another station worker at Mount Brisbane. The fighting men of the Dalla of the D'Aguilar Range and Yaggera would have to replace him if their campaign to remove the pastoral stations from their lands was to succeed. In outlook Dundalli hardly seemed the man to do it, despite his excellent physical attributes. Events from September 1841 to late 1842 appear to have unnerved the confident young negotiator of August 1841. On 15 November 1842 Dundalli returned an axe he had taken from missionary Johan Hausmann in March. Despite the great value of an axe in the forests of his homeland, Dundalli had scarcely used it, returning it in very good condition.[40] According to the mission diary Dundalli 'seemed to be very much afraid, regretting that he had stolen'. Perhaps his fear stemmed from the local people's belief that the missionaries' books were a source of sorcery that enabled the missionaries to see events happening far away. This belief had come about because of a discussion between two of the brethren, one of whom was reading a book at the time, about the theft of an axe belonging to a third missionary. When the man reading had been able to name the suspect without looking up, the Ningy Ningy had interpreted this mysterious power as coming from the book.[41]

To be able to fulfil the role as Commandant's replacement, Dundalli would have to undergo further training and mental preparation. It fell to a Bribie Island man of amazing strength, Cambayo, to coach Dundalli in the arts of law enforcement and refocus his attitudes now that all the peoples of the south-east were reassessing their opinions of the white presence. This included Deciby's people, who had worked so closely with the mission since 1839. They took Christopher Eipper and Johan Hausmann with them to Redcliffe on 22 November 1842. Eipper was optimistic at the start of the journey, reporting the men's attentive responses to Hausmann's evangelising, but the Ningy Ningy were becoming less tolerant of missionary demands. The clergyman sought to finish his report on a positive note about their religious efforts but even here he reflected that

> The intelligence of a squatter's dray having passed down to Wide Bay River [the Mary] was to them a matter of much greater importance than all the new & strange things we had told them; it crossed their conversation for two or three nights, while scarcely any mention was made of what they had heard from us.[42]

If Ningy Ningy generosity had been tested in November 1842 it was stretched to the limit by December. The excitement of the newcomers of mid-1841 had given way to disgust and horror at their violence.

The Bunya council of December 1842–January 1843 was eagerly awaited as a period to share information about them and deliberate on some of their transgressions of the past year. Unaware of the significance of this year's Bunya assembly to local Aboriginal people, three days after Christmas Reverend Schmidt and missionary Rodé set out for Toorbul with a heavy sense of Christian duty. The five Aboriginal men, one woman and one child who helped to carry their provisions and show them the way were also weighed down with internal tensions. They were concerned that no invitation had yet been extended to them to attend the Bunya meeting and festivities that were already underway and this exclusion aggrieved them. Among their group was Yilbung, who had cooperated with the mission only under Deciby's duress. By December 1842 Yilbung was beginning to win the debate among Deciby's people, who were no longer punishing him for offences against the mission. Schmidt and Rodé had concluded it was better to engage him as a bearer than to leave him at Girkum, where he was sure to steal from their houses and gardens.[43]

The missionaries were keen to get to Toorbul, where they were expecting to find a large gathering of coastal people, but their guides kept taking sidetracks. It seems that Yilbung and his friends had not bothered to explain to the missionaries that everyone was away at the Bunya gathering and as each day went by their tolerance of the missionaries dwindled further. The next morning they disrupted the Europeans' morning prayers, refusing to be silent, and smoking, laughing and doing 'just what they liked, so that we had to commence also this day with sorrow', Schmidt recorded. 'One even lifted up his tomahawk against me, when I told him to be quiet, whilst we were speaking with God.' That evening Yilbung refused to say grace as a condition of receiving some of the missionaries' provisions and defiantly informed Schmidt that God was 'not in the bush'. In response to the missionaries' complaints their guides led them on a particularly arduous route to Sandstone Point, which took them through river mud up to their knees and over long sandy flats. It was a hot and steamy December–January but they had no choice but to persist through thunderstorms and plagues of mosquitoes and flies. By the third day Schmidt's skin was covered in blisters from insect bites.

They were relieved to finally arrive at a permanent village with well-constructed huts, but disappointed to find only a couple of adults there. One was Deciby's friend and ally Dabianco, well known to the mission and brother to Rodé. He bore them bad news—Yilbung had been stealing from their provisions throughout the journey so that Schmidt was left with only a few cups of flour. Significantly, Dabianco did not seek to counteract Yilbung's influence over the group. When Schmidt fell ill and Rodé chose to confront Yilbung over his theft, the missionaries reached the lowest point of their journey. An unrepentant Yilbung used his fighting stick to challenge Rodé to fight and no one in the camp interfered but 'some rather followed his example in mocking at us'. There was one benefit from the journey. Schmidt finally learnt how the Ningy Ningy understood the Germans' evangelical travels: 'the adults suppose, we make journeys for mere pleasure's sake or to survey the land and to feast with them upon fish and oysters etc' he recorded. So dejected was he by the realisation of how little impact the mission had had after three years in the field that he was incapable of responding to this revelation with any feeling of gratitude or appreciation of the extraordinary hospitality and generosity shown to them by the Ningy Ningy, who had guided and fed nine missionaries on at least fifteen different journeys through their lands.[44]

There were clues as to other reasons why the Ningy Ningy were on edge over these weeks. After the evening confrontation with Yilbung over his refusal to say grace, the camp sang their 'Cry for the Dead', a mourning song, as the missionaries termed it, for 'a brother of one of our guides, who had died more than 9 months since'. Yilbung had been with the group who first brought news of the Kilcoy poisoning to the Ningy Ningy at Redcliffe on 16 March

1842[45] and it was natural that their thoughts would have returned to the Kilcoy killings, given that the proceedings in the mountains were probably reconsidering these matters at that very time. Finally, on the evening of 4 January, a messenger arrived from the Dalla to invite the last of the Ningy Ningy to the Bunya council. The Bora no longer regarded Yilbung and his supporters as personae non gratae. Excited and relieved, the group was keen to be rid of the missionaries, who were promptly returned to Nundah via shorter paths so they could get to the Bunya gathering.[46]

The Bunya Tour of December 1842–January 1843 was one of the largest ever. We know that distant peoples who had never come into contact with whites attended, because they visited Durundur Station where a female servant recorded a quite remarkable encounter with them. On 27 January she wrote in her diary:

> Today, when the men were all away, Binjy, one of our black boys, came shouting to me to 'look out.' I ran to the door, and saw about twenty blacks almost up the hill, and at the station. They were in full war paint, and carried spears, nulla-nullas, and waddies, and were quite naked. No gins were with them—they say that when the blacks mean mischief they always leave the gins at home—my knees quaked together. I begged Binjy to stay with me, and before I could turn round the blacks were in my kitchen, and the room was full of them. It was too late even for me to hide behind the door. They were the first naked blacks I had seen. Some of them were fine fierce fellows. Binjy was very friendly with them. I could see he was advising them to go away quietly, and avoid serious trouble. They pointed to me, and spoke about me, and Binjy described the wonderful strength of some man—my husband, I suppose. He lifted a chair, and threw it violently on the ground, and pretended to swing an axe round and round his head with terrible swiftness.

They laughed, and jeered, and pushed forward a big, powerful fellow. I never longed so much before to hear the stockwhips of our men coming home over the creek. The big man stepped back. Then Binjy said they wanted to see my hair. I took out the hairpins, and let my hair, long, fair, and wavy, fall about me. It caused a good deal of admiration. In the middle of it Binjy raised the alarm that the men were coming, and got the blacks outside. I flew to barricade the doors and windows. But Binjy came back soon to say he had got them away quietly by leading them with presents from the store. We had a great tale to tell when the men came home.[47]

We only have the young Scottish diarist's interpretation that these distant men 'admired' her hair but the interracial fascination and curiosity seem genuine. The body paint indicates that they were either on their way to or from formal proceedings and the date also fits with the winding up of that year's Bunya Toor. By 23 January Yilbung was back at the mission.[48]

It seems that the Bunya Toor had now agreed upon payback for the Kilcoy poisonings because 1843 began with a number of assaults upon whites. In March James Davis guided Commissioner Simpson and Reverend Eipper north along Aboriginal pathways to investigate possible new sites for a mission. In the region of present-day Gympie, Davis met Worumillo, an old Gubbi Gubbi friend, who informed him that now that the Bunya Toor was over, the process of evicting whites was to resume.[49] It had recommenced in February 1843 when a shepherd was killed at Kilcoy; the Gubbi Gubbi then killed four station workers at Eales' station at Wide Bay in April. (Another had been wounded in March but Reverend Eipper was remarkably unsympathetic—it turned out that the man had 'forcibly abused a Black woman'.[50]) In July the Yaggera killed a man named Worthington at John Canning Pearce's station at Helidon. Even the Archers were not exempt from Aboriginal justice. The spearing of a worker there in April in Dundalli's own country was the first expression of his new status and marked a turning point in his life.⁵¹

A cool and clear autumn morning dawned on 24 April 1843. William Vant's mate had already taken his sheep out to graze but Vant, as hutkeeper, was keen to keep the fire outside their hut stoked. At about eight o'clock Dundalli, led by the older Cambayo, a Joondaburri man from Bribie Island, approached the out-station. As Vant bent to put another log on the coals, Cambayo's spear struck Vant's left shoulder blade and penetrated diagonally through to his right hip. Dundalli immediately followed, throwing his spear at Vant. Vant claimed he was able to catch Dundalli's spear in his hand, although they were a mere eight feet [2.5 metres] apart. Perhaps Dundalli lost his nerve at the sight of Vant's gun leaning against the hut. The deed done, the two men hastily left for the coast. Injured, Vant could only wait for his mate to return and fetch help. Remarkably Cambayo's spear must have missed crucial internal organs. It took more than four hours for the shepherd to report the attack to the head station, just as the Archer brothers were sitting down to dinner with their guest Christopher Eipper. The clergyman headed out to the hut to dress Vant's wound and stay with him until he could be moved to the head station, where the Archers' neighbour and magistrate, Evan Mackenzie, issued a warrant for Cambayo and Dundalli's arrest.⁵²

Tom and David Archer did not commence a pursuit of the two men until the following day. Although they started out on horseback they sent their mounts back to the station after realising the two men had gone east into swampy country. A young Indigenous man from Durundur and 'Niguer' (probably the man the missionaries called 'Nicker') helped with tracking and discovered Dundalli encamped with several other Dalla from Durundur Station. Alerted to their approach, Dundalli took off and although Tom pursued, he admitted in his memoirs that he 'had not the faintest chance of catching' him.

Back at the camp, an armed and angry David Archer was informed by the intimidated Durundur men that Cambayo had headed in the direction of Mount Beerwah; they then agreed to accompany the brothers in storming Cambayo's camp. Tom's account, told with all the bravado of later years, does not hide the brutality of Cambayo's arrest, which included the colonial practice of tying a noose around his neck while his friends and family watched in 'petrified' horror because David Archer's gun was pointed at them.[53] In 1843 terms, and in contrast with most of his squatting neighbours, David Archer had made a legal arrest.

The next day Cambayo was taken by the Archer brothers to Brisbane for the committal hearing but as there was neither a gaol nor court facilities in Brisbane in 1843, he was then sent 1000 kilometres south to Sydney. In the 1840s the judges of the New South Wales Supreme Court travelled on circuit to the country towns of Maitland, Berrima and Parramatta and, as Maitland was the closest town to Brisbane, the authorities scheduled Cambayo's case to be tried there at the assize to commence on 13 September, even though it required another sea journey backtracking 250 kilometres northwards.

Cambayo's only support, or rather the only familiar face, at the trial was Christopher Eipper, who was subpoenaed to attend as a witness for the crown, not for Cambayo, but presumably it was the clergyman who acted as Cambayo's interpreter. His only recorded words in court were 'that he did not do it—white people told lies'. His defence counsel argued that since Vant's wounds had healed so well the charge of intent to kill could not be sustained, but the judge disagreed. The jury took only a few minutes to return a verdict of guilty and the judge passed a sentence of death.[54] Judge Stephen told Eipper that he was considering sending Cambayo back to the scene of the crime to be hanged at Durundur Station so that the gruesome death would act as a warning to others.[55] Cambayo awaited his fate in Newcastle Gaol. In the end the judge commuted the sentence to three years' gaol which, according to Police Magistrate Wickham, was served at Cockatoo Island. He was later joined there by the Yaggera man Mickey Mickey, who was found guilty of attacks at Tenthill Station in September 1843.[56]

However the Vant attack was viewed by British law, it also raises interesting questions about the processes of traditional law. Were eastern Dalla and Joondaburri payback for the Kilcoy poisonings now paid? It does seem that the Vant attack was an intentionally measured attack. The use of non-barbed spears and the choice of one Dalla and one Joondaburri man point to a symbolic value in the attack. Despite the close working relationship the Durundur Dalla had with the Archers, the Dalla clearly did not disapprove of the attack on Vant, as they had been happily encamped with Dundalli the following day. It is intriguing to note that the Archers were accompanied by Dalla men in the search and that Dundalli was alerted to their discovery of his camp, while the Joondaburri man was not so fortunate. Nonetheless, it was Tom who conducted the actual physical chase and capture. Assistance from Aboriginal people, including Paddy's people, was qualified. They did not disagree with the justice of Cambayo and Dundalli's actions and Archer's account makes clear the sense of threat that Aboriginal people experienced when armed white men rushed into a family's camp. The ability of Indigenous people to remain on good terms with Europeans yet happily endorse traditional payback against them would repeatedly perplex the Europeans, who persisted in branding it as treachery.

Unfortunately there is little further material to help interpret the relationship between Cambayo and Dundalli, but following Cambayo's arrest Dundalli became identified with the Bribie Islanders in the colonial literature. It was no longer safe for him to remain in close proximity to the Archers, or any other Europeans, and the island provided safe seclusion; in addition, the Joondaburri would have welcomed the addition of a strong young man such as

Dundalli in Cambayo's absence. The sources are contradictory in regard to the size of the community on Yarun, as its owners called it. John Uniacke, a member of John Oxley's exploration party, reported that they numbered just under seventy people in 1823[57] but Andrew Petrie, who first went to the island in 1837, made passing comment on how numerous the Indigenous inhabitants were.[58] Commissioner Simpson reported that their standard of living was higher than those of the inland, owing to 'more ample means of existence in the abundance of fish on the coast; they are consequently less migratory in their habits and in general of a more mild and humane disposition'. He estimated the Bribie people at 'about 200'.[59] The island stretches 34 kilometres north to south, with low coastal dunes and an expansive surf beach on the east. Just 8 kilometres to the west is Pumicestone Passage, which divides it from the mainland. This marine environment was rich in food sources—not just fish but also oysters, turtles and dugong. In the winter, the Joondaburri would move to their permanent village on the western side of the island where they lived on their bread cakes, made from flour ground from a native fern; a native fruit named dulandella; kangaroos, pademelons, possums and wild fowl.[60]

At the end of the long overland trek from the Castlereagh to Durundur, on a clear winter's day in 1841, Tom Archer was awestruck by the beauty of Bribie Island and the bay. His prospect was from the top of Mount Beerwah, where he had been led by a local Dalla man:

> Never have I forgotten the magnificent view that met our gaze, when, after half an hour's scramble, we reached the top. Nearly the whole of Moreton Bay district lay spread out beneath us, and about a dozen miles to the eastward of us was 'the sea, the sea, the open sea,' glittering in the sunlight, with Briby's Island, Moreton Island, and Moreton Bay to the south, and a hundred miles of coast stretching away to the north.[61]

The traditional owners of Yarun agreed that their island was 'a perfect paradise'—a sentiment which a naturalist, possibly the young Thomas Huxley or John MacGillivray, apparently shared.[62]

Bribie Island is important not only as Dundalli's new home but also as a gauge of changes in politics among the traditional owners of the region. In 1823 Uniacke had reported the generosity of the Bribie Islanders and their compassion for the castaway cedar-getter Thomas Pamphlett, so that the unexpected arrival of the explorer John Oxley—the surveyor general of New South Wales at the time—and his party on their island in November 1823 was met not with aggression but elation on the part of the Joondaburri. In his official report of his shipwreck and rescue, Pamphlett elaborated on the local people's warmth and hospitality: 'Their behaviour to me and my companions had been so invariably kind and generous, that, notwithstanding the delight I felt at the idea of once more returning to my home, I did not leave them without sincere regret.'[63] As a result of the Joondaburri's characteristic openness, Bribie Island was regularly visited during convict days[64] and Commissioner Simpson spoke favourably of their interaction with the Nundah Mission in his official reports.[65]

This view of the island was completely turned on its head as the 1840s progressed. Constance Petrie gives a number of instances of Aboriginal murderers fleeing to, or hailing from, Bribie Island in the 1840s and 1850s.[66] While in 1843 Commissioner Simpson had reported positively of the influence of civilisation on the Bribie Islanders, by 1847 he was acknowledging that 'the Aborigines of the Coast are less tractable & the German Mission & the three Stations nearest to the coast have all ... suffered from their marauding propensities'.[67] An 1848 gentleman visitor provides the most detailed account of how the outlook of the people of Yarun had changed. In this commentator's view,

> They are very selfish, more so, perhaps, than any of their countrymen, refusing to part with a single fish, which they catch in great

quantities with their tow-rows, unless they receive an equivalent in flour and sugar ... I lost nothing by them, though many things were, in the course of my three nights' stay, lying about in every direction. I do not think, however, that their ferocity has been misrepresented, and had we not exercised due caution, I have no doubt we should have been attacked ... The news of Government having given away blankets at the settlement seemed to please the natives very much; their greatest desire, however, was to obtain one or two harpoons, for the purpose of capturing the youngon, or sea-pig, which abounds in that part of the bay.

These parts of his description suggest a people worldly-wise to the exploitative ways of Europeans and only interested in trade on their own terms. The conclusion to the article returns to his theme of 'ferocity':

Visitors should be extremely cautious of venturing among the blacks who inhabit this part of the Bay, as the slightest indiscretion or want of proper watchfulness may cost the party their lives, for the tribe is fierce and treacherous; vindictive and cruel; they are, moreover, known to be exceedingly jealous of the intrusion of the white man on their territory.[68]

As the Joondaburri's political stance moved from enthusiastic accommodation to wariness toward the white newcomers, their relations with their southern neighbours were tested and their group cohesion strengthened. Joondaburri architecture was modified accordingly. Again the gentleman visitor of 1848 provides the best detail:

they have fixed habitations, dwelling in little villages of six or seven huts in a cluster. Some of them are of great length, extending upwards of eighty feet, and covering a considerable space of ground ... One of them was in the form of a passage, with two apartments at the end. The arches were beautifully turned, and executed with a degree of skill which would not have disgraced an [sic] European architect. In one of these apartments the chief of the family resides; in the other the married people, and the young men claim the passage as their proper dormitory ... It is in these snuggeries that the doings of the day, and the plans for the morrow are discussed and managed. Thus boxed up, morally and physically, secure from the intrusions of the white men, these blessed people build up a universe in their savage Lilliputian community. It is here they estimate their neighbours, white and black, by the only known standard, their own. The biggest man and the loudest talker is the greatest among them. These habitations serve their purposes admirably.[69]

This was the community that Dundalli joined in April 1843 after the attack at Durundur, and where his leadership would be developed.

In the remaining months of 1843, as Dundalli adjusted to his new life on Bribie, momentous events were unfolding in the Brisbane Valley. The great Moppy had died in a collision with whites. We have no precise account of when or where but legend says that even 'when mortally wounded he hung on to a sapling and waved his tribe on to continue the fight.'[70] Circumstances suggest this was sometime in mid-1842 but it could have been as late as mid-1843; his three sons vowed vengeance. From September to October 1843 it reached crisis point, with Commissioner Simpson reporting that the Yaggera men had 'formed a plan of intercepting all communication by the high road to the Darling Downs'. Their successes in the opening weeks of September increased their confidence so that by the 12th they had driven off fourteen white men employed to protect dray transports, seized three drays and appropriated the contents, and set up a blockade of the main road so that they could throw rocks at any whites who attempted to pass.[71] Three white men were killed at Tenthill and Tarampa stations in the same month, bringing the European death toll for the Moreton Bay district to ten, as well as four non-fatal spearings, in a twelve-month period.[72]

The governor responded quickly, authorising one sergeant and twelve men of the 99th Regiment to be stationed at Lockyer Creek, near present-day Helidon, on 14 October 1843.[73] However the Yaggera simply moved their attention to the east, focusing on European activity at Rosewood and continuing to harass the stations throughout the Brisbane Valley.

One who became caught up in the conflict was the explorer Ludwig Leichhardt, who had left Durundur Station on 24 October 1843 to collect natural history specimens and undertake geological exploration through the Brisbane Valley. On 28 October he was stuck at an out-station of the Bigges as 'the Blacks are making the whole area so dangerous that I risk no large excursions'.[74] The Yaggera, Dalla and Gubbi Gubbi were all cooperating in the attacks. The northern Dalla had made it clear as early as June 1842 that their intention was to 'revenge themselves on the whites, whenever they may happen to meet them'.[75] Now it seemed the Yaggera would reinforce this commitment after the death of Moppy. Commissioner Simpson blamed the 'Mountain tribes, perhaps not less than from 1500 to 2000 souls, extending from the Wide Bay Range to beyond Cunningham's Gap'[76] for the escalation of hostilities in 1843, which continued throughout 1844. That winter was a wet one, making it harder for the Brisbane Valley squatters to respond to the repeated dispersal of their stock.[77]

Nearer the coast, the mission was also feeling the growing hostility. Whatever had been decided at the Toor of December 1842–January 1843, it is clear that by the start of 1843 Deciby and the Ningy Ningy had withdrawn their protection of the Nundah Mission. The entries in the mission diary for January to July 1843 are a bleak account of its growing troubles: 'It is grievous to observe that no Nat[ives] approach our station, to assist us in our labour and to be instructed, but on the contrary that some are desirous to rob our gardens', Christopher Eipper recorded on 26 January 1843. For the next few months the mission had to call upon a small number of Aboriginal women to assist with station work as men were only occasionally recorded as present. By May the small numbers of Indigenous children about the mission were openly objecting to being forced to attend school and by June the ringing of the school bell was enough to send the children fleeing to the bush. The gardens were often robbed at night and the raids became more audacious. By May Aboriginal men were stealing potatoes from their field in broad daylight.[78]

The mission also survived 1844 despite internal dissensions, the dissolution of their Sydney support committee and the departure of Reverend Eipper. Their salvation was the arrival of four new missionaries from Germany who reinvigorated the group and inspired them to attempt an out-station to the north of the settlement.[79] The evident cooling of sentiment from the Indigenous community was misinterpreted as an effect of the expanding white township, with all its accompanying debaucheries. They hoped that a new mission in unsettled country close to the large coastal camps and villages to the north would revive their influence with the local peoples. In late 1844 they began clearing land, planting crops and constructing buildings with the help of Aboriginal people at this new locale on Burpengary Creek.

In early March 1845 the northern and coastal tribes gathered near Brisbane for a meeting and fight with the Brisbane and Logan (probably Yugambeh) peoples. To the white townspeople it was a great spectacle and several reportedly went out to watch.[80] The reports from the regions and discussions that were also a feature of these grand gatherings were generally impenetrable to the whites, and less

TOP LEFT: The only known images of Dundalli are believed to be the work of Silvester Diggles. This pen and ink sketch was made following Dundalli's trial in November 1854. JOHN OXLEY LIBRARY, STATE LIBRARY OF QUEENSLAND, NEG. NO. 11307

TOP RIGHT: A wood engraving published in the *Illustrated Sydney News*, 16 December 1854, page 440.

BOTTOM: Durundur homestead, painted by Charles Archer in 1843. The bark roofing was provided by the local Dalla people. JOHN OXLEY LIBRARY, STATE LIBRARY OF QUEENSLAND, REF. CODE 4624/1

TOP LEFT: Paddy, a head man of the Dalla, sketched by Ludwig Leichhardt while he was staying at the Archers' Durundur Station. MICHAEL AIRD, QUEENSLAND MUSEUM

TOP RIGHT: Charles Archer in 1853, ten years after he first arrived at Durundur.
JOHN OXLEY LIBRARY, STATE LIBRARY OF QUEENSLAND, NEG. NO. 13851

BOTTOM: Thomas Archer standing, second from left, with his younger brothers some 24 years after he unsuccessfully pursued Dundalli through wetlands east of Caboolture.
JOHN OXLEY LIBRARY, STATE LIBRARY OF QUEENSLAND, NEG. NO. 8875

TOP: The Blackall Range, with bunya trees in the foreground. This is Dalla country, where Dundalli grew to adulthood. PHOTO COURTESY OF NEIL ENNIS

BOTTOM: Obi Obi Creek in the Blackall Range, 1890s. SUNSHINE COAST LIBRARY

A rock gorge of the Blackall Range, Kondalilla National Park, 1924. SUNSHINE COAST LIBRARY

Kondalilla Falls (formerly Bon Accord Falls) in the Blackall Range, 1930. According to the Queensland Department of National Parks, Sport and Racing, *kondalilla* is an Aboriginal word meaning 'rushing waters'. SUNSHINE COAST LIBRARY

TOP LEFT: Willy McKenzie of the Jinibara in the 1950s. His tribal name was Gaiarbau, and his recollections, which were recorded in 1957, are a rich source of information on traditional Aboriginal life. SUNSHINE COAST LIBRARY

TOP RIGHT: Tom Petrie as a young man. JOHN OXLEY LIBRARY, STATE LIBRARY OF QUEENSLAND, NEG. NO. 12939

BOTTOM: Baroon Pocket Dam now covers the glade where the famous Bunya meetings were held. SUNSHINE COAST LIBRARY

TOP: Pumicestone Passage and the Glass House Mountains as seen from Bribie Island, Dundalli's home after April 1843. SUNSHINE COAST LIBRARY

BOTTOM: Tom Petrie's homestead, Murrumba Downs, its drive lined with native pines, including bunyas. JOHN OXLEY LIBRARY, STATE LIBRARY OF QUEENSLAND, NEG. NO. 284287

TOP: David and Mary McConnel, more than ten years after Cressbrook was established.
JOHN OXLEY LIBRARY, STATE LIBRARY OF QUEENSLAND, NEG. NO. 65979

BOTTOM: David McConnel's prosperous Cressbrook Station, with established bunya and other native pines in the garden, many decades after the killing of Commandant.
JOHN OXLEY LIBRARY, STATE LIBRARY OF QUEENSLAND, NEG. NO. 59732

TOP: The Stanley River, a headwater of the Brisbane River, in the vicinity of the original Durundur Station. PHOTO COURTESY OF NEIL ENNIS

MIDDLE: Tenthill Valley, home of Moppé's Yaggera people. PHOTO COURTESY OF NEIL ENNIS

BOTTOM: Mount Samson. Joyner and Mason's Samsonvale Station bordered Andrew Gregor's Forgie Station to the north. PHOTO COURTESY OF NEIL ENNIS

TOP: Johann Leopold Zillmann, one of the original missionaries who went on several expeditions with local Aboriginal people in 1839–41. The young Swiss and German missionaries were all in their twenties when they founded the Nundah mission in 1838.
JOHN OXLEY LIBRARY, STATE LIBRARY OF QUEENSLAND, NEG. NO. 16050

BOTTOM: The remains of one of the original German Mission cottages at Zion's Hill.
JOHN OXLEY LIBRARY, STATE LIBRARY OF QUEENSLAND, IMAGE NO. APE-032-01-001

TOP: Woorim, the eastern side of Bribie Island—Joondaburri country and Dundalli's home in the years 1843–54—looking across to Moreton Island. PHOTO COURTESY OF NEIL ENNIS

BOTTOM: The western escarpment of the D'Aguilar Range with Somerset Dam in the distance. The dam covers parts of Mount Brisbane Station and other stations in the Brisbane Valley. Multugerrah and his allies launched attacks on the stations then traversed the range to the coast to escape retaliation. PHOTO COURTESY OF NEIL ENNIS

TOP: Captain Wickham, police magistrate and later government resident for Moreton Bay.
JOHN OXLEY LIBRARY, STATE LIBRARY OF QUEENSLAND, NEG. NO. 8997

BOTTOM: A waterhole of the North Pine River, the country of Dalaipi and his people.
PHOTO COURTESY OF NEIL ENNIS

TOP: Ann Street, Fortitude Valley, 1858. In May 1854 Dundalli was arrested in nearby Wickham Street, near the crest of the hill in the background. Silvester Diggles, *Fortitude Valley* 1858, Collection: Queensland Art Gallery. IMAGE COURTESY QAGOMA

BOTTOM: A line drawing of the fight between the Logan people and the Bribie and Stradbroke Islanders in December 1853. It took place near today's Cornwall and Juliette streets in Brisbane. *ILLUSTRATED LONDON NEWS*, 17 JANUARY 1854, PAGE 575.

ABOVE: Aboriginal people gathered in front of the open doorway of the Old Brisbane Gaol, Queen Street, for a distribution of blankets in 1863. The gallows were erected in front of this entry for Dundalli's execution in January 1855. STATE LIBRARY OF QUEENSLAND, NEG. NO. 7773

OPPOSITE TOP LEFT: John Plunkett, attorney-general of New South Wales, who prosecuted three soldiers of the 11th Regiment for an attack on Daki Yakka's people in December 1849. STATE LIBRARY OF NEW SOUTH WALES, CALL NO. ML333

OPPOSITE TOP RIGHT: Charles Summers' bust of Sir Roger Therry, 1870, made sixteen years after he presided over Dundalli's trial. STATE LIBRARY OF NEW SOUTH WALES, CALL NO. XR31

OPPOSITE BOTTOM: Queen Street in 1870, with the old convict barracks on the far right, alongside new Victorian buildings. The Supreme Court sat in the old convict chapel on the top floor, and the Brisbane watch-house was in the northern corner of the ground floor. JOHN OXLEY LIBRARY, STATE LIBRARY OF QUEENSLAND, NEG. NO. 145370

On 5 January 2011, near what is now Post Office Square in Brisbane's CBD, a protest poster recalls Dundalli's execution 156 years before. A statue of General Glasgow in Anzac Square faces Central Railway Station where, on the day Dundalli was hanged, Aboriginal people sheltered in scrub. PHOTO COURTESY OF NEIL ENNIS

entertaining, so that regrettably we have no record of the proceedings which might have explained the ensuing events. But at some point in the week that followed the Brisbane meeting, the Ningy Ningy and Joondaburri opposition to the northern mission evolved into a plan of attack.

While the local Aboriginal people were down at the Brisbane meeting the lay missionaries Hausmann, Zillmann and Hartenstein were working at 'Nonga Creek', as the new mission was described in court records in the 1850s. By the turn of the century the general location of the northern mission had become known as Burpengary, and well into the twentieth century it was a pretty picnic spot alongside the Bruce Highway, demarcated by old and established native pines. The new site was more than 30 kilometres north of the old Nundah Mission although, travelling on foot and without established roads, the missionaries generally described it as 30 miles (54 kilometres) distant. Its advantage was that it lay close to Aboriginal pathways to Toorbul and Bribie Island, only 20–25 kilometres to the north-east.

With the Aboriginal gathering at Brisbane over, the missionaries unexpectedly had 'a great many men' whom they employed on this new station. In Hausmann's old age he claimed there were about 600 present, but in his court testimony in 1854 he gave a figure of fifty to sixty, which seems more likely.[81] They were sea coast men. Only two of them are named in any of the accounts: Trimberri and Dundalli. Hausmann sensed something was amiss and in the afternoon it was agreed that the other two missionaries should secretly return to Nundah for help while Hausmann would remain and guard the stores. The secrecy was part of a strategy of appearing strong and powerful and showed a good understanding of warrior culture. It was a value that Tom Petrie understood too, never backing down from a confrontation—although Petrie always went armed when travelling with his Indigenous companions and employees,[82] whereas Hausmann was not.[83] At sunset Trimberri called to Hausmann, who, maintaining the show of bravado, left the hut to talk to him. Trimberri, however, was a decoy allegedly set up by Dundalli to isolate Hausmann in order to rob the stores, plunder the fields and burn the building. When Hausmann refused to go into the bush to help Trimberri look for his dog he was struck by a nulla nulla, falling and breaking his hand in the process. As Hausmann retreated to his hut he discovered eight armed men were positioned behind trees between him and his shelter. He scrambled back but not before a spear pierced his back. Bolting the door, the 33-year-old Hausmann sat down and composed a farewell letter to his wife while his assailants outside began striking the slabs. When they finally broke in it was nightfall and Hausmann managed to escape undetected while flour, blankets and provisions were looted.[84]

In some of the accounts by mission descendants the purpose of the attack was to kill Hausmann, and Aboriginal men were said to have tracked him through the bush at night; however, he miraculously reached the Nundah Mission before they could complete the deed.[85] There are problems with this claim. Firstly, it seems unlikely that nine men surrounding a hut would have allowed one injured man to escape if assassination had been their aim. Secondly, it is improbable that Indigenous trackers could not have overtaken Hausmann, who had a broken hand and was bleeding from a head wound and a 12–13-centimetre deep spear wound in his back, as well as struggling to find his way through trackless bushland. Instead, the main focus of the raid appears to be the destruction of the crops and hut, which were raided then trampled and burnt. As Commissioner Simpson reported it, the missionaries had been 'ejected'.[86]

Dundalli and the coastal people appear to have been setting the limits to white settlement. They wanted to make clear that they would not tolerate any further loss of their lands. No doubt the attack was the subject of review and debate among their Jagera and Mianjin neighbours, who began gathering for another large pullen pullen on 17 March, just days after the attack, in the vicinity of Woogaroo and

Ipswich.[87] Later, in October of 1845, the Ningy Ningy were blamed for the death of a shepherd en route to Durundur Station, while to the west a few weeks later, at the pastoral station of Wivenhoe, the Dalla took the life of John Uhr, the young brother of pastoralist Edmund Uhr.

Uhr's death was symptomatic of the escalation of violence generated by the sustained pressure Moppy's kin was applying to the Brisbane Valley squatters. On 22 May 1844 David McConnel wrote to his brother William that he had gone out that day 'armed with full intentions to pepper some blackfellows', but despite a ride of 25 miles (40 kilometres) found none. He had more success in October. His superintendent, Mort, and five horsemen had discovered a large group of Dalla driving cattle up Sugarloaf Creek. They gave chase and in David's own words 'had a gallop & caught one gentleman; a few balls & two tremendous cuts with my sabre from a powerful arm would & did astonish him'. Later in the same letter he reassured his brother that two of his men who had been attacked had 'fired at & knocked down one old rogue, at which the rest (about 100) fled'. 'After shearing, we may quieten the blacks, & then have some fat cattle for next April or May', he wrote ominously in the same letter.[88] These events and any post-shearing 'pacification' make it easy to interpret the killing of Uhr and the lone shepherd as the execution of customary law. While McConnel writes with bitterness of the planning and organisation of groups of twenty, one hundred and even three hundred Indigenous men about his station and the theft of about thirty-nine head of cattle, in hindsight it is striking how measured the Yaggera and Dalla's response was.

In conveying the news of Uhr's death to Sydney, Commissioner Simpson wrote with growing frustration of the local lawmen and their accompanying young warriors. A corporal and eight infantry had been sent to Fairnie Lawn Station, belonging to Major North, a magistrate, and to Ferriter and Uhr's Wivenhoe Station solely to 'calm the fears' of pastoral staff and their families since 'the aggressive party has crossed the D'Aguilar Range & is actually now engaged in spearing Messrs Joyner & Mason's cattle', he informed the colonial secretary's office.[89]

By the end of 1845 the old leadership of men such as Ubie Ubie in the mountains and Deciby on the coast, who had been in favour of beneficial contact with the Europeans and had successfully moderated anger over European infringements, had been surpassed. The new leadership enforced the laws of retaliation against neighbours and trespassers irrespective of race. On the coast Dundalli successfully moved to Bribie Island, and from there his influence among the Dalla and Joondaburri grew to encompass the Gubbi Gubbi all along the coast from the Brisbane to the Mary rivers. At Durundur, Paddy and the local tribe succeeded in remaining on good terms with the Archers but also with their coastal neighbours to the east and other Dalla to the south and west.

The geographical meeting point for these two powerful groups was the Pine River Valley, just to the south of the Archers' property. When Dundalli led a multigroup assault on a station there in 1846 it would reverberate in the community for many years to come.

4

THE ATTACK ON GREGOR'S STATION

Today when you stand at lookouts dotted along the D'Aguilar Range at places such as Mount Nebo and further north at Mount Mee, and look east towards Bribie Island and Redcliffe, or south to the city of Brisbane, you get a sense of why the Pine River Valley was so important to Dundalli. From these heights, above the cars and traffic, it retains its delightful scenic aspect: lush, green lowlands falling gently to the coastal edge. It was essential to traverse this valley to access important meeting and ceremonial sites on the Pine, at Toorbul, Bribie Island and Redcliffe and further south at Nudgee, among others.

The valley is bounded on the north by the Caboolture River, which marks the start of Dalla country, but its lushness is also maintained due to it being watered by two branches of the Pine. Today the Pine River is dammed and the dam waters partially cover two of the first stations established after the district was opened to free settlement in May 1842. The Pine Rivers district was within the former 50-mile limit of restricted settlement so it was not until after May 1842 that the Archers had any European neighbours to their south-east—due south were the mountains of the D'Aguilar Range and due east were the Glass House Mountains and then the sandy coastal plain, neither suitable for squatting.

The first to take up land here was Andrew Gregor, a 28-year-old Scot from Aberdeen.[1] He chose the nearest land to the Archers but his station was still 40 kilometres across mountainous country from the Archers' Durundur head station. His lease included the foothills of Mount Mee and a small creek that is the headwaters of the Caboolture River. According to the Archer family correspondence he moved on to the land in 1842, but crown lands records indicate that he did not take out a licence until 1845. He named the station 'Forgie' after his family home at Forgieside in Aberdeen.[2] His parents, James and Janet Gregor, despite having only a modest farm of 40 acres, managed to send three of Andrew's five brothers to King's College, University of Aberdeen, but it seems there was little financial support for young Andrew as his pastoral lease was under-capitalised. Although there were three other stations in the Moreton Bay district as small in size as the 25 square miles (65 square kilometres) of Andrew Gregor's Forgie Station, none had as little stock or as poor a dwelling. From October 1845 through to February 1846 Commissioner Simpson visited every station that comprised his pastoral district; all were making do with slab huts, some with shingles, others with bark roofing, but only Gregor was residing in a bark hut and with only a young Aboriginal boy, Ralph Barrow, for company.[3]

His poverty may have been the reason for his lack of hospitality. To refuse refreshment or even a bed for the night was not well regarded in these frontier districts. Gregor's run was on the main road from Brisbane to Durundur, and young Tom Archer complained to his mother that Gregor was 'mean and stingy', never had 'a decent morsel to offer a traveller' and used his saddle cloth for a sleeping blanket.[4]

Perhaps Andrew's need for moral and financial support was why his eldest brother, the Reverend John Gregor, accepted a posting to Moreton Bay upon his ordination as an Anglican priest. University-educated

John was originally enlisted as a 28-year-old Presbyterian minister by John Dunmore Lang when Lang was in the British Isles as part of his recruitment drive for ministers for the colony in 1837. This was the same trip during which Lang had recruited his German missionaries for Moreton Bay, although they arrived via a different ship a month later.[5] Reverends Lang and Gregor soon had a falling out over internal Presbyterian matters and by 1841 Gregor had made the decision to convert to Anglicanism. In September 1842 the first Anglican Bishop of Australia, William Grant Broughton, welcomed him by ordaining him deacon and priest the following December.[6]

Brisbane was not a strong posting for an Anglican priest. Although the area was declared open to free settlement in May 1842, it was still defined by the Church of England as a 'Mission beyond the boundaries of location'. This rough pastoral district was a strange appointment for a minister whom Bishop Broughton had described as 'one of the best qualified ... in terms of literary and scientific requirements'.[7] Nevertheless, in January 1843 the Reverend Gregor boarded the Brisbane steamer *Shamrock* at Newcastle, joining the passengers from Sydney en route to Brisbane. Among them were Brisbane's newly appointed police magistrate, Captain John Wickham, and his party of town constables, headed by Chief Constable William Fitzpatrick.

The bishop had been giving moral support to Apsley, William Watson's breakaway mission to the Aborigines in the Wellington Valley on the Macquarie River, and had visited it in May 1841.[8] Perhaps this was when he christened a young Wiradjuri boy, Ralph Barrow, who was subsequently sent to be educated at the Anglican school at Narellan, near Camden. How he had come into the hands of the bishop is not clear but Broughton now made the decision to send the boy 1000 kilometres north to the care of John Gregor. Although Ralph could read and write well, he never knew what year he was born; however, by the end of 1842 he could not have been more than seven years old. He could have been as young as five.[9] How and when one small Aboriginal boy made his way to Brisbane from Sydney to join John Gregor remains a mystery. Whatever the case, he was destined to become a momentous figure in Dundalli's life.

In December 1842 Bishop Broughton made another puzzling decision when he decided to send John Gregor north. One Moreton Bay visitor summed up John Gregor as 'very suitable for a fashionable church in Sydney, but most unsuitable for making headway among a lot of wild bushmen'.[10] He nonetheless diligently set out on three arduous tours of his far-flung district from August to September, September to October and October to December 1843. He wrote detailed reports for the bishop of his visits to the Moreton Bay pastoral stations, where he 'exhorted' the station workers 'to do their duty to God, themselves, their masters, and their neighbours'.[11] Rather than winning their hearts, young Gregor's refinement and conservatism sparked a quite different reaction from colonists, who were in the exciting grip of a newly won right to vote for part of the Legislative Council and were already beginning to press for self-government. Tom Archer found him insufferable, complaining many years later: 'When I ventured to advance the axiom "Vox populi, vox Dei," he answered, "No, sir! Vox populi, vox Diaboli!"'[12] Strangely, on his first tour to the north of Brisbane, Gregor did not record calling in on his brother but went directly from the German mission to Durundur. Nor did his young charge, Ralph, accompany him—Gregor hired a manservant for his journey so by this time Ralph had probably already been sent to Andrew Gregor's isolated station.[13]

In October 1843, when Captain Francis Griffin took up 25 square miles (65 square kilometres) of land along the North Pine which stretched to the coast and which he named Whiteside, Andrew Gregor acquired a European neighbour 19 kilometres to his southeast. The two enterprises were a marked contrast in terms of personnel. Griffin was soon joined by his brother William and his wife; his parents, George and Jane; and his youngest brother, John.

The station was always on the lookout for labourers for clearing land for cultivation, constructing houses, shepherding and harvesting, so it is not surprising that the commissioner of crown lands recorded ten residents there during his inspection tour in February 1846.[14] It was not a happy family enterprise.[15] Nonetheless the station was prosperous, with small herds of sheep, cattle and horses and 10 acres of cultivation already underway by the time of the commissioner's visit.[16]

A second neighbour took out a pastoral licence on 1 July 1845.[17] William Joyner was a gentleman and about to marry when he and William Mason took up Samsonvale Station to the west of Whiteside and south of Forgie.[18] Like Gregor's, their station included the foothills of the D'Aguilar Range and was predominantly a cattle station. Mason managed the station with three staff while Joyner spent most of his time in Sydney until his untimely death in the shipwreck of the Sydney steamer *Sovereign*, in Moreton Bay in March 1847.[19] Samsonvale was only 3 kilometres from Whiteside but relations between the two stations did not always run smoothly.[20]

These European settlers, preoccupied with their own domestic problems as well as the religious and political divisions of colonial society, were for the most part unaware of the larger legal and political system that continued unabated in this valley. Its heavily wooded foothills and creek flats hosted Aboriginal gatherings large and small that were occasionally given a passing reference in George Griffin's station diary. Commissioner Simpson was more alert to the significance of this country for the local peoples, although even he had only a one-dimensional view of it, representing it as a refuge for young warriors who launched assaults in the Brisbane Valley before retreating east across the range.[21]

Commissioner Simpson visited these stations only two months after the killing of John Uhr and was alarmed to find Andrew living alone with just young Ralph Barrow, now about ten years old, and whom Simpson referred to as 'hutkeeper'. He warned Andrew that he was a target for Aboriginal attack. In Simpson's view the stations required a minimum of two men for security. Perhaps young Tom Archer's assessment of Gregor was misplaced because Gregor appears to have heeded the commissioner's advice; in the next few months he employed Thomas and Mary Shannon to assist him and built a second bark hut on his station for them and their three daughters—baby Eliza, three-year-old Mary Ann and five-year-old Margaret.[22]

The high country of the Brisbane Ranges belonged to different family groupings of the Dalla but the lowlands, where Samsonvale and Forgie had been established, belonged to Pine River people, one of whose elders was the renowned Dalaipi. To the east were Ningy Ningy lands and Bribie Islander country, so the valley was important as a pathway to friends and allies on the coast as well as a meeting place for regional groups.

At first the Pine River people were not overtly hostile to the white newcomers. As with their neighbours they watched to see whether a beneficial accommodation with these settlers could be reached. By the mid-1840s Aboriginal people were exchanging goods and services with the Europeans when it suited them, and the Griffins and Gregor employed Aboriginal people to collect bark for their roofing and housing, to deliver letters and messages to neighbours and to herd cattle. An Aboriginal–European economy had begun to develop, with Aboriginal people regularly providing fresh fish to the settlers.[23] These exchanges meant that Aboriginal people were often around the stations in the years 1842 to 1846. At Forgie, by October 1846, Gregor had one Aboriginal man living on the station as well as young Ralph; an Aboriginal boy who was helping Shannon is also mentioned in court transcripts.[24]

Familiarity was by no means submission. Commissioner Simpson had played down the killing of John Uhr in the Brisbane Valley in December 1845, reporting to superiors that in his view it had been an accident: the Aboriginal group involved had merely intended to rob Uhr's hut of provisions when Uhr's intervention led to a violent exchange resulting in his death. By mid-1846 the commissioner's correspondence was more pessimistic. Almost every station in the district had suffered Aboriginal raids on cattle but he named three in particular—Major North's near the Rosewood Scrub, Dowse's in the Logan district, and Joyner and Mason's in the Pine River Valley—which suggest that Aboriginal actions were a continuation of the pattern that began with the Great Bunya Toor of the summer of 1842–43. In December 1844, in his annual report on the state of Aborigines, Simpson had acknowledged the systematic nature of the attacks on Europeans on the main road to the Darling Downs and on the stations of the Brisbane Valley to the north, blaming the sons of the great Moppy, who had made clear they were methodically exacting compensation for their father's death.[25] The attacks on the Logan and the Pine suggest how far the regional agreement about enforcing payback on vulnerable Europeans extended. In July 1846 Simpson had issued six warrants, attempting to home in on the young warriors who he believed were the ringleaders, and this action by Simpson undoubtedly contributed to the collision that took place on Coutts' station at Rosewood in September 1846.

From July to August 1846 a man known by the Europeans as 'Jemmy Cambell' was said to have led raids on Coutts' cattle at Rosewood Station. In the first week of September the *Moreton Bay Courier* claimed that five hundred Yaggera had gathered at the Rosewood Scrub, about 20 kilometres west of Ipswich. On the Saturday evening Cambell is said to have led a party of twenty men to demand money and provisions from Coutts, who refused. Later that night three neighbouring squatters joined Coutts and spent the night in his hut. The Yaggera were possibly unaware of the arrival of so many armed men, for Coutts claimed that at sunrise Cambell's men attacked the family's hut and were only repelled after 'three or four volleys' were fired. Coutts' letter to the commissioner of crown lands appealing for police assistance made no mention of Aboriginal deaths, but Aboriginal people at Commissioner Simpson's headquarters informed the commissioner that Jemmy Cambell had died and two or three others had been wounded.[26]

Neither Commissioner Simpson nor Coutts carried out an inquest so there are few sources to help shed light on these events. It was a terrible blow to the traditional owners of the Brisbane and Lockyer valleys. 'Cambell' was Moppy's leading son, described by Frederic McConnel as a good-looking young man;[27] he had undergone name exchange with the pastoralist John Campbell sometime around August–September 1841. His tribal name was Multuggerah and he was a young Yaggera warrior when he interacted with Campbell in his country, the foothills of the Great Dividing Range. In response to the Ugarapul's sustained campaign to drive the Europeans from the Lockyer Valley, including successfully blockading the main route to the Darling Downs in September 1843, a military post comprising a sergeant and twelve men of the 99th Regiment had been established at the foot of the range at Helidon on 18 October.[28] Moppy's men countered by simply concentrating their attacks further to the east— northwards of the Rosewood Scrub. The years 1844–45 were wet ones and Simpson complained that these 'mountain men', as he referred to them, drove cattle into swampy ground and used the wet conditions, which put the Europeans at a disadvantage, to evade capture.[29] John Campbell linked the assault on John Uhr to an overall campaign, which Multuggerah had warned him about, that involved attacks on horses, drays and rations aimed at starving the Europeans and disrupting their traffic along the main road to the Downs.[30] Of Multuggerah, he wrote, 'Under my name young Moppy became rather a celebrated character', presumably meaning among the traditional owners, for in the view of the local paper, he was the 'notorious black "Campbell" '.[31]

Like Dundalli, Multuggerah had been a young man when the European pastoralists arrived in 1841. If they had shared the Bora ceremony as youths they would have had obligations of brotherhood to one another despite their membership of different tribal groups. Certainly reports of how easily the Lockyer Valley men crossed the range after attacks indicate that Dundalli and Multuggerah knew one another and their respective feats. Also like Dundalli, it appears that Multuggerah had an important standing in his community. There is no doubt that Multuggerah's death was a blow to the broader Aboriginal community of south-east Queensland. Commissioner Simpson makes no mention of the fate of Multuggerah's two brothers but Campbell believed that Multuggerah had been given leadership status after the death of his father and one of his brothers.[32] If his biological brothers had predeceased him, then his uncles and tribal brothers would have borne the responsibility to exact payback under ancestral law for his untimely death, adding another layer to Aboriginal grievances.

This was the context for a gathering in the foothills of Mount Mee five to six weeks after Multuggerah was shot by settlers at Coutts' station. We know little about the proceedings of this assembly other than what can be gleaned from the hostile British court transcripts arising from events on the morning of Sunday, 18 October 1846. From about Monday, 13 October, large numbers of Aboriginal people began to gather on Dalaipi's lands at Forgie Station. Dundalli was among them. The local whites went about their regular duties, blissfully unaware of the grave deliberations taking place nearby. Only Thomas Shannon, unnerved by the presence of large numbers of Aboriginal people about the station for a week, had taken the precaution of carrying a gun with him when he went out on the following Sunday.

That morning, at about 9 a.m., three pairs of Aboriginal men separately approached the station. Andrew Gregor had crossed the road in front of his hut to his stockyard; his female servant Mary Shannon was tidying her hut, and his new station hand Thomas Shannon was on his way to a waterhole about 200 metres from Gregor's hut. Gregor stooped to inspect some bark that Aboriginal workers had collected for him earlier that morning, and the first of the warrior band, Dick Ben and Jacky, struck. Andrew Gregor was hit with ferocious blows that killed him instantly, dislocating his left eye from its socket and fracturing his skull so badly that his brain protruded on the right. At the same time two men, whose identities were disputed, fatally struck Mary Shannon with tomahawks to the left side of the neck and head as she stooped to pick up a broom from the front of her hut. The two men sent to dispatch Thomas Shannon mistimed their approach, for Shannon had turned when he heard his five-year-old daughter Margaret scream and was heading to the hut when a spear was thrown at him; he then fired at another assailant but as the first man was now pursuing him, he ran for his life in the direction of the Griffins' station, 20 kilometres away. In the meantime 'a great number of Blacks' ran from the creek to the huts on the call of one of the assailants.

Eight kilometres down the road Shannon was lucky enough to come across the pastoralist William O'Grady Haly on his way to Gregor's. Haly mounted Shannon on his horse and immediately headed back to the Griffins' for help, leaving a small Aboriginal boy who had fled with Shannon to run along behind. Fortunately for the latter, by chance they came upon two bush workers along the road, so Shannon dismounted to allow Haly to gallop to Whiteside Station. The three Griffin sons were all at home and they promptly armed, mounted and charged back with Haly to Gregor's, arriving to find the last two of the Aboriginal men removing goods from Gregor's hut. They unsuccessfully gave chase as the men took to thick scrub. The Griffins and Haly removed the bodies to Gregor's hut and soon after Haly headed to Brisbane to report on the events to the police magistrate.

The next morning Captain Wickham, accompanied by a medical doctor, arrived to conduct the inquest, and also sent word to Commissioner Simpson. The same day, a man called Jemmy Perowa reached Durundur Station and began making inquiries of Paddy, the local head man. Perowa is not identified in the court transcripts but his initiative in heading to Paddy's camp on Monday suggests that he might have been one of the mounted Aboriginal troopers who had been attached to Commissioner Simpson. Constable, a Dalla man who had been living at Gregor's, arrived at Durundur Station on Tuesday, 20 October, wearing a shirt that had belonged to the Reverend John Gregor and also showing awareness of the assault on the station. Simpson didn't arrive at the Archers' until Thursday, 22 October, when he placed Constable under arrest.[33]

The inquest on Monday, followed by Constable's committal hearing a fortnight later in Brisbane, quickly established a frontier mythology of Aboriginal treachery and savagery. Witnesses testified that Gregor and his brother John had employed different Aboriginal men and had treated them kindly, which the *Moreton Bay Courier* echoed. This was the first time a white woman had been killed, and the fact that Mary Shannon had been pregnant added to the image of Aboriginal betrayal and mercilessness. However modest a pastoralist Gregor had been, the fact that he was a squatter and the brother of the district's Anglican clergyman added more emotional fuel.

The facts, though, were surprisingly scant. Only the older children—ten-year-old Ralph Barrow and five-year-old Margaret Shannon—were able to identify individual culprits. Thomas Shannon had been running away, and some years later, when court cases associated with the attack were still being pursued, the attorney-general noted that Shannon had been too traumatised by the attack to be a useful witness.[34] Between them, Ralph Barrow and Margaret Shannon named twenty-seven Indigenous men and one woman who had been involved in either assaulting Gregor and Mary Shannon or removing goods from the huts. This was not the full complement of people involved—Thomas Shannon had remembered 'a great number of Blacks' coming up from the creek. Some seven years later, when Frederick Walker, the commandant of the newly reconstituted

Native Police, objected to the number of warrants he had been given for Aboriginal men associated with the attack, he claimed that all Aboriginal men, women and children on surrounding stations were implicated, and unsuccessfully demanded an amnesty on all prosecutions arising from the attack.[35] So there is no doubt that large numbers of local people had participated in the meetings prior to the attack and in raiding the station afterwards.

This was not just local payback but an action involving inter-tribal cooperation, since men whose country was up to 200 kilometres away were mentioned in the children's evidence. According to Barrow, Dick Ben and Jacky killed Andrew Gregor, and Moggy Moggy and Millbong Jemmy killed Mary Shannon. Young Margaret, however, believed that Millbong Jemmy had struck Gregor and that a different 'Jemmy', a Ningy Ningy black, had killed her mother. Additionally, a fortnight after the attack, when he was brought into court for the committal of Constable, Ralph was asked to name those he had seen stealing provisions from the hut:

> I saw Davy and Larry they were standing near the Door . . . The other blacks were on the road looking on. I saw amongst them Simon, Constable, Miller, Dandalli was standing near the hut at the time. Jemmy Solomon was standing near the hut. Tear was standing in front of the hut. Jemmy Parsons was at the hut.[36]

At this point the boy told the court that he could not remember any more, but the police magistrate needed names for warrants so he helpfully pressed on:

> After the blacks had killed Mr Gregor they went into the hut and took Tobacco, Sugar, Tea, Blankets, Coat, Teapot, Red Shirt, Flour in 4 bags, and carried them into the scrub in so doing they came nearer to me and I could see the things in their hands.

Jackey had tobacco in his hand. Dick Ben & Jemmy Parsons had sugar. Millbong Jemmy had tea. Dundalli had blankets. Moggy Moggy had a coat. Jemmy Solomon had the tea pot. Tear had the red shirt. Davy, Simon, Beddy and Constable were carrying flour. Brandy Brandy was carrying sugar. Mickey was carrying flour. Nicker was carrying tomahawks, Carabine and two pistols. Dick Ben had a pint pot & 2 tea pots. Merriman had flour. There was another Mickey took sugar. Billy Quart Pot took Gregor's packing needles and thread. Sampson had flour. Billy Barlow was carrying sugar. Bono had flour. Billy Gray had flour; he is Constable's brother.[37]

Again at this point the boy told the court 'I do not know the names of any more', and again he was pressed further to clarify the respective roles of those who did the killings. Margaret had only lived on the station for less than seven months so not surprisingly could not add many names, but distinguished between those who were normally around the station and the 'Saltwaters'—the Ningy Ningy and Undambi from the coast. Interestingly she noted the involvement of a woman, 'Old Mammy', who she said carried away two guns.[38]

The children's comments provide enough evidence to show that there was a variety of tribal groups involved. As well as local Pine River people such as Brandy Brandy, Dick Ben, Jemmy Parsons, Mickie and Billy Quart Pot, there were men associated with Durundur such as Nicker and Bono; a group of Dalla from beyond Durundur, which included Dundalli, Constable and his brother Billy Gray; Jacky and Beddy, who appear to be Ningy Ningy; Moggy Moggy, who was a Gubbi Gubbi man from the Sunshine Coast–Cooloola region (usually described by whites as Wide Bay); and lastly, Millbong Jemmy (Yilbung, who had caused the German missionaries so much grief).[39] Of course there is uncertainty about evidence taken from two young children who had just experienced extreme trauma. In fact,

Tom Archer was able to provide an alibi for Bono, who was actually with him, helping to set up a new station in the Burnett district.[40] Nonetheless Ralph's identification of the actual killers is substantiated by authoritative Aboriginal evidence. Jemmy Perowa had gone to Paddy, the nearest elder not implicated in the attack, who spoke with certainty as to those responsible. The boy was correct—Dick Ben and Jacky had killed Gregor, but Paddy also named 'Moggy Moggy—Marmoulli brother belonging to Dandalli—Dandalli stop in scrub. Jemmy—Moggy Moggy kill white Mary'.[41] So Moggy Moggy was given a more central role and there is confusion about 'Jemmy', given that the boy had named Jemmy Parsons and Millbong Jemmy. Of these names, only those of Jemmy Parsons and Moggy Moggy would be tested in a court of law—Moggy Moggy and Jemmy Parsons were among many names ascribed to a young Gubbi Gubbi man and were the subject of cross-examination at a court hearing in 1851.[42]

Paddy's views are important in providing insight into traditional decision-making. Paddy's certainty about who was responsible is an indication that there were clear ties of obligation determining who would have carried out these killings. Without more information about these individuals and their specific responsibilities as brothers and uncles we cannot be sure whose deaths were being legally avenged according to ancestral law. Paddy's ready divulging of information suggests that there was no shame attached to the attack as far as Aboriginal people were concerned.

We also know that the action was planned. Aware that white people did not understand the local laws, in the interests of honour Aboriginal people repeatedly sent messages to white friends and even intended victims when an attack was about to take place. This was the case with both the squatter John Campbell and Andrew Gregor. On the Tuesday before the attack Constable, who had been living at the station, had told Ralph what was planned. The men responsible for the executions had also discussed it openly while camped near Gregor's hut on

Friday, 16 October, according to Ralph, who had informed Gregor of what he had heard.[43] In tribal settings this meant the accused could defend himself or seek refuge elsewhere but Europeans invariably did not understand this process and ignored warnings, as appears to have happened at Forgie.

It is also important to note that while European settlers were horrified at the brutality of this scene, it was actually a measured response. The plan appears to have been to take out the adults and destroy the huts. At no stage were the children threatened. Ralph said he sat watching on his horse from the creek because he was worried that the horse would be under attack, rather than him personally. Margaret Shannon screamed the moment her mother was assaulted but she and her two younger sisters remained unmolested in the hut while Aboriginal people ransacked it.

Nevertheless, the trauma of a five-year-old at witnessing such shocking adult behaviour still comes through the records in her colonial accent, as she describes their destruction of both Andrew Gregor's belongings as well as her parents':

> All the blacks run into the hut and began to rob it carrying away flour tea blankets bedcloathes and everything and smashed every ha'porth ... The salt water blacks tore up my mother's bed ... The looking glass was broken by the blacks. Jemmy and another black fellow came to the hut after the others had gone and took _our_ looking glass.[44]

Nor was it a sign of treachery that men (and presumably women) who had worked with the Griffins, the Archers and the Gregors had participated in this attack. Once a meeting had decided on a guilty party, it was irrelevant whether one liked or had a relationship with them. Australian anthropology recognises how 'retribution may fall on the kinsman or kinswoman of an offender, or a person of the same

Table 4.1 Names of men alleged to have killed Andrew Gregor and Mary Shannon[45]

Witness	Murder of Andrew Gregor		Murder of Mary Shannon	
	Inquest, 19 October, Forgie Station	Committal hearing, 3 November, Brisbane	Inquest, 19 October, Forgie Station	Committal hearing, 3 November, Brisbane
Ralph Barrow, 10 years old	Dick Ben Jacky	Dick Ben Jacky	Moggy Moggy Millbong Jemmy	Millbong Jemmy Jemmy
Margaret Shannon, 5 years old	*Not interviewed*	Millbong Jemmy Did not know other's name	*Not interviewed*	Jemmy
Paddy of Durundur (according to Jemmy Perowa)	*Not interviewed*	Dick Ben Jacky Marmoulli Moggy Moggy	*Not interviewed*	Jemmy Moggy Moggy

shared identity, rather than the offender'.[46] What was important to Aboriginal people was not the individual but the restoration of social, political, community balance. 'The emphasis was on the continuity of life as it was experienced. The status quo must be preserved. If the actions of individuals or groups disturbed the balance of life there must be a corresponding action to rectify this and restore the balance.'[47] The legitimacy of these practices was not questioned within the Aboriginal community, for they were religiously ordained. Ancestral law was the 'proper way' shown by totemic ancestors so that people knew their obligations to kin and their 'connections to and rights in land, waters, and their resources'.[48]

Dalaipi, an elder on whose land the attack had taken place, sought to explain this legal system to a young Tom Petrie when he criticised

Aboriginal people for killing Europeans who were innocent of any offence against them. Dalaipi actually spoke in pidgin English but Constance Petrie gave his words greater dignity in the eyes of her Edwardian readers by transcribing them in formal English:

> The missionary and white fellow tell us that if a black fellow kill a white man they catch him and kill him by putting a rope round his neck; and if a white man kill another white fellow, they do just the same. That is your law. Well, the black fellow is different. We do not blame the man we see killing the other, but go by the cracking of the dead man's bones. And when we get a chance we do not put a rope round the murderer's neck, but kill him with a waddy, a spear, or a tomahawk. That is the difference, and we do not see any harm in killing that way. It was our law before the white fellow came among us to teach us all sorts of things. Why did the white man not stop in his own country, and not come here to hunt us about like a lot of kangaroo? If they had kept to their own land, we would not have killed them.[49]

Given the recent killing of Cambell and the wounding and possible deaths of two or three of his allies by whites, there is no doubt that this attack was legal under Aboriginal laws of payback, but it is impossible to be sure whether this was the precise cause, or whether the attack was part of the implementation of a much longer regional inquest process related to payback over the Kilcoy poisonings, as some settlers believed.

There is one more important insight that can be drawn from the courtroom and Paddy's evidence. It is interesting to note the pairing of men with responsibility for wielding the fatal blows. Jacky and Millbong Jemmy were older men, known about the district, while Dick Ben and Moggy Moggy (assuming he was actually Mickaloe, which was much debated) were young men, suggesting the attack was also used as a system of warrior training. Marmoulli was named not by the children but by Paddy, so he had possibly been assigned to dispatch Thomas Shannon, who said he came under attack by two men.

For the first time we have some fresh evidence about Dundalli and his new role in Aboriginal politics. Although Ralph Barrow would later declare that Dundalli had actually struck blows against Gregor, that was not part of his evidence in 1846, and Paddy of Durundur was very specific about Dundalli's part: 'Dandalli stop in scrub'. At first it appears as if Paddy specifically wanted to exonerate Dundalli since he had not been named as a significant player by any of the Europeans at this point, but Paddy was unlikely to have been aware of the detailed descriptions the children were providing to the makeshift court that morning 40 kilometres away. Rather, it seems that Dundalli had a specific role in the attack and that Perowa and Paddy understood why Dundalli had stopped in the scrub. When Hausmann was required to swear on oath about the details of the attack on the missionaries in March 1845 he could not ascribe specific acts to Dundalli either, other than that he had heard Dundalli outside talking during the attack on the hut: 'Dundalli was chief talker there he seemed to be the principal one there'.[50] So perhaps Dundalli was in the scrub at Gregor's station to direct proceedings, just as a battle leader or lawman might do and in the same way that he had supervised events at Burpengary. Although there were no European eyewitnesses to accuse him of any direct role in the attack, Europeans came to blame him as the central figure and, as the years went by, young Ralph's testimony reflected that hostile community opinion, varying his statements enormously from trial to trial.

In the immediate aftermath of the attack William Mason, from neighbouring Samsonvale, bravely volunteered to spend the night at Forgie to guard the station and cattle from further assault. Presumably he slept in the Shannons' now pillaged and dishevelled hut, since the corpses of Gregor and Mary Shannon were in the other. Where the traumatised Thomas Shannon, the Aboriginal boy Ralph and the three little girls slept that night was not covered in any court transcripts. The bodies were buried at the station on the Tuesday after the inquest had been finalised on site.[51] In the days that followed, Shannon headed to Sydney to enrol his three daughters in the Female Orphan School.[52]

Reverend John Gregor, who was away on one of his tours, visiting his scattered congregation, returned to Brisbane early in November, and then only briefly.[53] So it is not clear where Ralph Barrow, now without a guardian, spent these weeks. Reverend Gregor had lost his residence in Brisbane when the government decided to put all the former convict buildings in Brisbane up for auction.[54] His supporters had rallied, holding a meeting to raise funds for a church and parsonage just days before the attack on his brother's station, but this was a long-term plan.[55] In the meantime he joined the former German mission community at Nundah. The uncertainty regarding his home must have added to the trauma for the young boy, who was again now in John Gregor's care. Barrow was a crucial witness who would be called upon in no less than nine court proceedings in the years ahead, a gruelling experience which could only have intensified his insecurity and which would have calamitous results for Dundalli.

The loss of the young brother of a squatter, a squatter and a female servant all within a ten-month period greatly disturbed the white community. Ludwig Leichhardt, then on the Darling Downs in preparation for his 1846–47 expedition to the Swan River in Western Australia, wrote anxiously to his good friend David Archer, on whose station he had spent many productive months in 1843. Leichhardt had worked in the field with Dalla and coastal men learning about local botanical specimens, so he knew some of those involved in the attack and its proximity to Durundur. 'Gregors death has alarmed me if not for your personal security, but for that of your stock; the time of hostility and war is approaching fast and I fear you will have your share of it.'[56]

War was indeed on many settlers' minds and its pursuit would be mired in controversy.

5

WHITE POLITICS AND BLACK POLITICS

'Hostility and war is approaching fast'—as Leichhardt was writing to David Archer at Durundur, David's younger brother Tom Archer, now twenty-three years old, was also putting pen to paper to discuss Dundalli's attack on Gregor's station. He wrote to David from one of the Archer brothers' new makeshift sheep runs in the Burnett district.

> What are you all going to do in the present case? Surely not sit still and allow yourselves all quietly to be murdered. I am so convinced that something must be done that either Charlie or I will be down someday soon to try and get up a party or I am convinced that part of the country will be impassable and untenable.[1]

The attack on Forgie Station provoked passionate debate in both the black and the white communities of south-east Queensland. The question about how European and Indigenous should relate to one another and deal with brutal infractions of each other's law was brought to a head as a result of the attack. The arguments reflected larger political differences within both societies. On the Aboriginal side, Dundalli came to lead one powerful division, which sometimes crossed tribal lines, blurring allegiances. As his leadership came to the fore and his stature rose among the Aboriginal peoples of south-east Queensland, his fearsome reputation among settlers grew.

Among the Europeans were many who wanted retaliatory action in open defiance of their own law. Others, convicts and officials alike, advocated an equally brazen and violent form of vengeance while manipulating the appearance of legality—knowing how difficult it was for Sydney officials to enforce the law on this remote frontier. Only a minority believed that Europeans should behave lawfully and respect human rights.

From what we can perceive of the debate inside Aboriginal society, its politics were just as sophisticated. In the summer of 1842–43 all the south-east Queensland peoples had agreed that the settlers were base and ignorant people whose unlawfulness could not be tolerated. The question was how best to respond to them. Should the old ways of ancestral law continue to have primacy when Europeans were so lacking in the courtesy and honour that Aboriginal law required? Europeans had powerful technology and no sense of proportion, so their vengeance lacked all subtlety—it would be wreaked upon those living in close proximity to European settlement and would always escalate disputes. Those who persisted in asserting that traditional ways were sacred and immutable could flee to their mountain fastnesses and island homes. In the 1840s any regions without roads or accessible waterways generally remained safe for Aboriginal people.

The Stradbroke Islanders, Mianjin and Jagera of Ipswich and South Brisbane did not have such easy sanctuary. Since they coudn't avoid them, they preferred to exploit naive Europeans to settle their own scores. Settler understanding of Aboriginal politics was crude, and at times it was easy to persuade them to act against one's opponents, whether they were European wrongdoers or Aboriginal rivals or offenders. For, just as Europeans were preoccupied with their own national and family problems at the same time that they were debating frontier relations, Aboriginal law and politics continued to be about more than just the malevolence and savagery of Europeans. It was Aboriginal-focused, not European-focused.

Naturally the sources are scant on Aboriginal internal politics. The tensions between romantic love and the enforcement of arranged marriages that honoured old debts and upheld the authority of the elders was one of the Aboriginal political fractures that European witnesses understood and continued to refer to in the 1840s and 1850s. The laws of marriage made women political players, but their aims and motives remain even more difficult to discern than the politics of their men.

To understand some of the Aboriginal responses to the Europeans, and to appreciate the levels of violence emanating from each society, it is important to look at the political dissension among the Europeans in the Moreton Bay district before looking in some detail at the Aboriginal politics resulting from violent interracial episodes.

Tom Archer's thoughts of vigilantism were very much in keeping with the attitudes presented by the *Moreton Bay Courier*. In a passionate editorial in mid-November 1846 it lambasted a 'one-sided' British law, which it claimed protected 'native ferocity'. It refused to acknowledge the integrity of Aboriginal culture; the fact that Aboriginal people met and planned responses to infringement of their law was used as proof that *all* Aboriginal people were criminals, not just the warriors who carried out the agreed actions. The paper wanted all local Aboriginal people punished—a mass retaliation. British law was the declared enemy of the Moreton Bay settlers, who must go beyond its bounds.

> The crimes of a tribe of savages, whom no kindness can conciliate, are treated as the crimes of a single individual, and

his equally guilty compeers are suffered to escape! ... 'Oh, Justice, Justice, what absurdities are perpetrated in thy name!' ... what is to be done? Because the question is surrounded with difficulty, are we to remain without protection, waiting to be cut down like ears before the sickle—bound hand and foot by the terrors of a one-sided law, which in our relations to the blacks, threatens instead of protecting us?

Clearly not. This editorial four weeks after the Forgie Station attack urged the 'authorities ... to shut their eyes while we take the law into our own hands'.[2]

An aggrieved John Gregor had already written directly to the colonial secretary in a private and personal letter, urging that the military be allowed to become involved in the capture of his brother's murderers. In dreadful handwriting that no doubt reflected his emotional state he appealed to Sir Edward Deas Thomson to offer a reward to convict and free alike, and begged that the military also be allowed to claim it, 'if military law permits of such a course being pursued'.[3] The newly appointed governor, Sir Charles FitzRoy, had to authorise any official response and he would not concede to the latter; since 1831 the British government had refused to endorse military incursions against the Indigenous peoples of Australia. In the intervening years there had been instances where governors had resorted to military action against Aboriginal people and they invariably became mired in controversy. The British government's claim was that Australia was settled, not conquered, and Aboriginal Australians were supposed to be without any sophisticated polity capable of waging war against a European power. Declaring martial law would imply Aboriginal people had sovereignty and were as able as any other peoples at violently resisting the appropriation of their lands. In spite of numerous references from settlers and officials alike to living in war-like situations on the frontier, London and Sydney refused to endorse it. Governor FitzRoy willingly agreed to Gregor's other suggestion, however, and promptly posted a reward of £25 for free persons or a conditional pardon for any convicts 'who may bring to justice the murderer or murderers' on 9 November 1846.[4]

It was an old remedy under British law and one seemingly suited to this attack, for Reverend Gregor also complained in his letter about the return to the Pine Rivers district of an Aborigine who had served a criminal sentence for a past attack: 'From inquiries made by myself on the spot, I have every reason to believe that this now accomplished miscreant was one of the prime instigators to my brother's murder.' In Gregor's and most settlers' eyes there had to be an individual—an Aboriginal battle leader or lawman—responsible for the instigation of criminal acts. A little over two weeks later the *Courier* had reached the same conclusion but was more passionate in its denunciation of the government. Its editorial mocked how

> Our humane government recently forwarded to this district at the public expense, an Aboriginal black who had undergone a term of incarceration of three years on Cockatoo Island. With a multitude of European vices grafted on his native ferocity, his presence in this district is already disastrously felt. Led on by him, the Brisbane and Pine River tribes, have become so daring in their depredations that no person now ventures to trust himself unarmed beyond the precincts of the town.[5]

It was a reference to Cambayo, who had given Dundalli his martial training and led him in the attack on William Vant in April 1843; Cambayo had also issued threats to David Archer at the time of the Gregor attack.[6] The problem was that no witnesses had named Cambayo as part of the attack so no warrant could be issued in his name—even if they had had any hope of finding him in the wilds of the Caboolture–Sunshine Coast hinterland. And warrants were what even the lowest felon in the district knew were legally necessary in order to claim any reward.

The colonial government's response to Gregor's letter—the posting of a reward—was so rapid that it pipped private residents of Brisbane who had also decided on that course of action. These private residents were still calling for subscribers for their proposed reward of £10 per accused when the government's notice appeared. Two days later their advertisement offered £10 'to any party who apprehends the following Aboriginal Natives, viz.:—Jackey Jackey, Dick Ben, and Moggy Moggy, the murderers of the late Mr Gregor and Mrs Shannon; and Horse Jemmy, the principal in the murder of the late Mr Uhr'.[7] The use of the name 'Jackey Jackey' is puzzling—none of the witnesses had used this name at the original inquest or at the committal hearing for Constable on 3 November. Jackey Jackey had been known since penal settlement days and appears to have come from Limestone but all of the witnesses at Forgie Station had used the name 'Jacky' and referred to him as a man who had undertaken work for Reverend Gregor.

To understand the mayhem that followed, the value of £10 to the shepherds and labourers of Moreton Bay needs to be appreciated. Unlike a government reward, private subscribers were not going to fuss about refusing payment to a convict nor would they require a legal apprehension and conviction in a court of law. Most station hands were working for board (usually a rough bush hut), rations and £25 per annum, so this sum was equivalent to more than four months' wages. It was more than seven weeks' wages for Brisbane's chief constable and more than three weeks' wages even for Captain Wickham's clerk.[8]

Nor were the working men of the Moreton Bay district the type to be repulsed by the risk and brutality required to deceive and entrap. The official census of 1846 recorded a non-Indigenous population for North and South Brisbane of 960 people, but males outnumbered females almost two to one and a quarter of all males were of convict background. When Ipswich was included there were almost

1600 non-Indigenous residents in the region,[9] most of whom were single working men. This number was regularly augmented by Sydney convicts given tickets of leave for Moreton Bay. Additionally the government retained a small convict workforce to maintain agricultural plots, cattle and other infrastructure that remained from penal settlement days. In 1846 John Kent, the officer in charge of the Government Stock and Agricultural Establishments, was responsible for more than twenty-two convicts, many of whom were 'lifers', at the Stock Establishment at Ipswich and at what became known as the 'Ploughed Station' at Bundamba. Serving convicts also comprised the boats crew for the pilot station on Stradbroke Island and assisted the government surveyors.

In 1844 a letter complaining of the lack of law and order at Ipswich from William Dorsey, the first medical doctor to practise professionally in the north, was read to the Legislative Council. When called upon by the colonial secretary's office to explain, John Kent admitted that many of the convicts still employed by the government at Bundamba and Ipswich were Norfolk Island expirees with bad records, but in defence of his convict staff he itemised all the offences known to have been committed in the area to show that most had been perpetrated by free men and by ticket of leave holders assigned to the district's pastoralists. As he explained to his Sydney superior, 'In a place like Ipswich unprovided with Police the resort of all the idle and dissolute of the district with the usual accompaniments of Sly Grog Shops and Illicit Stills the prophecy of Mr Dorsey may be accomplished without the aid of a Government convict Establishment in the neighbourhood.'[10]

These were the kinds of men who were drawn to the frontier districts. They took up the offer of monetary rewards, however brutal and bloodthirsty the work, with relish. Nonetheless, 'government men', as the convicts were euphemistically referred to, played leading roles in some of the killings that ensued.

Clearly Gregor's private letter to Thomson had become the talk of the town, for excitement about a possible reward swept through the community within days. Gregor dated his letter 2 November, the colonial secretary's office did not draft a notice until 9 November, and the *Government Gazette* that announced it was published on 16 November,[11] whereas the first killing resulting in a reward took place on the morning of Friday, 6 November.

Yilbung did not venture into Brisbane until seventeen days after the attack at Gregor's, when he was seen with a group of Aboriginal men at Breakfast Creek. From there local settlers gave chase until the group fled across the river. They apparently spent Thursday in the bush near what are now the suburbs of Murrarie and Lytton, near Bulimba Creek, but on the Friday morning Yilbung approached the hut of some sawyers. None of the surviving evidence is clear about how many workmen were at this camp. We have the names of three who were involved: Richard Bickerton, who fired the fatal shot; James Smith, a former convict, who was illiterate; and his co-worker Joseph Liddiard. In the version of events that the sawyers gave officials, Yilbung was pestering them for food, and when a bullock driver and one of the sawyers entered the hut, Yilbung became violent, striking one of the men with a waddy. One of the men later gave a quite different version of events to Tom Petrie, admitting that the sawyers had heard the talk of rewards and intentionally lured Yilbung to their camp with offers of tea and food. Once Yilbung was seated and had begun eating they attempted to secure him; as he struggled on the ground one of the logging party shot him in the head. Clearly this shot was not sufficient to kill him because the talk of Brisbane was that even after three shots Yilbung was alive when the men threw his body on a dray to bring him in to Brisbane. Petrie says he died on the road, while the *Moreton Bay Courier* simply reported that it took two hours for him to expire. Police Magistrate Wickham immediately held an inquiry and the *Courier*'s weekly Saturday issue devoted a paragraph to this 'justifiable homicide', which began, 'we have something like satisfaction in informing our readers the hand of retributive justice has reached one of its victims'.

Yilbung's body was not returned to his people for the women's funeral rites; instead it ended up at the hospital where, Petrie said, the head was cut off and boiled down so that a cast could be made of his skull. In Brisbane the private subscribers promptly paid a £10 reward and, despite the fact that Paddy of Durundur had not even named Millbong Jemmy as one of those involved in the Gregor attack, and that the children had disputed his role in it, his brutal death was not questioned by authorities. The *Moreton Bay Courier* hoped that it had taught the 'natives . . . a lesson they will not soon forget'.[12]

The ready payment of this first reward and the sly and brutal entrapment of Yilbung added to the district's excitement. Out at Ipswich, Kent had instructed the overseer of the Stock Establishment to privately inform the convicts that warrants had been issued for Aboriginal men who were accused of spearing government cattle. At this point there was still no announcement of a government reward, but Kent promised that he would use his influence to recommend pardons for any men involved in their capture, and talk of the collection of the private reward for the Gregor and Uhr assailants was already circulating among the convicts. The warrants had been issued for Aboriginal men who were well known around Bundamba and Ipswich but the men's restless talk meant that the locals soon knew what was afoot and left the district.[13]

Yilbung and his friends had entered Brisbane a few days after a large pullen pullen of Stradbroke Island, Bunya Bunya and Yaggera peoples had been held at Bundamba, less than a fortnight after the Gregor station attack; now, as elders departed homewards from this meeting, they found themselves confronted by white authorities. Mulrobbin, the acknowledged elder of South Brisbane, was arrested on 18 November at about the same time that Commissioner Simpson's

Border Police were at Redbank securing Wunkermany, a Jagera man who was just as prominent among the Mianjin and Ningy Ningy. These men were no longer leading warriors—they were now older men, elders whom Brisbane authorities recognised as influential.

The charges against them were flimsy. Major North, who had conducted the inquest on John Uhr, had reached a finding of 'murder against blacks unknown'[14] because there were no surviving European witnesses, so warrants should not have been issued for his death. Wunkermany's charge stemmed from an attack, allegedly by dogs belonging to him, on a government steer back in June 1846. The intent behind these warrants, which were issued for a long list of Aboriginal men for the attack on the cattle, seemed to be to capture as many influential men as possible and then seek to associate them with more serious charges such as the killings of John Uhr, Andrew Gregor and Mary Shannon.[15]

Two weeks after Mulrobbin and Wunkermany's arrests, word reached Ipswich that a large group of Ugarapul was encamped at Rosewood Scrub for a wallaby hunt. Keen for monetary reward and government pardons, three convicts from the Stock Establishment prepared to add to the tally of Aboriginal captives. On 27 September 1839 Daniel Doyle and John Lindon had landed in New South Wales on the convict ship *Blenheim* after being tried in Dublin City on the same day six months earlier; both men had been given the same sentence of ten years' transportation. Their companion at Rosewood was another Irishman, John Reynolds, who had landed the year before with a sentence of fifteen years. None of them had good records in the colony. Over a seven-year period they had received additional cumulative sentences of 100, 172 and 150 lashes, respectively, as well as time in the cells, on the treadmill and in ironed gangs, before being sent to the Moreton Bay Stock Establishment between 1839 and 1845. The colonial government was keen to be rid of the responsibility and cost for these men but inquiries as to their fitness for tickets of leave had seen John Kent evaluate Reynolds' and Lindon's records at Ipswich as 'bad' and Doyle, the leader of the group, as 'indifferent'. In other words, none of these men was deemed fit to reside as a free man in British society. Despite their police histories the Stock Establishment overseer not only gave them permission to go to the Aboriginal camp at Rosewood some 21 kilometres away but also to carry firearms. When they headed out on 30 November 1846 they also had copies of warrants for three Aboriginal men provided by Overseer Thomson.[16]

Their target was Waakoon, a Ugarapul man known by the Europeans as 'Horse Jemmy', whom Doyle claimed to know well. Like the Yilbung attack, this supposed capture was marked not by an honourable warning, so common to Aboriginal protocol, but by deception. Arriving at the scrub to find at least two hundred people encamped, Lindon and Reynolds stayed out of sight while Doyle approached Waakoon to tell him that there was flour for him at a nearby cedar loggers' camp. Waakoon was in company with one of his friends, John Mayhall, but after 40 or so metres something alerted Mayhall that all was not well; perhaps he saw the outline of two pistols Doyle had secreted in his shirt, because after some words from Mayhall, Waakoon refused to go any further. Doyle then grabbed both young men and told them they were under arrest. Mayhall successfully broke free while Waakoon and Doyle struggled on the ground. As Waakoon made a break Doyle took out his pistol and shot the young man as he fled. Lindon and Reynolds also fired shots, causing a general panic among the hunt participants, which allowed the massively outnumbered convicts to claim Waakoon's body. The young man died as they carried him to Major North, a magistrate and the owner of the nearest station.

North, who immediately carried out an inquiry on the body, was cautious enough to give a finding of 'shot by Government men' but the *Moreton Bay Courier* made the tenuous claim that clothing and items belonging to both John Uhr and Mary Shannon were found upon Waakoon, thereby supposedly establishing the young man's guilt, not of spearing government cattle, but of murder. The assault upon Mayhall and the shots fired by Lindon and Reynolds were also conveniently overlooked by the *Sydney Morning Herald*, which repeated the claim about Uhr's clothes.[17]

Two men dead, two elders in custody and random firing at an Aboriginal gathering. By 16 December complaints were starting to filter through to Sydney about the all-out mayhem being inflicted on Aboriginal people in south-east Queensland. A letter to the *Sydney Chronicle* in early December provided a little more context to the sawyers' allegations that Yilbung had approached them—in fact parties of whites had been shooting at Aboriginal camps near Brisbane using the pretext that they were seeking to arrest individuals. Yilbung and his friends had probably decamped to Bulimba Creek for safety. Two weeks later editorial comment in the same Sydney paper objected to the Moreton Bay practice of allowing convicts to be armed and unsupervised on these raids and called for an inquiry.[18]

Its timing was apt. As the *Sydney Chronicle* was coming off the printing press on 16 December a regional meeting of Aboriginal people was gathering at York's Hollow near Brisbane. Unconcerned by the disquiet that was brewing in the south, Brisbane police used convict and Aboriginal informants to hatch a plan for a night raid on Daki Yakka's village. Despite being close to Brisbane, where there was a resident magistrate as well as a chief constable who could have formally visited the Aboriginal camp to assist in making any arrests, two constables instead chose to make up a party with Grattan, a convict belonging to the local government surveyor, and three Mianjin men: Paul Paul, Mooky and Jackey. They had equipped Jackey with a noose to slip over their suspect's head and waited until late in the evening— they thought it was about 11 p.m.—before sneaking up to the hut of Jackey Jackey, the man they were seeking. All the men were armed, the police constables and Grattan with carbines and Jackey with a pistol. It was a showery summer evening so when things went wrong and

Jackey Jackey escaped the noose and ran, Constable Murphy's carbine misfired, as did Grattan's. Jackey fired his pistol at a dog that rushed him, leaving Constable Connor to fire at the back of the fleeing Jackey Jackey, less than 50 metres away. The shootings aroused the whole village and up to four hundred men, women and children, young and old, pregnant and infirm, fled in panic. That left Connor, Murphy and Grattan free to go through the huts, burning and breaking weapons and stealing any goods they fancied, until dawn.

The next morning James McAllister, a boatman in the customs department, was at Connor's house, where Murphy boasted of how Jackey Jackey had screeched and fallen from Connor's shot. Without a body though, Connor and Murphy could not claim the reward, so at eleven o'clock that morning they returned to York's Hollow. They claimed they could find no traces of blood, let alone a body, which in the event of complaint would allow them to deny anyone had been wounded.

And complaint there was. Without a body there was no need for Police Magistrate Wickham to initiate an inquest, and without an Aboriginal arrest there was nothing for the local paper to report. However, the Mianjin elder Daki Yakka conveyed what had taken place to William Duncan, the newly appointed sub-collector of customs at Moreton Bay.[19]

Prior to taking up his appointment, Duncan had been the editor of a progressive newspaper in Sydney, the *Morning Chronicle*, which had supported Governor Gipps's land reforms and earned Duncan the enmity of the squatters. He had become insolvent rather than accept a bribe from the Pastoralists' Association to change his editorial position. It was a tough decision for a man with a young family and Governor Gipps, with the support of the Colonial Office, rewarded him with the Brisbane appointment. Duncan's politics were also influenced by his religious affiliations. He had migrated to Sydney from Aberdeen in Scotland as a Catholic schoolteacher in 1837 but soon took up a position as editor of the Catholic newspaper, the *Australasian Chronicle*. This brought him into a network of educated and articulate Catholics that included professional men such as Roger Therry, who became Judge Therry in 1846, and John Plunkett, attorney-general of New South Wales. Therry and Plunkett had excellent records when it came to defending Aboriginal rights in the colony. Soon after Governor Gipps's arrival in the colony the two young barristers had responsibility for the prosecution of the Myall Creek trials, the only successful trial of whites for a mass killing of Aboriginal people in Australia's history.[20] These three men would all come to play pivotal roles in Dundalli's fate.

By the time of the York's Hollow raid, Duncan could no longer call on the support of Governor Gipps—his term had ended and Gipps had departed for England on 11 July 1846; but Duncan still knew the Sydney newspaper scene and he formally wrote to the executive government. Given the subject matter, his anonymous letters to the editors of newspapers were sure to have been read by the attorney-general. On 2 January 1847 the *Sydney Chronicle* published information about the York's Hollow attack of 20 December, and in an editorial comment referred to the quest for the murderers of Gregor and Uhr as but a 'pretence' to go out and shoot Aborigines at Moreton Bay. The *Courier* fought back with a long letter signed 'Anti-Humbug', which attacked the *Sydney Chronicle* letter writer and defended the killing of Yilbung by giving a long and exaggerated list of his aggressions towards whites dating back to penal station days. 'We have seized their country by the right of might, and by the right of might the whites will continue to possess it', the paper defiantly assured its readers.[21] It was not a response designed to allay the concerns of the attorney-general. Captain Wickham was instructed to chair an inquiry into the Waakoon and the York's Hollow shootings.[22]

Wickham was hardly an impartial adjudicator of these events. The Gregor attack had led him to urge drastic action, writing to Colonial

Secretary Deas Thomson just days before the entrapment of Yilbung, insisting he was not a 'blood thirsty' man 'but I think they want a severe dressing, and that a few months of martial law and wholesome discipline, would bring them to their senses'.[23] Perhaps that is why the inquiry into the shooting of Waakoon and events at York's Hollow comprised a panel of four local magistrates—Wickham was required to sit with Lieutenant Blamire (in charge of the small military detachment at Moreton Bay), Major North (who had conducted the Waakoon inquest) and Commissioner Simpson.

The inquiry took place sporadically over a three-week period, commencing on Monday, 25 January 1847, and hearing the last witnesses on Saturday, 13 February. After listening to the evidence of the first few days Duncan realised that local officials were 'stacking' the inquiry by calling only those witnesses whose conduct was being investigated. He asked to be allowed to appear which, as he recalled in his memoirs, Wickham conceded 'with a very bad grace', but it did enable evidence of harassment of Daki Yakka in the aftermath of the Gregor attack to be presented, as well as testimony from another customs department employee, James McAllister. A Brisbane constable, Jerry Scanlan, admitted that he had tried to frighten Daki Yakka from the town and when he did not leave, shot at him while Daki Yakka was cutting wood in a neighbour's yard. Duncan also presented information about the death of Daki Yakka's daughter Kitty and news from the Quandamooka warrior Canary, who accused a sawyer, Dick Smith, of taking his wife, and the pilot's boat crew of abducting young women from Stradbroke Island at gunpoint.

In the end, however, given the contradictory evidence and the lack of certainty regarding Jackey Jackey's death, and local officials' support for Doyle, Lindon and Reynolds, the colonial secretary's office accepted that no further action could be taken. Colonial Secretary Deas Thomson later reassured Duncan that he supported his action in reporting events.[24]

Not so the *Moreton Bay Courier*, which continued its newspaper war against Duncan and the *Sydney Chronicle*, with the occasional contribution from the *Sydney Morning Herald* on the side of the *Courier*. The *Courier*'s 6 February editorial complained of spies, toadies and pseudo-philanthropists, exaggerated the number of whites who had been killed by Aborigines at Moreton Bay and launched an attack on the attorney-general for ordering the Waakoon and York's Hollow inquiries when he had done no such thing over the killing of whites in the district. These claims were ludicrous given that European deaths had been investigated by the executive government in late 1844, six Aboriginal men had died as a result of official action, including a public hanging at Brisbane's Windmill, five had undergone terms of incarceration, and a military detachment had been stationed at Helidon to prevent further Aboriginal aggression there. It was a very high rate of official measures, all the more so given the remoteness of the district.[25]

But the editorial did not end there. It also attacked the heart of Aboriginal society and governance by citing Reverend James Günther's reply to the 1845 Select Committee on the Condition of the Aborigines. The committee had sent a questionnaire to clergymen, commissioners of crown lands and benches of magistrates. Some of the replies showed sympathy and insight into why Aboriginal people opposed the British presence. New South Wales' first Catholic Bishop, John Polding, for example, was examined by the committee in person, and summed up the source of Aboriginal disaffection.

> There is established in the mind of the black population a sentiment that the whites are essentially unjust; there may be exceptions as they find individuals who are good and kind to them, but ... that is the leading idea, founded on the fact of the whites coming to take possession of their lands, without giving them what they deemed an equivalent; ... to trespass upon the

hunting grounds of another tribe is deemed by them a cause of war; and for one tribe, through mere wantonness, to invade the grounds of another, must necessarily be considered by them an act of spontaneous injustice.[26]

In his reply to the committee Reverend John Gregor, too, opposed the proto-Darwinian position that was rife in the community. Three years before his brother had come under attack he had written to his bishop, urging an Aboriginal mission on Fraser Island, and he included this letter as part of his response to the Select Committee. It was a letter that borrowed its cadences from Shylock in *The Merchant of Venice*, as he explained that Aboriginal

> physical and spiritual constitutions are as perfect as ours ... they have a will, and are free and voluntary agents; that they learn reason and judgment, and exercise them in drawing conclusions and in forming and executing designs; that they discern moral distinctions, and do know good from evil; that they have and exercise all the better affections of love, kindness, tenderness, and gratitude; that they are led by the same crimes as we are, that they yield to the impulses of the same appetites, and that they are but too subject to the same evil passions of anger, hatred and revenge; ... barbarous and uncultivated as they are, they nevertheless form an integral portion of the great family of human kind ...[27]

Gregor, the university medal winner in natural philosophy, had concluded that Aboriginal people and Britishers shared a common humanity.[28] That was not the message the *Moreton Bay Courier* wanted to give its readers. It preferred Günther's views of their inferior disposition and his much shorter assessment that they would always 'return to the savage life', and cited his claim that Aboriginal people were 'more devoid of reflection than any other known race of the human species'.[29] This notion of Aboriginal racial inferiority was warmly pursued by some members of the Select Committee. It was still fourteen years before Charles Darwin published his *Origin of Species* and although this notion was not yet fully established as the scientific orthodoxy, it was a powerful weapon to use against Christians and missionaries who insisted that Aboriginal people had souls and therefore rights as human beings.

James Günther had been missionary at the Church Missionary Society Wellington Valley mission when Reverend William Watson had walked off the mission, taking all thirty Aboriginal residents with him in 1841, including the young Ralph Barrow.[30] The only way to civilise, according to Günther, was compulsion—he wanted every man not in employment penalised under the *Vagrants Act* as idlers; he also wanted the rule of the old men banned by government decree and to outlaw their 'warlike preparations and demonstration, from settling their own disputes and taking revenge by feuds and duels'. It would put a stop 'to their frequent excursions and ... produce more steady habits', according to Günther. In effect, Günther had, in a distorted way, identified the basis of Aboriginal law and governance and wanted the colonial government to destroy it completely—a project with which the *Courier* enthusiastically agreed. That was the way to respond to 'pseudo-philanthropists'.[31]

The following week, when it became clear that the inquiry would not result in any legal action against those involved in the attack at Rosewood or the attack at York's Hollow, the *Courier* was triumphant. Its report would be '"gall and wormwood" to the writers ... in the Sydney journals', it crowed, especially since the *Moreton Bay Courier*'s report of the hearings was truncated, omitting much of the evidence from Duncan and McAllister. The *Sydney Morning Herald* joined in, publishing commentary that was hostile towards Duncan and his evidence to the inquiry. The *Sydney Chronicle* replied calmly, pointing out that the evidence was disturbing and recommending the removal of convicts from government departments at Moreton Bay. It also published a letter from Duncan which made the rather obvious point that had been overlooked in both the *Sydney Morning Herald* and *Courier* reports: that shooting did not constitute 'apprehending'.[32]

In April the media war extended to include the *Australian*, another Sydney paper, which criticised the *Moreton Bay Courier*'s biased reporting of alleged Aboriginal threats to whites without ever reporting on European aggressions towards Aboriginal people. It focused on the fact that the *Courier* had made much of an assault on shepherds at Whiteside Station in November and a threat to Captain Griffin in January, but had failed to inform its readership of another poisoning of Aborigines by shepherds at Griffins' station.[33] An employee of Whiteside had come forward to report to Brisbane officials that two fellow shepherds had intentionally left flour poisoned with arsenic at their hut, knowing that it would be consumed by Aboriginal visitors.[34] Forewarned, Captain Griffin had galloped back to his station to warn his two accused men, who willingly came down to Brisbane to testify that they had merely left flour in a hut along with a disused vessel that had been used to mix arsenic—no actual poisoned flour had been left by them at all; at least that was the version the *Moreton Bay Courier* reported. The newspaper spent more time denouncing 'tattling, tale-bearing, eaves dropping and other anile vices' than it did on the credibility of the two shepherds or on the seriousness of another case of attempted mass poisoning in the district. The correspondent to the *Australian* was clearly a 'viperous calumniator' and a 'masked coward'.[35]

Sadly the evidence from the *Australian* was true. According to Petrie, Aboriginal men had used the flour to make damper; several became sick and three of them died before the rest of the flour was discarded. There were other violent assaults committed on Aboriginal people on this station that were similarly never reported.[36] Clearly the editor of the *Courier* intended to intimidate any whites thinking of coming forward with evidence of atrocities. In October it even editorialised against the annual general meeting of the Aborigines Protection Society held in Crosby Hall, London. 'What a pity it is for the cause which those kind-hearted gentlemen espouse, that the gentle savages of Moreton Bay cannot read the newspapers,' it sneered. In shrill tones it declared that it was the white settlers who were 'disappearing' from the 'murderous assault of the natives' and reminded its readership of the 'murdered victims who are yet unavenged on the Pine'.[37]

The events 'on the Pine' had certainly not been forgotten. Despite the controversies of the Waakoon and York's Hollow 'captures', there was one more night-time assault by police on Aboriginal people camped near Brisbane in the 1840s. It was every bit as brutal as that of December 1846, but Captain Wickham remained unmoved by the questionable tactics of using Aboriginal and convict informers or of police entrapment. Following this raid of May 1848 he went so far as to apply for the payment of a government reward to the Aborigines and former convict who assisted, praising their conduct and that of the police to the colonial secretary in Sydney. Wickham, the most senior government representative in the district, played a central role in what ensued as Aboriginal and convict informants approached him on the morning of Saturday, 27 May 1848, to tell him that Oumulli, Dundalli's brother, was encamped at Spring Hollow. Although the child witnesses to the Gregor attack had not named Oumulli as a central player, in broken English Paddy of Durundur had named him in a way that seemed to suggest he had contributed to the assault. Wickham's clerk had then recorded his name as 'Marmoulli'.[38] The former convict Eugene Doucette and his Aboriginal friends from Stradbroke Island gave the information to the police magistrate on Saturday morning, but Wickham's instructions to his constables were to wait until evening to approach Oumulli at Spring Hollow. Waiting until nightfall and sending junior constables in the company of Aboriginal informants? Wickham was endorsing what could at best be described as unorthodox police procedure.

Spring Hollow is still visible in the dip between Wickham Terrace and Leichhardt Street in Brisbane; in 1848, before Brisbane residential development had spread to Spring Hill, it was bushland not far from the customary camping place of the Stradbroke Islanders and Logan people, at what are now the heights of the Roma Street Parklands.[39]

As in the slaying of Jackey Jackey, there was no attempt to make any arrest. According to Petrie, the constables hid in the scrub while Doucette and two of the Stradbroke Islanders approached Oumulli's hut with half a pint of rum to share. One of the Stradbroke Islanders, Bobby Winter, was prepared with a noose hidden in his shirt, and while Oumulli was preoccupied with Doucette, Bobby threw the rope over his head and held firm. This evidence is in stark contrast to the testimony of the constables at the inquest held on Monday morning, when they claimed they had surrounded Oumulli as he lay on the ground, then Doucette grabbed him by his hair and declared him to be the murderer while Constable Ramsay snapped handcuffs on his ankles. Doucette and the Stradbroke Islanders supposedly then carried Oumulli up the hill towards Queen Street. A more accurate account comes from Petrie, who tells us that Oumulli was dragged along the ground with the rope still tight about his neck. Somehow his strangulated gurglings were eventually heard by his friends, who attacked the police party, but the police were armed and returned the attack of waddies and spears with gunfire.[40] The constables claimed on oath that no one noticed that Oumulli was dead until they reached the lockup at the southern end of Queen Street, more than a mile away.

True to the required form, the inquest held on Monday morning concluded that Oumulli had died 'resisting lawful apprehension ... on a charge of murder'.[41] Had Brisbane officials let the matter rest, it is possible that there would have been no further scrutiny. However, the forms of law having been duly followed, Wickham had the audacity to apply for the Gregor reward on behalf of those involved in Oumulli's capture.[42]

Only sixteen months after the York's Hollow inquiry, here was another death of an Aboriginal man supposedly evading capture in Brisbane. Attorney-General Plunkett passed a critical eye over the request. For the most part the response was typical of Plunkett, incisively exploring the legal details and argument. The only hint of his own feelings on the matter was his description of the carriage of Oumulli's body to the watch-house: 'a rope was put about his neck and arm, and he was dragged by that rope a considerable distance; and <u>until</u> he reached the Watch House, the Constables did not perceive that he was actually dead from strangulation' (Plunkett's emphasis). The only clear legal deficiency, however, was that Oumulli had not been named as one of the accused at the original Gregor–Shannon inquest; the accusation that Oumulli was implicated in the attack on Gregor's station came only from an unsworn Aboriginal witness. Plunkett had legitimate grounds for denying the payment of the reward, which he did, and took the opportunity to add that not only had the constables not taken proper care during the arrest but also 'they cannot be regarded as entirely guiltless of having unnecessarily caused his death'. Governor FitzRoy added his agreement with Plunkett's findings and ordered the full response to be forwarded to the police magistrate in Brisbane.[43]

Just as the Europeans focused on receiving justice for their dead—Uhr, Gregor and Shannon—naturally the Aboriginal nations had similar feelings over the repayment of the deaths of warriors in their prime. In stark contrast to the convict and police raids that resulted in indiscriminate shooting as 'captures' got out of hand, the attack on Gregor's station had been controlled and precise, with no more than threats issued to David Archer to the north and to George Griffin to the east by departing warriors.

The pullen pullen held at Bundamba on 30–31 October 1846 had been an opportunity for the Ipswich Jagera, Dalla and Stradbroke Islanders to assess the legal situation. Had the attack by Dundalli's party avenged their loss of Multuggerah and the wounding of his brothers at Rosewood in September? Was payback still outstanding for their many losses since August 1841? Had the attack on Gregor and Shannon been done 'proper way'? Unfortunately the newspaper correspondent who reported the meeting left no account of its deliberations.

Whatever its assessment, the Jagera's plans were soon overtaken by the shocking news and manner of Yilbung's death. From their arrival the Britishers' refusal to share when they were on his land had disgusted Yilbung. When Aboriginal elders had reached a reluctant accommodation with the settlement in the mid-1830s, it mattered nought to Yilbung, who soon had a reputation for theft among the soldiers, settlers and convicts.[44] Even when elders such as Deciby had subjected him to severe traditional punishment for his thefts from the missionaries, he had maintained his defiance while appearing to cooperate. What a triumph the regional agreement for retaliation over the Kilcoy poisonings and Moppy's death must have been for him, despite the lateness of his invitation to that Bunya gathering in January 1843.

Defining Yilbung's position within traditional society is difficult. The mission diaries show that he mixed freely with Aboriginal people from Durundur Station in the north, Toorbul in the east, Tingalpa in the south and of course Brisbane. He also readily visited Stradbroke Island, where the Nunukul emblazoned him with their body scars in the hope that it would confuse the British as to his identity. Yilbung's fresh tribal scars suggest that he had high standing among the Nunukul, which fits with claims that he had supported them in the Stradbroke Island conflict with the military back in 1832.[45] Yet settler claims about his violence do not withstand scrutiny. He had been punished in penal station days for a knife attack on a constable at the Windmill but this 'attack' was so light that it was deflected by the constable's overcoat. He had lost the fight with Dabianco when Deciby had challenged him over his theft from the mission. Nor was there anything suspect about his activities at Breakfast Creek in early November 1846 beyond his well-known practice of stealing food from settlers' gardens. It was his embodiment of Aboriginal values of sociability and generosity that explains his popularity among all the peoples of south-east Queensland. Whenever he acquired food his largesse in hosting night-time feasts was renowned, and his generosity shored up his Aboriginal support. He never seems to have lacked Aboriginal companions, although Petrie emphasised his bravery in being prepared to travel alone at night, which he said was unusual.[46] His 'cheekiness', including his dismissive attitude to settlers, probably also endeared him to his many supporters.

His role in the Forgie Station attack is puzzling. Both children claim to have seen him participate but as his damaged eye made him a memorable character for Europeans it is understandable they could both name him. On the other hand they disagreed about whom it was he struck—a crucial fact when you are seeking to indict someone for murder. Furthermore, the Aboriginal evidence from Paddy of Durundur omitted him altogether, unless 'Jemmy' was meant to refer to him. It fits the Europeans' image of Yilbung that he would have wanted to be involved, despite his lack of any convincing record of violent assault.

Whatever his involvement in the attack, Yilbung's personality, sociability and reputation for upholding the Aboriginal values of sharing food meant that his death, like Waakoon's, was not one the Aboriginal community would take lightly. The *Moreton Bay Courier* sneeringly referred to him as one of the Aboriginal community's 'pet chiefs'.[47] 'Chief' does not appear to be the right term but he was undoubtedly someone who was valued and whose death would need to be avenged. The failure of his closest male relatives to enact payback would severely undermine their status in Aboriginal eyes.

The man who we know took the first action and who is likely to be his elder, if not a direct relative, is Daki Yakka. On the Tuesday after Yilbung was killed, Daki Yakka, accompanied by two or three younger men, came into the township of Brisbane and approached several inhabitants, trying to induce them to come into the bush. He told them he knew where the Gregor murderers were but that it would require white people to bring them in. Given the mood of the township and the eagerness to 'capture' those involved to claim any rewards, it is strange that no whites believed him—according to the *Courier* all refused his entreaties. While Duncan described Daki Yakka as a friendly old man, it seems others in the town were less sure of his loyalties. In the weeks that followed he was met with abuse from the town police. In fact when questioned by Constable Scanlan about the Gregor attack, Daki Yakka claimed he had no idea who the murderers were because he was not there. At least this was part of Scanlan's defence before the York's Hollow inquiry as he explained why he had been verbally abusive to Daki Yakka and 'accidentally' fired his pistol while cleaning it near him.

Before any of the Mianjin had been able to take action for the killing of Yilbung came the unsettling news of the killing of young Waakoon and the shootings by convicts at the Rosewood wallaby hunt. Here was a promising young man whose death must be repaid, but elders such as Mulrobbin and Wunkermany were now in custody. Although charges could not be sustained against Mulrobbin, Wickham held him in the local lockup while he supposedly awaited advice from the attorney-general. Wunkermany was forwarded to Sydney but he also was deemed to have no case to answer and was returned to Brisbane after a lengthy period in custody in Brisbane and Sydney; not surprisingly, he was much embittered by the experience.[48]

This was the context for the meeting of 'four tribes' near Brisbane between 16 and 20 December 1846. It seems to have fallen to Daki Yakka to host, given the losses to the Rosewood Ugarapul–Ipswich

Jagera. There would have been much to discuss. Had the four tribes reached a decision about who was responsible for payback for Yilbung and Waakoon? Had those who carried out the Gregor and Shannon killings done things 'proper way'? The Brisbane police claimed that representatives from the Forgie Station attack were present so it seems likely that it would have been reviewed, if only as an example of how its prosecutors believed lawful payback should be enacted. On the other hand, there were those among the Mianjin and Quandamooka who believed that using Europeans for Aboriginal payback purposes was less risky. According to the town police waiting in the bush on a rainy Sunday night at the height of summer, when Brisbane mosquitoes are usually at their worst, the tribes argued for hours. They estimated it was 11 p.m. before the debating stopped, the elders retired and they could approach Jackey Jackey's hut.

The police shootings that night cut short the Brisbane meeting. The evidence at the subsequent inquiry hardly helps to unravel the machinations of Aboriginal politics—if anything, it adds to the confusion. William Duncan's autobiography provides a few leads. Duncan explains that the police informant Jackey, who was given the task of throwing the noose over Jackey Jackey, wanted to marry Jackey Jackey's wife and that she was actually already in police custody the night of the attack on York's Hollow; she was to be the reward for Jackey from the Brisbane police. So Jackey, whose tribal identification is unknown, had a personal agenda. Mooky and Paul Paul are more complicated. They were both leading Mianjin figures, so why they were absent from the elders' debate on the Sunday night is puzzling unless they too had reason to want payback against Jackey Jackey. Years later, Mooky (whose name is rendered as 'Murki' by Tom Petrie) became a focus of Joondaburri payback, although none of the white sources shed any light on what the original point of dispute was. Mooky's assistance in the police raid against Jackey Jackey adds weight to the circumstantial evidence that the attack on Forgie Station reinforced the traditional political factions that divided some members of the Mianjin and Quandamooka from the North Coast and Dalla peoples.

It is important not to imagine that because Daki Yakka and Canary sought the support of William Duncan that they were somehow 'good' Aborigines, who were loyal to Europeans and recognised European authority. The main game was Aboriginal politics. What they really wanted from the Europeans was help with regaining their political ascendancy among their own people. William Duncan and his friend, the local Catholic priest Father Hanly, never really understood this dimension of Daki Yakka and the younger Canary. Paul Paul's disdain for Europeans was made clear by 1850. In that year he was arrested for working with a group of three other Mianjin men to rob a brickmaker of his tobacco and money at the northern end of Queen Street. The court found him guilty and he was sentenced to six months' hard labour, which he served in Sydney.[49] And what of the role of Daki Yakka's daughter, whom the Europeans called 'Kitty'? Duncan and Hanly, knowing that she had lost her baby in the aftermath of the police raid on York's Hollow, despite being almost full-term, had assumed that it was as a result of the police shooting and ensuing panic. She refused to submit to European doctors at Brisbane hospital, however, and Aboriginal testimony at the York's Hollow inquiry claimed that Jemmy from Limestone had assaulted her after the police raid for being an informant. Was she friends with Jackey Jackey's wife? Did the Mianjin women side with young Jackey's claims over the older warrior Jackey Jackey? Aboriginal women had reported Jackey Jackey to Ipswich police for his involvement in the killing of a white toddler in April 1843,[50] so while Aboriginal lawmen might have given him a leading role in the Gregor station attack, his standing among Aboriginal women seems to be contentious. The colonial racism that leaves us so few names for Aboriginal women and such nondescript men's names as 'Jemmy from Limestone' and 'Jackey Jackey' casts too many shadows for further analysis. However,

Jackey Jackey was associated with Limestone so it makes sense for a Limestone man to have exacted payback on Kitty for his death. Perhaps the history of overt aggression towards whites by the Ugarapul could well have led the Limestone people to side with their western neighbours and the northern coastal peoples on the issue of enforcing payback 'proper way' and to reject the Mianjin's use of Europeans in their internal politics.

Other Aboriginal deeds confirm Duncan's testimony regarding events that culminated in the violence of that night. The Stradbroke Islanders were staunch allies of Daki Yakka and the Brisbane Mianjin and traditionally opponents of the Bribie Islanders and 'Saltwaters' of the north coast, but Canary's actions indicate that, whatever the basis of the differences between these traditional enemies, European unlawfulness disgusted them both and they found ways to repay it. We have one clear example of the sexual abuse of a young Stradbroke Island girl, consistent with Duncan's broad testimony regarding mistreatment of Stradbroke Island women. Even told through the euphemistic language of the nineteenth century press it is shocking.

A former convict by the name of Peter Glynn was a crewman on David Peattie's cutter, *Nelson*. Some time prior to November 1846, Peattie, his crew and boat were hired by David and John McConnel for an overnight expedition to Stradbroke Island. On the return journey Glynn sexually assaulted a ten-year-old Stradbroke Island girl who had been taken on board so she could join her mother at Kangaroo Point. Peattie and the McConnel brothers tried to intervene but Glynn repelled them at gunpoint. Incredibly, on returning to Brisbane neither Peattie nor either McConnel brother thought it appropriate to have Glynn charged with rape, carnal knowledge, assault or abduction; instead David McConnel had him charged with 'misconduct while in his service'. Glynn was able to call a man to testify that Glynn was technically still his hired servant on the night in question and the case was dismissed.[51] Duncan's evidence to the inquiry had been that ten young women had been abused; the Brisbane magistrates had failed to offer the protection of British law to even one little girl.

Canary—and Aboriginal law—saw the situation differently to the Brisbane magistrates. A Catholic mission had been established at Dunwich on Stradbroke Island by Bishop Polding in June 1843. Disputes among the four Italian and Swiss Passionist priests had led to several of them leaving, so by early 1847 only one missionary priest, Father Raymund Vaccari, remained to carry on its work. Father Vaccari, as the sole European at Dunwich, became the focus of Canary's anger against the European presence. While relations between the mission and local Aboriginal people had initially been warm, in August 1843 the locals had become concerned about three children taken by Bishop Polding back to Sydney to be educated; they threatened to kill the missionaries unless they were returned 'by the next steamer', so Polding relinquished the children from the Sisters of Charity in Sydney and sent them back immediately.[52] Vaccari thus had direct experience of the seriousness of Aboriginal threats long before William Duncan had arrived at Moreton Bay. In early 1847 the priest sent messages to Father Hanly, the Irish Catholic priest in Brisbane, pleading for some support given the repeated threats he was receiving from Canary. The irony was that Hanly and Duncan were friends and it was to Duncan and his customs department staff that Canary had given information about the treatment of the Nunukul women, possibly when he was in town for the York's Hollow pullen pullen of 20 December. His conversation with Duncan could have been a warning according to Aboriginal protocol. Hanly and Duncan, however, naively failed to understand Canary's obligations as an Aboriginal man and refused to believe that Vaccari could be in genuine need of protection from him. Father Vaccari had no doubt about it; Canary's hostility towards him had come to physical blows; faced with further threats of violence from Canary, in April 1847 Vaccari took the mission boat, bypassing Brisbane, and headed straight to

Tweed Heads.⁵³ For the second time Europeans surrendered Dunwich to its traditional owners, this time because of direct physical threats from a Nunukul man.⁵⁴

The police contribution to the killing of Jackey Jackey and Canary's successful eviction of the Catholic mission undoubtedly left some of the Mianjin and Nunukul confident of their ability to manipulate the Europeans, but by September 1847, Yilbung and Waakoon had still not been avenged. Aboriginal women must have also been wondering whether the removal of one largely inoffensive Catholic priest constituted sufficient retribution for the abduction of Nunukul women. It fell to Dundalli to enact this payback.

On a clear frosty day in late June 1847, John Griffin was herding cattle on the coastal parts of the Whiteside run when he came across a large pullen pullen. Some weeks later his father recorded in the station diary that there were about ten or twelve men 'in the scrub with the sawyers'. Sawyers were on the station fairly permanently in 1847 to construct a new house,⁵⁵ and George Griffin had also been employing one of them to assist with ploughing in early September.⁵⁶ One of these men was James Smith, who had participated in the assassination of Yilbung near Bulimba. It is also possible that Duncan misnamed the sawyer responsible for the abduction of Canary's wife at the York's Hollow inquiry. He had given the name 'Dick Smith'— had he confused Richard Bickerton and James Smith, two of the confirmed participants at Bulimba? Dundalli suspected this Smith of abuse of Aboriginal women. So these reports should have given the Griffins some concern; they, however, were too preoccupied with their own internal tensions to keep abreast of Aboriginal activities unless they directly affected the station. In fact George Griffin employed an Aboriginal man on the station in August, oblivious to any Aboriginal friction.⁵⁷

The Griffins should have been more alert to the democratic and lawful nature of traditional Aboriginal society. The gathering witnessed by John Griffin in June 1847 appears to have been a continuation of the disrupted pullen pullen of 20 December 1846—held in the safer vicinity of the coast—which was taking up where it had broken off: canvassing responses to Yilbung's murder and the abduction of the Nunukul women, and agreeing on appropriate payback. Certainly it was preparation for the events of September on Whiteside Station. The presence of the ten or twelve Indigenous men at the sawyers' camp, as recorded by George Griffin, was to reconnoitre and plan the administration of punishment in accordance with customary law.

On 10 September 1847 the station awoke to a dull, cloudy day. The youngest son, John, had finally been alerted to planned Aboriginal aggression on the station—he had received word that the Ningy Ningy were planning to spear his cattle and so spent the morning 'cleaning up the small arms'. The station diary did not record who had provided the information, but it was typical of Aboriginal protocol to issue a warning to one's adversaries. John seems to have misconstrued what was planned. At lunchtime, instead of spearing cattle, an intertribal group of men exacted payback on the sawyers. The three men—sawyers James Smith and William Boller and a labourer by the name of William Waller assisting them—were working near the Pine River when a group of Indigenous men attacked them. James Smith survived and made it to the head station, where the alarm was raised at 2.30 p.m. George Griffin immediately 'sent all the disposable force I had to bring the [other] man in'. This was Smith's mate, the sawyer William Boller, who had survived multiple spear wounds but could not make it to the station unassisted. Boller must have had internal injuries, for he was very weak and passing blood.[58] Griffin also sent a party to search for the cook, William Waller, who was already dead; Waller's dog led station staff to his body the next day.

Whiteside Station was not a happy family enterprise and the family's response to an Aboriginal attack on their station was confused. Assistance eventually arrived at 4 p.m. the next afternoon when Wickham, a medical practitioner named Dr Cannan and a constable rode into the station. But it was too late for Boller, who died in Brisbane Hospital the next day.[59] The Indigenous men involved were now presumed guilty of two murders as well as the assault of Smith.

Like the Gregor attack, the confrontation with the sawyers must have been the subject of discussion and planning, for the Pine River people at Griffins' station had not been present at the attack but were able to tell police afterwards who struck the blows. Participation by up to twenty men again crossed tribal boundaries, with Gubbi Gubbi, Dalla and Joondaburri given prominent roles in colonial records that were otherwise poor at identifying individuals. As is so often the case, the Aboriginal version of events can only be reconstructed through the distorted lens of the records of criminal cases in which Indigenous men faced capital convictions.[60]

Commissioner Simpson was one official who recognised the likelihood of Aboriginal payback and refused to succumb to the chest-beating of the *Moreton Bay Courier* over this group attack on three whites. 'As they were sawyers, a class of men but too apt to give provocation, it is difficult to say who may have been the aggressors', he noted in his annual report.[61] James Smith, the only man to survive the attack, naturally emphasised that the sawyers had been on friendly terms with their assailants, who had visited the loggers' camp a fortnight earlier, and again the previous day when a Gubbi Gubbi man, Mickaloe, had offered them fresh meat. Intriguingly, Smith also testified that on one of these visits Dundalli had asked him 'where the jins were' though in the courtroom neither the prosecution nor the defence pursued this line of questioning. Dundalli appears to have linked this sawyer named Smith to the theft of women—surely this is the Smith whom Duncan complained of at the York's Hollow inquiry?

Smith's testimony also provides evidence that links this assault with payback for Yilbung. In seeking to reassure the court that his identification of Mickaloe was accurate, he told how he had met young Mickaloe in the days that followed the Gregor murders when he was working with a group of sawyers near Bulimba.[62] Smith's own testimony places him as a sawyer in the scrubs east of Brisbane at the time of the attack on Yilbung. Not only were Smith and his sawyer companions the obvious target for retributive justice but also, as he and his companions came under attack and his offers of food or any goods they possessed were rebuffed, Smith claimed to have asked why they were being assailed. Dundalli was said to have stepped from behind a tree and answered in his own language. But Smith did not understand him so the words could not be recorded by the court.[63] From the meeting in June through to Dundalli's declaration in the midst of the raid, Aboriginal protocol appears to have been followed.

In one swift encounter, Dundalli and his supporters had dramatically avenged Yilbung and probably too Waakoon, Jackey Jackey and the Nunukul women, according to customary law. The rise in Dundalli's prestige must have been disturbing for his political rivals. No doubt they would have felt that the Bribie Islanders and their Dalla allies needed to be brought back down to earth, but a direct confrontation would have been unwise. Dundalli was a powerful man who had proved his skills as a lawman; now his reputation as a renowned fighter was growing. A better course of action was to weaken his northern base of support. In May 1848, Oumulli, Dundalli's brother, presented their opponents with just such an opportunity. One of the advantages for the northern Dalla and the Bribie Islanders was that they did not spend enough time in the township for settlers, and especially the police, to be able to readily identify them. Perhaps that is why Oumulli confidently camped near Brisbane on 27 May 1848, underestimating how fiercely the Stradbroke Islanders' longstanding antagonism still burned. Certainly the timing of his death appears to link this customary retribution on Oumulli to his brother and to the ongoing conflict between the Bribie Islanders and the Moreton and Stradbroke

Islanders that was remarked upon by many contemporaries, and which at times encompassed others in the region.[64]

Oumulli could not have been captured without the assistance of Eugene Doucette, a former convict originally from Mauritius and now living at Amity Point on Stradbroke Island,[65] and a friend of the traditional owners of the island. Doucette had been one of fifteen convicts transported from Mauritius to Van Diemen's Land in December 1839 and then transferred to Moreton Bay. This French-speaking group were sometimes described as 'Negro', although at least one of them was originally from India and Doucette was officially listed as a 'half-caste'.[66] Doucette had been an assigned servant to the Brisbane businessman and storekeeper Le Breton, and in that capacity had given evidence favourable to the Brisbane police at the York's Hollow inquiry in February 1847.[67] Granted his ticket of leave in 1847, he had obtained a boat and commenced a shell and oyster fishing business with a crew of Quandamooka men.[68] In May 1848 Doucette was keen to win the favour of an Aboriginal woman described by the *Moreton Bay Courier* as a member of Oumulli's own tribe. She was said to have told him where Oumulli was encamped.

The police may have viewed this as the successful application of British law, but the involvement of some Nunukul, including the well-known Bobby Winter, is a sign that Oumulli's 'arrest' was probably a product of traditional law as much as British colonial justice. Although the *Moreton Bay Courier* praised Doucette for assistance to the Brisbane police,[69] it seems he was abetting Winter and the Nunukul as much as the town police, and it was Doucette and Winter who applied the rope to the upper part of Oumulli's body. In fact, given the central roles played by Doucette and Winter, primacy should surely go to it being an enactment of Aboriginal law and politics. Once again a parallel system of law and justice was being performed under the very noses of the settlers without their comprehension. We may never know what infringement of ancestral law that the Nunukul had decreed Oumulli guilty of, but according to anthropologist Ian Keen, the strategy of a night attack was by no means unusual in other parts of Australia.[70] Constance Petrie includes this modus operandi specifically in her discussion of punishments ordained in south-east Queensland Aboriginal inquests:

> Perhaps some night [the accused] would be curled up asleep in the dark, when suddenly he was pounced upon and put out of existence; or perhaps he would be innocently engaged at some occupation when a dark form, sneaking up behind him, would send a spear through his skull, or otherwise do the deed. A death always roused great desire for revenge, and the friends of the deceased would watch and plan in every way till at last their end was accomplished.[71]

Bobby Winter certainly does not appear to be viewed by the traditional owners of the mid-nineteenth century as some kind of lackey of the town police, for according to Constance Petrie his own unexpected death later became the subject of a corroboree performed throughout the region.[72]

For all of Captain Wickham's official praise for Eugene Doucette in 1848, it counted for nought in 1850 when he was living with Aboriginal people at Kangaroo Point. He was arrested for 'being continually with the blacks and having no place of residence'. Doucette explained to the court that he had a new boat but was having difficulty in getting another Aboriginal crew together. Although a Mr Beard had offered him work at the Pine River, his involvement in the killing of Oumulli made it impossible for him to take the job. 'The Blacks there would kill me ... I once took a Blackfellow & if they got me in the bush they would spear me', he explained. It seems the gratitude of the criminal justice system at Moreton Bay was short-lived, for the court was unmoved by his explanation; he was sentenced to three months' hard labour in the newly opened Brisbane Gaol.[73]

The killing of Oumulli retipped the balance of Aboriginal politics in favour of the Mianjin and Nunukul's way of enforcing Aboriginal law—that is, by manipulating the Europeans to do it for them—but it was a risky strategy. In November 1849 it went terribly wrong.

The Colonial Office would not define conflict with Aboriginal people as war but the European residents of Brisbane still lived with a sense of siege almost twenty-five years after white settlement. Late on the night of 28 November 1849 the residents of Brisbane believed they were about to come under mass attack from the traditional owners. When word reached the chief constable he ordered one of his men to go straight to Ensign Cameron, the commander of the local detachment of the 11th Regiment. On this hot summer night Cameron was found fishing down by the river only a few hundred metres from the military barracks at the southern end of Queen Street.[74] He immediately called out his troops, who within the hour were dressed, armed and marching in formation to the Aboriginal camp on the northern edge of the town. Once again the York's Hollow camp was to ring out with gunfire in the middle of the night. When the troops were approximately 400 metres from the camp Cameron ordered them to load, and divided them into two flanks to surround the unsuspecting, sleeping Mianjin. The camp soon woke in alarm to find British redcoats, soldiers of the world's then leading military power, lined up in battle formation with muskets pointed at them. Their fear must have been palpable; today it would be like waking in the middle of the night to find US Special Forces had surrounded your home. Remarkably, while the majority awoke and fled towards Breakfast Creek, two incredibly brave warriors had the composure and presence of mind to fight back. A boomerang and a waddy were allegedly thrown that night. Although no order was given, some of the soldiers opened fire.[75] Three of the troops were subsequently charged with shooting 'at an aboriginal native with intent to do him some grievous bodily harm' and subpoenaed to appear at the first ever sittings of the Supreme Court on circuit to Brisbane in May 1850.[76]

It is important to pause here and again consider the impact of these events on white politics before returning to the implications for the region's tribal nations. This was an important moment in this city's frontier history, for it marked a turning point in the administration of criminal justice in the north.

As the 1840s progressed, an increase in criminal cases from Moreton Bay and the Darling Downs had convinced the judges of the New South Wales Supreme Court of the need to hold criminal trials in the northern district. Rather than requiring defendants, police and witnesses to travel to Sydney or Maitland, a judge and his staff, along with the crown prosecutor, would travel to Brisbane to hold Supreme Court hearings twice a year. This arrangement was referred to as the 'Supreme Court on circuit' and the first sitting was due to be held in Brisbane in May 1850.[77]

The prosecution of British soldiers was a difficult case for the attorney-general, and for the presiding judge at the historic first sitting of the Supreme Court in the northern districts. The local white community already held the British army in high regard and also respected the prompt reaction of their small garrison, however ill-founded their rush to beat to arms had been that night. Judge Therry naturally wanted this assize to reinforce to Brisbane locals the importance and majesty of his court, but this case could undermine respect for the law and lead the *Moreton Bay Courier* on another of its defiant rants about the absurdity of British law. Judge Therry showed his displeasure by giving his view that the soldiers should have been dealt with by military officials at courts martial.

The attorney-general, however, took the opportunity to make official policy very clear in a district with an appalling record of shooting at Aboriginal people. Plunkett insisted on his right to prosecute the case; he rejected the notion that there had been any provocation towards the soldiers or the residents of Brisbane and again stressed the equality of Aboriginal people before the law. On this point his address to the court was impassioned.

> A black man's camp is as much his castle as a white man's house and if he found it invaded at night by an armed and hostile force, he would be justified in throwing a boomerang ... He would have been highly culpable if he had neglected to institute this prosecution. If offences like these could be committed upon the blacks, with impunity, it must be conceded that an armed military force might be called out to any place where large numbers of white people were assembled:—to the race course for instance—into one of the tents, where numbers of people might be assembled, drinking, and perhaps intoxicated, and that they might fire upon those people. Who was there present who would not shudder—the hair of whose head would not stand on end at such a monstrous proposition? When he had placed the evidence before the jury he should have done his duty, and no doubt the jury would do theirs.[78]

The jury found only one of the men guilty and that was of common assault. Additionally they made a recommendation for mercy; Therry obliged by sentencing him to six months' imprisonment in Sydney.[79] It was nonetheless an unequivocal message about the unacceptable level of violent policing being directed at the local Aboriginal community.

The involvement of the military in these events led to further official reflection and reports. Major-General Wynyard, commander of the British regiments in New South Wales, commented on the Brisbane events in his six-monthly confidential report to British headquarters. He placed the blame on the only magistrate resident in the town, Dr Ballow, for a failure of judgement as to whether the military should have been called out in the first place, and then for failing to accompany them to the scene:

> The civil authority having taken up the matter, I have not deemed it necessary to institute further proceedings but intend to make it a subject for animadversion when [Cameron] rejoins his Head Quarters and at the same time instruct the young officers of the Regiment how they should act under similar circumstances.[80]

The Brisbane detachment of the 11th Regiment was withdrawn in June 1850 and not replaced. Young Cameron perhaps concluded these events had not helped his career prospects, for within the year he transferred to another regiment.[81]

The magistrate resident in the town, Dr Ballow, certainly received public criticism but the local inquiry headed by Police Magistrate Wickham focused its displeasure on the chief constable.[82] William Fitzpatrick had been the first chief constable appointed to the township and had arrived on the same vessel as Captain Wickham in January 1843. The chief constable's failure to leave his bed during a presumed crisis for the town was deemed deficient in the leadership and diligence required of his position.[83] The most senior police officer in the district was dismissed within days of the finalisation of Wickham's inquiry.

While Captain Wickham laid the blame on the chief constable, the *Moreton Bay Courier* sought to scapegoat the Mianjin for the attack—it was all the fault of Aboriginal 'cunning', their extreme 'duplicity and treachery'.[84] But no matter how much the *Courier* might have wished otherwise, the upshot of it all was that in 1850 senior military and civilian officials accepted that Aboriginal people had rights before the law and due process must be followed.

In some respects these events at Brisbane are as deserving of scholarly attention as the Myall Creek massacre trials, for they were both highpoints of evangelical humanitarian influence in colonial policy. Plunkett was at the centre of both decisions. No wonder otherwise liberal men such as Plunkett and Duncan had major qualms about colonial self-government.[85] In only six short years New South Wales, including the districts that were to become the new colony of Queensland, had a locally elected parliament which replaced a frontier policy of rule of law with, in the words of the second premier, Charles Cowper, 'exemplary punishment' and 'just retribution for [Aboriginal] barbarity'.[86]

The uproar in the town says much about white anxiety regarding Aboriginal agency and dominance in the district in 1849. But how it came about also throws light on Aboriginal politics. A young Mianjin boy, Wamgul, who was about fourteen years old, had been disciplined that afternoon by a female elder at the York's Hollow camp. Bitter over his treatment, he had concocted a plan to agitate their nearest European neighbour against his elders. Just on nightfall he had gone to the home of Humby, a brickmaker who was the first European to build his house in the Hollow, and told him that the Mianjin were in the process of killing one of Mr Petrie's cattle, which grazed nearby. Humby became paranoid and, believing that he was being watched by the Aborigines, waited some ninety minutes before sneaking out his back door to report the incident. When he found the town's night watchman he was said to have told him two bullocks had been killed and that he had had to escape from his hut to come into town. From there the story spread like wildfire. By the time the news reached Constable Conroy, it had inflated to: 'Aborigines were surrounding the Petrie's home'. It grew even further: when Lieutenant Cameron approached Magistrate Ballow a second time for instructions, the sergeant was beating to arms and 'people were running about in a state of much alarm'. Not surprisingly, Dr Ballow told him to proceed.

Wamgul had followed Daki Yakka's strategy: he had sought to use whites in his own personal power play with a female elder and it had all gone terribly wrong. Three of the Mianjin men received injuries, including two with gunshot wounds, as did Wamgul—although the medical doctor's testimony was confusing on the latter point. Initially he testified that Wamgul's injured thigh was caused by gunshot, but under cross-examination he conceded that it could have been a result of an Aboriginal weapon and inflicted more recently than 28 November. While it is certainly possible that Daki Yakka and the female elders might have been responsible for inflicting his injury—wanting to impose a tough lesson on young Wamgul, who was not yet a kipper—Petrie makes clear that the boy was one of those shot that night.[87] While Wamgul may have interpreted his elders' methods with a serious lack of sophistication, the unpredictability of the British settlers had yet again highlighted the weakness of some Mianjin-Quandamooka strategies; the settlers were unreliable allies in Aboriginal politics. It was all too easy to lose control of both them and the situation.

What did the mountain and north coast peoples make of these events? The terror of 28 November strengthened the argument for respect for law in both the Aboriginal and European communities. At about the time when Cambayo was sent south to Sydney to serve his sentence for spearing William Vant in April 1843, a songman of the Sunshine Coast hinterland was composing a new corroboree. Ludwig Leichhardt witnessed him performing it in the weeks following the Bunya council of December 1843–January 1844. He recorded in his diary how

> The Blacks living in the bush find fault with those who join the Whites and live close to the stations. In the war song he reproaches those, who no longer come to hunt kangaroos, and to catch possums, and who don't take part in the battles, and are rendered weak from living too much with the Whites. Then he sings: 'Why do you not give me women, kangaroo skins, pipes and tobacco and hatchets! I gave you all these and you give me

nothing'. The accused answers usually with an excuse: 'I do not live in the dwelling of the Whites; the Whites are angry with me: I have no pipe, no tobacco, no hatchet; I live in the bush'.

Reflecting on this corroboree Leichhardt noted that 'As long as the Black, who enters into communication with the Whites, exposes himself to the criticism of his brothers, the less is to be hoped of his attachment [to Europeans], that is as long as the wild population in the scrub remains isolated from the Whites.'[88]

As the 1840s drew to a close, the 'wild population' of northern coastal and mountain peoples and their Bribie Island allies had the strongest commitment to the old ways. Dundalli's success in upholding Aboriginal law against Aboriginal and European offenders alike contributed to his growing stature. The death of his brother must have brought home to him, however, the effectiveness of the Mianjin–Nunukul way. Dundalli the diplomat and negotiator and Dundalli the lawman understood the desirability of avoiding situations that brought the British directly into his world. The political debates continued.

6

ATTEMPTS AT CONCILIATION

The Dundalli of court reports and newspaper columns in the years 1846 to 1849 appears as a young man maturing as a leader. The attack on Vant back in 1843 and on the German mission in 1845 were restrained, however terrifying they must have been for the victims. In contrast the Forgie Station and sawyer attacks of 1846 and 1847 were decisive and unequivocal in their enforcement of Dalla law. It would be wrong, however, to conclude that Dundalli was inflexible or rigid in his imposition of local law. The years 1851 to 1853 reveal his attempts to limit and constrain conflict. We also have fleeting glimpses of the more wholistic aspects of traditional leadership through Dundalli's protection and training of youths in 1849 and 1852.

According to Gubbi Gubbi oral history Dundalli was a 'kooringal'— a man charged with carrying out the instructions of the Bora council.[1] The old men knew the hereditary laws but they required someone of 'conspicuous courage and force of character' to enforce it.[2] At times being a tribal lawman had required him to act as battle leader and by 1851 he was clearly a head man among the Joondaburri. The Brisbane and Stradbroke Island tribes certainly viewed Dundalli with fear,[3] which suggests that he might have had some connection with the Bora men, whose severe enforcement of the law was dreaded.[4] There is no indication that he was feared by the Bribie Islanders, however, and by 1850 he was still only approximately thirty years old, so it is difficult to find any definite label for him based on the documentary sources. Complicating the interpretation of who Dundalli really was is the fact that he was coaching two young followers by this time—Mickaloe from Wide Bay and Billy Barlow from Bribie Island—and their hostile actions were then attributed to Dundalli by European settlers and the press, whether or not they acted with his approval or knowledge. What can be deduced from Dundalli's actions in the years 1849 to 1853 is that he sought to defuse conflict, although he never resiled from protecting his people.

Debates within the European community about how to police the northern frontier did not abate after the withdrawal of the 11th Regiment in 1850. The regular presence of the New South Wales Supreme Court on circuit from May 1850 restrained the questionable policing practices common in the 1840s, but the law proved to be a blunt instrument when it came to responding to frontier violence. Caught between the pastoralists' and settlers' demands for action, and the need to abide by fundamental legal processes requiring credible witnesses able to swear an oath, colonial law also had the moral problem of sentencing young men to death for participating in group actions in which they were honour-bound to perform. The result was aggravation all round.

The northern tribes, of which the Bribie Islanders were an important part, were increasingly affected by British criminal justice in the years 1849–53. Aboriginal regional politics also continued to be enmeshed in colonial politics, although neither side appreciated the extent or agency of the other. When these parallel moral and spiritual universes collided, there were often dire results. Making peace with his Aboriginal neighbours became a priority for Dundalli. At the same time he and his allies tried to limit any further incursions by settlers in the Pine River Valley and the coastal flats between Bribie Island and Brisbane.

In July 1849 Dundalli was blamed for the death of a settler, Charles Gray, but the report of the inquest indicated that the Joondaburri, on whose behalf Dundalli was acting, had intended to negotiate with the victim, who panicked. The only account of the inquest comes from the *Sydney Morning Herald*, whose Brisbane correspondent was Thomas Dowse. In contrast to the first report of the episode itself in the *Courier* almost a fortnight earlier, Dowse's report of the coronial inquiry provides enough evidence to show that in fact Gray had been the aggressor. Intent on making some money from the prolific oyster banks of northern Moreton Bay, he had sailed his ketch *Aurora* to Bribie Island, employing William Boddin and two unnamed Aboriginal youths. One Sunday in July 1849 they took the rowboat to collect shells on a sandbank when the notoriously cantankerous Gray threw an oyster shell at one of the youths, cutting his head. Both youths then downed tools and left. Later that day they returned with seven to eight Joondaburri. They were unarmed but as they tried to approach Gray, he and Boddin panicked and tried to launch the *Aurora*'s beached rowboat. As one man came near, Gray swung an oar at him; another of the Aboriginal men then picked up the remaining oar and knocked Gray to the ground. Boddin did not hang around to find out what happened next. He took to the water and swam to a small mangrove island, remaining there for the rest of the day and night. On the beach the next day, he found Gray lying dead, and the sails and provisions removed from the *Aurora*, still moored off the island. Boddin then took the small boat and rowed to the Brisbane River where he found a customs department boat crew. They sailed up to Bribie Island, recovered most of the provisions from the Bribie Islanders and returned the undamaged ketch to Brisbane.[5]

Dundalli, now a recognised leader from the island, was presumed responsible for Gray's death but the details suggest that it was not planned payback—simply a desire to parley that went wrong when Gray swung his oar at their spokesman. The group was unarmed; there was no fair warning and no evidence of aggressive preparation. There was no mutilation of Gray's body—although his clothes were removed—and no damage to the boat. Boddin was allowed to swim away.

The Bribie Island men were already partly incorporated into an Aboriginal–European economy; like the Quandamooka, they formed boat crews and sold fish to the settlers as it suited them. By 1848 they were known as canny negotiators with a keen awareness of monetary values when they engaged in such transactions. They were remote from the settlement and confident in their own homelands. Out here the message to Europeans was: 'This is our country and sea. We want the benefits of your new tools and goods but we will do it on our terms.' Dundalli endorsed this approach. In 1853 he worked on the ketch *Aurora*, which by then belonged to a fisherman named William Wilson, but he set certain conditions—Dundalli first underwent name-exchange with Wilson so that the European was brought under Aboriginal law and ties of obligation. Under these circumstances Dundalli worked with Wilson for twelve months learning his European ways of boating, sailing and fishing, travelling with him throughout the bay and its islands. As a blood brother he probably also shared important Aboriginal knowledge about fishing and hunting in this environment.[6] The Moreton Bay marine economy was as much an Aboriginal economy in these years as it was a European one.

So the Bribie Island men undoubtedly knew the labour value of the two young men whom Gray had employed and wanted to discuss his treatment of them. Three separate sources from the period more or less acknowledge that Gray had been the cause of his own problems. In the local people's justification of this event conveyed by Petrie, the boy had been 'beaten unmercifully'. Petrie ends his very brief account of this incident with confirmation that Gray 'was a very cross old man, and many a slap on the side of the head I got from him when a boy'.[7] Commissioner Simpson also affirmed the locals' position. In his annual report for 1849 he again obliquely recognised the fairness of Aboriginal laws, reporting of this killing simply that 'from the known character of the man [it] was probably occasioned by his own misconduct'.[8] Even Dowse—who had sided with the *Moreton Bay Courier* in its newspaper war against William Duncan in 1846–47—reported: 'I fear that Gray has become a victim to his violent temper; for, from all I can gather there does not seem to have been any premeditated intention on the part of the blacks to become the aggressors'.[9] It is extraordinary to find then that the Brisbane coroner reached a verdict of 'murder'.

Although none of the specific accounts of this attack actually named Dundalli, the *Moreton Bay Courier* subsequently attributed Gray's death to him; it was added to a long list as proof of his bloodthirsty nature. Later Aboriginal accounts told to colonial businessman and amateur historian Thomas Welsby gave a little more information: this was not Gray's first assault of an Aboriginal boy; he had also assaulted some young Joondaburri who had been assisting him with his oyster business some months earlier. The 'king' of Bribie Island had sought to speak to him on that occasion but Gray had taken off; the Bribie Islanders had not forgotten his mistreatment but bided their time.[10] There are inconsistencies between the later account and the report of the coronial inquiry. Yet, this readiness to parley on behalf of young men—kippers, in Welsby's account—and anthropological assessment of traditional authority is consistent with Dundalli's leadership. As has been noted in other parts of Australia, the leadership role of older male kin as protectors and sponsors of the young kippers was a feature among the Bribie Islanders and the Undambi of Moreton Bay.[11]

In July 1851 another instance arose in which Dundalli sought to defuse the tensions of a situation but his gesture was again completely misunderstood. In that month he sent an emissary to the naturalist Frederick Strange, challenging him to a fight.[12] Strange had spent the years 1850–51 collecting natural history specimens in south-east Queensland, and had been developing his collection of marine and coastal artefacts around the islands and fringes of Moreton Bay.[13] The naturalist's exploration with a boat and crew near Bribie Island clearly led Dundalli to believe that he was seeking to capture him. Dundalli's challenge to hand-to-hand combat was a method of dispute resolution according to traditional law[14] and common in south-east Queensland.[15] His preparedness to confront his adversary was probably protective of the Bribie Islanders; far better to confront Strange head on rather than face an armed party landing on the island which would in all likelihood provoke violent group confrontation. It was also a way of saying to Strange that while you are in our sea country you must follow our legal processes.

The *Moreton Bay Courier* preferred to interpret this challenge as proof that Dundalli was an 'irreclaimable ruffian' and used it to remind its readers of his involvement in the Gregor attack. It also made clear Dundalli's standing among the traditional owners by 1851, for it claimed: 'it has always been considered an object of great importance to the tranquilizing of the hostile blacks of his quarter, to seize him and deliver him into the hands of justice'.[16] It wasn't so much his involvement in the Forgie Station attack that bothered the *Courier*—by July 1851 the white community had already taken the lives of three men and imprisoned another for that attack, although the desire for vengeance persisted—rather, it was his influence over, and leadership of, the hostile northern tribes who refused to recognise the 'supremacy' of British law and British ways.

The Bribie Islanders' anxiety about Strange's presence on their island was understandable. It coincided with Mickaloe, a young Gubbi Gubbi man who had spent time in Brisbane and worked with Dundalli, being taken into custody by the Native Police at Wide Bay in June 1851 for participation in the attack on Gregor's station. The news of his incarceration appeared to have reached the island as rapidly as it reached the township of Brisbane.[17] The only European township at Wide Bay was a small community at Maryborough, about 250 kilometres north of Brisbane, with no direct shipping to connect them, so Mickaloe had been sent to Sydney, then in August transferred to Brisbane, where he was incarcerated in Brisbane Gaol to await trial at the November 1851 assize. First the local magistrates had to prove to the crown law officers that there was sufficient evidence for him to face a criminal trial, and that required a committal hearing. According to James Davis's testimony at Mickaloe's committal, Mickaloe was a very young man; the clerk at the gaol had entered his date of birth as 1836, although Davis's comments suggest it was more likely 1829. If he had participated in the attack on the sawyers in 1847, as the ex-convict sawyer James Smith insisted, it could not have been many months since he had been through the kipper ceremony. But he was one of two young men who were portrayed as followers of Dundalli and his arrest caused much excitement in Brisbane.

As soon as Mickaloe had been transferred from Sydney to Brisbane Gaol, the *Moreton Bay Courier* called for witnesses to come forward.[18] The paper wanted to pin the Gregor murder on him but he had been arrested under the name of 'Paddy Shae'—although the clerk at Brisbane Gaol conveniently entered him in the prison register as Paddy alias Jemmy Parsons (who had been named as a participant in the attack) alias Mickaloe, the name he insisted was his actual name. Furthermore, the northern tribes were much less well known in Brisbane and the two child witnesses from Forgie Station had disagreed over who had perpetrated which crimes at the original inquest; five years later details would need to be firmly established before the attorney-general would proceed to trial.

Rather than transport Mickaloe a kilometre or so down Queen Street to the courtroom in the old convict barracks, the presiding magistrates, William Duncan and J.S. Ferriter, held the committal hearing in the gaol itself on 15 August 1851, on the Friday after

Mickaloe's transfer to Brisbane. Ferriter had been business partner and co-owner of Wivenhoe Station with Edmund Uhr—the station where Uhr's younger brother had been killed by Aborigines in December 1845—but he had sold his share in March 1849 and now resided in Brisbane, where he sometimes acted as police magistrate when Wickham was on leave.[19] However personally unsympathetic Ferriter might have felt towards the accused, Duncan was not going to allow any abuse of legal process to falsely commit a young man. Ironically, Duncan's staunch commitment to Aboriginal legal rights would itself produce a harsh and unreasonable penalty on another young Aboriginal boy, Ralph Barrow.

The hearing began with Ralph Barrow, now about fifteen years old, confidently taking his oath on the Bible. The boy's life had not been any easier since Andrew Gregor's death. When members of the divided Anglican congregation of Brisbane succeeded in driving Reverend John Gregor from his home in George Street,[20] he took up residence at the German mission sometime in late 1846 or early 1847. Gregor was given practical as well as personal support by the German community and Ralph Barrow also lived in this community, which included young people, the eldest of the German community children being only two years younger than Ralph. However, his stable home life was not to last. John Gregor died unexpectedly in January 1848 while bathing in a lagoon at Nundah.[21] Barrow was not yet twelve and found himself again without home or guardian in traumatic circumstances. He was now dependent on the small German community and was still living there in 1852, when he gave his occupation as 'stockkeeper'.[22]

Having lived with a priest and former missionaries for five years, it is not surprising that Barrow was confident as he made his oath on the Bible. Soon after his opening words, however, his nervousness and the pressure he was under to make sure Mickaloe was sent to trial became apparent. The precise details of his testimony in August 1851 varied significantly from what he had given in October and November

1846 when he was only ten years old. No doubt he had picked up the mood of the town, for he ascribed both the killing of Gregor and of Mary Shannon to Mickaloe, whom he identified as 'Jemmy Parsons'. William Duncan knew the town wanted young Mickaloe to hang. He quizzed Barrow from the bench on a number of points. The court report is brief but in response to a series of unreported questions by the magistrates, Barrow directly contradicted evidence he had given five years earlier. Then Mickaloe cross-examined him in broken English before the bench again asked more questions of him. To the boy it must have felt like an interminably long time on the stand. Finally the magistrates called for the bench books that contained the record of the Gregor–Shannon inquest to be produced and asked further 'searching' questions about his testimony without allowing Ralph Barrow to hear or read what he had said five years earlier. As Ralph's responses became more inconsistent they cautioned him that he had sworn an oath; the pressure was too much for the youth and he began to cry while still in the witness box. He then denied crucial points he had made at the start about Mickaloe's actions during the Forgie attack. Under pressure from Duncan, the town's crucial witness fell apart. Duncan consulted with Ferriter and they sentenced the boy to seven days' imprisonment 'for prevaricating in his evidence'.[23]

Although Ralph Barrow was Aboriginal, even the *Moreton Bay Courier* thought his treatment was unfair. Its editorial argued that Barrow had the right to hear his deposition from five years earlier in order to refresh his memory since 'we are ... left in doubt whether the discrepancies ... arise from his own falsehood, his comparative ignorance at the time, his fear of the blacks, his want of memory, or any mistakes in taking down his former evidence'. It might have added: community pressure readily inflamed by the press. Its editorial waxed further about the parts of Barrow's testimony that could be relied upon—it still wanted a committal—with no further consideration of the cruel punishment to which the magistrates had just subjected Barrow.[24]

To understand the severity of Barrow's sentence requires consideration of the state of Brisbane's first gaol in 1851. The first prisoner was incarcerated in Brisbane Gaol on 3 January 1850. Previously all prisoners sentenced for more than a month from the lower courts or held awaiting criminal trial had been sent to Sydney to serve their terms. The decision to extend circuit courts to Brisbane in 1850 required a secure gaol to hold prisoners awaiting trial, and Wickham had been approached for advice about suitable buildings as early as December 1846. He had urged the construction of a substantial prison but instead the colonial government opted to modify the disused female factory from Brisbane's penal settlement days.[25] It stood a kilometre away from the main township at the northern end of Queen Street, with scrub still standing between it and the Petries' residence further north at Petrie's Bight. Today the site is in the heart of Brisbane's CBD. In the 1850s it was surrounded by a high brick wall with residential quarters for the gaoler, matron and principal turnkey, and a gaol office built adjoining the western wall and front entrance gate. Within this large compound was a central building, constructed around 1829, with divided yards that were also walled. Male prisoners were held in two large wards, and there was a smaller ward for women; each opened to yards, with toilets at the end of each enclosure under the northern wall. This main building of the old female factory also included a chapel and five cells for solitary confinement. Poor Barrow's ordeal as a witness presumably took place in the chapel, although it was only marginally larger than the gaol entrance room.

Throughout the 1850s the gaol struggled with problems of overcrowding. It had only been built to hold thirty to thirty-five persons at most, but Gaoler Feeney confidently reported to Sydney that his prison could hold forty-five prisoners in wards and solitary cells. In May 1851, just before the sitting of the May circuit court, inmate numbers peaked at seventy-six. These large numbers and too few wards meant that it was impossible for Gaoler Feeney to impose any sort of classification of prisoners. The 1846 gaol regulations stipulated that prisoners should be divided on the basis of whether they were insane (for there was only one 'lunatic asylum' in the whole of New South Wales, so those suffering mental illness were imprisoned until a transfer could be arranged); unable to procure bail; awaiting trial; convicted of a misdemeanour; or convicted of a felony. There was no separation of children, and women were sometimes incarcerated along with their offspring. So the chances are that young Ralph Barrow, who had been raised on a mission and reared by a priest, found himself incarcerated in a large musty ward with twenty to thirty former convicts. There was also a high chance that he would have had to share a ward with the man he was accusing, young Mickaloe, who was not yet convicted of any crime. The only free men—men either born in the colony or who had migrated as free men—incarcerated the week Ralph was in the gaol were Mickaloe and seven Chinese labourers sent from the Darling Downs for breaching the *Masters and Servants Act*.[26]

At least he would have briefly had the company of James Davis (Duramboi), although he was a notoriously truculent individual. Davis had also been subpoenaed to attend Mickaloe's hearing as court interpreter, and upon his arrival in court Mickaloe had greeted him warmly. When the magistrates had instructed Davis to swear the oath he had flatly refused unless his court expenses were paid, so Duncan and Ferriter had sentenced him to twenty-four hours' imprisonment for contempt.[27]

The imprisonment of the first two who took the stand certainly helped to clarify events and personalities for the next two who were called. Margaret Shannon and her sister Mary Ann had been rescued from the Orphan School by David Peattie and his wife and were now living in Brisbane. The court deemed Mary Ann too young—she was now eight years old—but Margaret, who was ten, was subpoenaed. She bluntly told the court that she could not identify anyone involved in the attack on her mother. The next witness was Tom Petrie, who testified that Mickaloe looked nothing like Jemmy Parsons and that he knew him by the name of 'Cowander'.[28] The case against Mickaloe was crumbling. Some in the town blamed Duncan, who had to endure correspondence in the *Moreton Bay Courier* claiming he was neglecting his customs department duties.[29]

In fact the police case against Mickaloe was not yet over. The legal proceedings resumed on Monday, 18 August, when the examination focused on whether Mickaloe was the Jemmy Parsons accused of involvement in the Forgie murders. James Davis was more cooperative this time, but while his testimony was insightful regarding the naming of Mickaloe at childhood, kipper and adult stages of life, he had never heard Mickaloe go by the name of Jemmy Parsons. The next three witnesses were very willing but the problem for them was that during Mickaloe's incarceration in Sydney the authorities had cut his hair and dressed him in prison garb. The Aboriginal men of south-east Queensland wore their hair twisted almost into dreadlocks, which were fixed on the crown of the head with a bird feather. Mickaloe's shorn head and working man's smock made identification difficult for Europeans, although Tom Petrie's older brother, John, and another witness, Henry Chambers, nonetheless confidently asserted that he had participated in the Gregor attack and another alleged attack between Brisbane and the Pine River in 1845.[30]

This second hearing closed without any firmer evidence, leaving the Brisbane constables anxiously looking for further witnesses. The situation was saved by the ex-convict sawyer, James Smith, who asked to see Mickaloe at the gaol and claimed to recognise him from the 1847 attack on the sawyers at Pine River.[31] So a fortnight later Duncan and Ferriter again headed to the gaol where Smith took the oath. Smith verbally quaked before Duncan, nervously repeating 'says I' throughout his testimony. He nonetheless held firmly to his claim that Mickaloe's name was Moggy Moggy, that he had always been known to have been involved in the Gregor attack and that he had seen Moggy Moggy spear his mate 'Bowler' in September 1847.[32] Mickaloe cross-examined Smith in broken English, denying that he had ever gone by the name of Moggy Moggy or participated in the Pine River attack, and naming the Aboriginal men who were. The only name the *Courier* 'could catch was Dundalli'. The bench believed that it was sufficient to commit Mickaloe for trial for the murder of William Boller.[33] The attorney-general agreed—Barrow's evidence was too unreliable to sustain a trial for the Gregor murders but he would proceed against Mickaloe for the murder of Boller at the forthcoming November circuit court.[34]

The Brisbane circuit was a most uncomfortable one for the colonial legal establishment; it often took up more time than scheduled owing to storms and other weather conditions delaying the passage of the steamer from Sydney.[35] The range of accommodation at Brisbane was also limited. The hotel with the best reputation was so rudimentary, with neither locks on the doors nor coverings for the windows, that Mary McConnel, David McConnel's genteel Scottish wife who arrived in the colony in 1849, refused to stay there.[36] It was also deemed inappropriate for the judge to take hotel accommodation with other members of the bar, further limiting options for everyone involved. It might seem unnecessary to state that for the accused awaiting trial it was even worse, not least because the Brisbane Gaol was so inadequate for its task that in the weeks just before the assize it often held two or three times the number of prisoners for which it had been designed. It is hard to know how men found sleeping space on their hard bed boards in the cramped wards.[37] Nor was it a lucrative circuit, despite the large number of criminal trials at each sitting. At Brisbane the expense of the voyage and accommodation made it hard to bring in sufficient income, so few barristers bothered to attend. Not that many of the ex-convicts, working poor, Chinese and Aborigines who made up the majority of the accused could have afforded decent legal representation anyway. Judge Therry allowed solicitors to appear at the first circuit, and they were again allowed in November 1852 owing to the absence of barristers in private practice. The only two members of the Sydney bar to appear with any regularity were William Purefoy and the new colonial arrival Peter Faucett.[38] Purefoy was a senior member of the New South Wales bar by this stage,[39] and Faucett later became solicitor-general and judge of the Supreme Court of New South Wales.[40]

The 10–15 November 1851 assize at which Mickaloe was to stand trial was the fourth since the Brisbane circuit commenced, so it again fell to Roger Therry to preside as judge. Attorney-General Plunkett and the criminal crown solicitor, John Moore Dillon, usually alternated to undertake prosecutions for the crown and this November it fell to the latter. By 1851 it had become established practice in New South Wales to insist upon interpreters for Aboriginal defendants, and the judges usually called upon any member of the bar who was available to take their defence. Mickaloe was on trial for murder—if found guilty he would hang, so he was fortunate to have William Purefoy assigned to him by Judge Therry. There was little time to prepare but Purefoy naturally seized upon James Davis's testimony to call into question the reliability of Smith's identification of Mickaloe. Despite having such an experienced defence lawyer, and although Therry 'summed up with great care', as so often happened with the 'hanging' juries of this era, the jury took only 'a few minutes' to return a guilty verdict. The judge called for silence. Angee, a Chinese shepherd from the Burnett district, had been found guilty of murder the day before and Therry spoke of his feelings of distress 'to pronounce the last dread penalty of the law against two beings in a state of heathen darkness' before declaring the death sentence.[41]

We know that Mickaloe's people lived more than 150 kilometres to the north of Brisbane, that he was a Gubbi Gubbi man and that he had been arrested by the Native Police near Maryborough, but his precise country is unknown. During his committal hearing he had told the court he 'belonged to Wide Bay' but that could mean anywhere in the Mary River Valley, from the northern Sunshine Coast and hinterland to Maryborough. He and his brother, Burra, worked closely with Eumundi's men, probably Dulingbara people, whose lands were the Noosa lakes region.[42] The traditional owners still controlled these lands despite British claims to sovereignty over the entire east coast more than sixty years earlier. Europeans had resettled Maryborough after Eales's disastrous squatting efforts at Tiaro on the south bank of the Mary River in 1843, when five of his men were speared, four fatally. In May 1851 the commissioner of crown lands for Wide Bay, John Bidwell, attempted to blaze a land route, but his party was attacked by the Gubbi Gubbi and he became lost in scrub near the Blackall Range. By 1851 Europeans commanded only the sea routes to Wide Bay and the small town of Maryborough—so all European communication to and from Maryborough was still by sea—while the Wakka Wakka and Gubbi Gubbi contested the pastoralists' occupation of their lands in the Burnett to its west, and the coastal lands south to Brisbane remained the sole domain of the Gubbi Gubbi and their neighbours.[43]

Wherever his people were from, the shocking news that Mickaloe had been sentenced to hang electrified the traditional owners and it spread far and wide, just as the authorities of Brisbane had wished. It had reached the people of the Cooloola coast north of Noosa by April 1852, when it proved to be fatal intelligence for a party of white shipwreck survivors. The barque *Thomas King*, en route to Manila for a cargo of sugar, was wrecked on Cato Reef near Keppel Bay on 17 April 1852. The main part of the crew was left on an island that had no fresh water while their captain, James Walker, five crew and one passenger set out in a small boat for Moreton Bay in the south to try to organise a rescue. Walker could not have predicted that rain would fall on the island only two days later and that a whaling vessel, the *Lady Blackwood* was in the area. By 27 April the whaler had returned the main part of his crew to Moreton Bay where they immediately transferred to a coastal steamer, which landed them in Sydney on 9 May 1852.[44]

In the meantime Walker and his small party found they were most unwelcome in Gubbi Gubbi country. They made it as far as the Inskip Peninsula when damage to their boat forced them to continue on foot. At the north shore of the Noosa River, they met a group of Aboriginal people who tried to warn them not to continue, but Walker could not understand their miming of a hanging. Mickaloe's brother, Burra, was at that moment gathering a 'war' party to assist him to avenge his brother's death, and Walker and his crew had just walked into his country.

Burra, determined to exact payback for his brother, caught up with the bedraggled unarmed survivors at nightfall just to the north of Mount Coolum. Walker's men had seen Burra and his men with spears and other weapons in the distance and, certain that they were about to face serious attack, they hid in thick scrub. It posed little hindrance to Burra and his warriors. Walker heard two of his men being clubbed to death as he lay quietly in the brush.[45] He and one other survivor, Seaman Sherry, separately and slowly made their way south over many weeks, surviving hunger, severe sunburn and exhaustion to rejoin one another at Deciby's village at Sandstone Point, where Aboriginal people finally took them to Brisbane.[46]

When Walker and Sherry arrived at the Aboriginal village at Breakfast Creek, white authorities were immediately alerted. While the two men recuperated in Brisbane Hospital a search party left for the coast; its Aboriginal guides recovered much of the property of Walker's small group but the party was otherwise unsuccessful.[47] It took a second search party, again largely composed of Indigenous men and women, to recover the bodies near Coolum in June. The Sunshine Coast was an alien land to the whites, who simply set up a depot on Bribie Island, then based themselves at Caloundra while sending the Indigenous members of the party to the north.[48] On their return the Aboriginal guides reported that the remaining crew members had died of starvation and exposure, not murder as Captain Walker had claimed, and remarkably this evidence seems to have been accepted by the Europeans. Equally remarkable was the absence of any attempt to arrest Burra when he appeared at the Caloundra base camp; perhaps the white men 'leading' the search party knew too well that they were on Aboriginal territory, not European, even here at Caloundra in mid-1852.[49]

Burra and the Dulingbara did not know that Mickaloe was in fact still alive. He was being held in Brisbane Gaol while officials prevaricated over his fate. Six months earlier Judge Therry, reflecting on the contradictory evidence concerning young Mickaloe's identity, had asked the police magistrate to make further inquiries and provide him with more definite evidence but Wickham could throw no further light on the matter. At the meeting of the Executive Council in December 1851, Therry's advice was that Mickaloe should be reprieved but that 'the prisoner is to be detained in the Brisbane Gaol ... three months and then sent quietly to Wide Bay to join his own Tribe with an intimation that his life would be endangered if he return to the neighbourhood of Brisbane'.[50]

From the British perspective, Therry's solution was inventive. Getting Mickaloe out of Brisbane would placate local Europeans, and returning him to his people would evoke gratitude among the Aborigines, in accord with the age-old deterrence model of British criminal justice. However, the decision met with opposition from leading settlers, who did not endorse any expressions of mercy from the courts. Francis Bigge, a Brisbane Valley landholder who happened to be in Sydney at the time of the Executive Council decision, took the opportunity to lobby the colonial secretary. He was concerned that such a journey would be deemed a 'special mark' that 'would only embolden the Aborigines of those districts & probably lead to further loss of life'.[51] Police Magistrate Wickham was troubled by the logistics of how he was to get Mickaloe to Wide Bay—the only available sea passage between Brisbane and Wide Bay was via Sydney—and recommended that he be released from Brisbane Gaol to find his own way home. The colonial secretary's office consented to this in April 1852,[52] just as Captain Walker and his party were still struggling to make their way along the coast to Brisbane. It was not soon enough to save them.

The self-interested *Moreton Bay Courier* was furious about the Executive Council decision and editorialised against it. Quoting Aboriginal testimony only when it suited its purposes, it claimed the local Mianjin 'almost unanimously' identified Mickaloe as the murderer of Mrs Shannon. However, this doesn't so much prove Mickaloe was at the Gregor attack, but rather confirms the ongoing political enmity between the Gubbi Gubbi and Mianjin, and the fact that some Mianjin were still keen to use Europeans in their disputes with their northern neighbours. Talk of the release of 'Cowander', as the Mianjin knew Mickaloe,[53] clearly disturbed them. 'If you let go Cowander, he will kill more white fellow' was said to be the advice from York's Hollow.[54]

Despite the fulminations of the press, on 26 May 1852 gaol officials at Brisbane finally released Mickaloe in the township with a warning. The news did not reach Burra until 14 June, when he was at Caloundra to meet the second party that had set out in search of any *Thomas King* survivors. The democratic and communal nature of traditional law was evident in the reports of this second rescue expedition. Two of the Toorbul women who had accompanied Captain Walker to Brisbane gave the Sunshine Coast people the news of Mickaloe's reprieve. The coastal people, the newspaper reported, 'had been quarrelling and fighting... because news had been brought that... Make-i-light ... was not to be hanged, but was on his way to rejoin his tribe; and some of the blacks seemed to be quarrelling with others who had taken revenge without cause'.[55]

Unlike young Mickaloe, who had visited Brisbane on several occasions, Burra and his people had consistently eschewed contact with whites in the towns and on the stations, preferring the wilds of the Cooloola coast. This would suggest that Burra was traditional in his attitudes, and that his guiding values were those of ancestral law and the Bora. In a rare concession by the Europeans, Burra's actions were acknowledged as payback in early Queensland historiography.[56]

The colonial historian J.J. Knight, who drew heavily upon the *Moreton Bay Courier*, was not always consistent in recognising the operation of the ancient laws of south-east Queensland. For example, when some Bribie Islanders attacked the Mianjin man Mooky, it was dismissed as a grudge by the paper and a feud by Knight. While Mickaloe was still being held in Brisbane Gaol and news of his fate was still unknown to the Joondaburri, a group of Bribie Islanders came to town to enact payback law. Billy Barlow, a young Bribie Islander[57] soon to be almost as celebrated as Mickaloe among the Gubbi Gubbi, was assumed by the whites to have acted with Dundalli's blessing. His target this evening was Mooky or 'Murki', whom he struck on the back of the neck with a tomahawk. Despite the severity of the wound, Mooky was able to escape by swimming across the river. Mooky had been one of the Mianjin working with the constables the night of the police attack on Jackey Jackey in December 1846,[58] so this was part of the longstanding dispute between the northern peoples and the Mianjin and Quandamooka.

Billy Barlow's attack on Mooky re-inflamed tensions. By the start of February the *Moreton Bay Courier* was claiming that the Ningy Ningy and Bribie Islanders were intent on waging a 'war of extermination'. A Mianjin man by the name of Mickey had been killed and his people had headed to the Logan either for refuge or to convince the Logan people to join with them in the dispute.[59] It is tempting to see these conflicts as indirectly related to Mickaloe's arrest and incarceration, with Billy Barlow seeking to display northern power and authority in the face of Mickaloe's absence. His message: You can use the whites to take out Jackey Jackey and they now have Mickaloe but we northerners are still strong and one of your warriors will pay for the loss of any of ours.

When the Brisbane sheriff finally released Mickaloe on 26 May 1852, he had been continuously in custody—held by the Native Police, in Darlinghurst Gaol and in Brisbane Gaol—since June 1851. Just four days earlier two other Gubbi Gubbi men who had been tried at the May assize and found not guilty had also been released, so there was much for the friends and allies of the Gubbi Gubbi to celebrate. Mickaloe's liberation even led to a general, if temporary, conciliation, with exuberant celebrations by the Mianjin when he joined them at their camp near Breakfast Creek.[60]

There were two large-scale assaults to the north of Brisbane in the weeks that followed Mickaloe's release. The press reported both as evidence of Mickaloe's revenge for his time in gaol but there are enough details to suggest a more interesting situation. In the first assault, Mrs Cash, the wife of cattle station owner James Cash, claimed that up to two hundred people participated in the attack on their small station in the Pine River district on 19 June 1852.[61] Although Mary Cash was struck by a nulla nulla, it was a comparatively mild strike between the shoulders in order to wrest a gun from her. An Aboriginal child was present, whom the elder Tinkabed sought to calm and to assure that he was not in any danger. Once these two hundred people had stripped Cash's hut of food, clothing and valuables, all but three young men moved on to the surveyors' camp 270 metres away. It is a little unclear from Mary Cash's evidence but it seems that those who remained were propositioning her— she made reference to the fact that they wished her to go into the bedroom with them—but no one laid hands on her and she was able to leave and run towards the surveyors.[62] The number of people involved, the lack of physical violence, the presence of children in the 'attacking' party and the close supervision by an elder all make this a most unusual incident.

The bare wording of the court transcripts makes it impossible to be certain what was happening here, but three weeks later a report in the *Moreton Bay Courier* gave one more clue. It noted that 'from all that can be gathered it appears that the greater part of the blacks concerned in the late outrages were young men, or kippers'. The Cash's station, now identified as Cash's Crossing at Albany Creek, is only 16 kilometres north of Brisbane and 5 kilometres due north of a Bora ring at Keperra. Historian John Steele records another Bora ring to the west of Cash's Crossing. The presence of at least one young boy during the Cash station attack, its low level of violence, the very large number of males said to be involved and the young men pressuring Mrs Cash to go into the bedroom leave open the possibility that this 'attack' was one part of a much longer kipper-making ceremony in the region.

Mrs Cash's testimony caused outrage in the town, although she admitted that these three 'did not lay a hand on me'.[63] Senior men involved in the attack appear to have moderated the young men's behaviour in the Cash and surveyor harassment. As well as Tinkabed's intervention, in a rare concession the militant *Moreton Bay Courier* credited Dundalli with preventing harm: 'The notorious Dundalli has also figured in the late attacks, according to the accounts of his countrymen; although it is said that he for once performed an act of mercy, having saved the life of Mrs Cash, which the blacks had intended to take.'[64]

Since neither the hutkeeper at the surveyors' camp nor Mrs Cash were seriously threatened, the notion that murder had been contemplated by any of the main lawmen involved in these ceremonies seems very remote. It is much more likely that Mickaloe and the other released Gubbi Gubbi, Perika and Darryguree, having joined the kipper ceremonies, had urged a revenge attack for their incarceration, which was refused by the Bora and other leading men. Perhaps archaeological astronomy will one day solve this mystery, for the kipper-making ceremonies were called when particular constellations, deemed to be sky Bora rings, revolved to the same north–south axis of the earthly Bora rings in the region.[65]

Rebuffed by Dundalli, Mickaloe and his fellow inmates then sought out Billy Barlow over their payback plans. They found him a few days later working on Darby McGrath's station, known as The Gap, now a northern suburb of Brisbane. On the morning of Sunday, 27 June, Mickaloe, Perika and Darryguree, Billy Barlow and five or so other local men launched an attack on one of McGrath's outstations. The hutkeeper, Edward Power, survived the assault but the hut was robbed of all its provisions. The shepherd Michael Halloran, working some distance away, was killed by a severe assault to his head. The evidence indicates that robbery was not the motive—his body was not stripped, there was still cash in his pockets and none of the sheep were taken. So this assault, rather than the events at Cash's station, suggests payback for the three young Gubbi Gubbi men's arrests and long incarceration. Billy Barlow was learning from the militancy of his northern brothers, but the group dispersed soon after and the young Gubbi Gubbi returned to the north.[66]

The remainder of 1852 and the year 1853 did not get any better for Dundalli's people in terms of relations with the British criminal justice system. One after another men from the Pine Rivers, from the northern Gubbi Gubbi and from Bribie Island were detained by authorities in Brisbane's gaol and watch-house. Tinkabed was arrested under a charge of robbery with violence on 8 September 1852. Informers—presumably local Mianjin—had told the Brisbane police that he was camped near Breakfast Creek, and Chief Constable Sneyd along with three other constables snared him at 2 a.m., catching him and his friends completely off guard.[67] He was tried by Judge Dickinson at the Brisbane circuit court in November 1852, sentenced to five years' hard labour on the roads or public works, and was promptly transferred to Sydney on 29 November.[68] He would have briefly shared the ward for men awaiting trial with Mickaloe, who was rearrested in September and by 31 October 1852 was back in custody in Brisbane Gaol.

It was Edmund Uhr who engineered Mickaloe's second arrest. He had sold his Wivenhoe Station in the Brisbane Valley where his young brother had been killed and established a pastoral station and boiling-down works near Maryborough. While on his way to his factory he had come across Mickaloe with a group of Gubbi Gubbi friends. While chatting to the young man Uhr noticed he was wearing a gold band. Thinking it had come from one of the murdered crew of the *Thomas King*, Uhr had the Maryborough chief constable make inquiries of the Brisbane police, who advised it belonged to Mrs Cash. This enabled the Maryborough bench to recommit Mickaloe. Uhr, a material witness for the crown, could not make the November assize and so Mickaloe was held over in Brisbane Gaol to wait another six months for the May 1853 circuit.[69] On 25 November Mickaloe was joined by a young Pine Rivers man, Mickie, who had been named by Ralph Barrow as a participant in the Gregor station attack six years earlier. He and Billy Quart Pot had been arrested by the Native Police, but town police released Quart Pot while Mickie was committed for trial.[70] Nine weeks later, on 1 February 1853, the Brisbane police picked up Billy Barlow. He was remanded to 9 February while the police tried to find firm evidence of his involvement in the attacks on Halloran and Power at The Gap, then again to 16 February, until he was finally released from the gaol on 22 February into the hands of the police who had been unable to build a case against him.[71]

Their months in the small ward and yard for men who had been committed for criminal trial must have been distressing for Aboriginal men used to the freedom of the bush. They shared it with Norfolk Island convict runaways and a white man who had been committed for the murder of his Aboriginal defacto wife. These men were awaiting trial for crimes punishable by death and were desperate; on 31 March five of the white men attempted a break out, which was rapidly suppressed by the turnkeys securing the yard and bringing in arms. No wonder the gaol clerk recorded Mickaloe as 'orderly' in the Prison Register.[72]

On Wednesday, 18 May 1853, Plunkett opened the case against Mickie at the Brisbane circuit court. This circuit court was mired in frontier politics as the *Moreton Bay Courier* notched up its attacks on the attorney-general and his defence of Aboriginal rights before the law. It again fell to Judge Therry to preside over the sittings. Plunkett was reluctant to try Mickie for murder. He had not been named as a central player at the original inquest and Plunkett was all too aware of the faltering recollections of the sole witness, Ralph Barrow. On the day of his trial the young Mickie was placed in the dock for theft from Andrew Gregor's station in 1846. Barrow was again extremely nervous but, 'being treated kindly by the Judge', gave his evidence 'plainly'. Peter Faucett took Mickie's defence, and his cross-examination of Barrow highlighted discrepancies between Barrow's evidence at Mickie's committal in December 1852 and on this evening sitting of the court. Mickie was nonetheless found guilty, but neither his nor Barrow's court ordeal was yet over.

The next day was to be Mickaloe's turn on the stand, but Plunkett was forced to concede that he could not proceed with Mickaloe's indictment for theft from Mrs Cash as Edmund Uhr, an essential witness, had once again not arrived from Maryborough. The disappointment among many of the townspeople was palpable. The pressure Plunkett was under for the Mickaloe decision was made clear on the last day of the criminal trials. On Friday, 20 May, he reversed his position and ended up bringing a second indictment against Mickie for the wilful murder of Mary Shannon, after all. He opened the case passionately, complaining of 'outrages which... were perpetrated upon the aboriginal natives by the European settlers'. However he was also personally on the defensive, alluding to

> the accusations that had been brought against him of eagerness to prosecute whites for acts against blacks, and reluctance to proceed against the aborigines for outrages on the whites. These accusations he indignantly repudiated, and declared his full determinat[ion] at all times to act legally and according to the dictates of his own conscience.[73]

Peter Faucett and his assisting local solicitor, Robert Little, were now fighting for Mickie's life. In his final address to the jury Faucett was reported as 'dwelling with much force upon the evident defects of memory in the only witness, and upon the probability, even if the prisoner had been present, that he had no part in the intention to murder'. The jury took about an hour to reach their verdict of guilty but Judge Therry, alerted by both the attorney-general and the defence to the weaknesses of the case, refused to pass sentence of death. As was the custom of the day, Therry instructed that 'death recorded' be entered in the Judgment Book, meaning that Mickie's actual sentence would be decided later by the judge upon his recommendation to the Executive Council.[74]

Plunkett's second prosecution of Mickie did not spare him from political attack. The following week the *Moreton Bay Courier* sneered in its editorial over the attorney-general's 'tone of deep feeling' in his address to the court. Overlooking the severity of Mickie's treatment, the editorial went on to complain about the release of Mickaloe, 'once more turned loose upon society, to continue his career of crime and blood, should his savage nature prompt him to do so'. Its conclusion bewailed 'the amiable philanthropists' and hoped that they would 'transfer a portion of their compassion from the murderers to the murdered'.[75] It was a sentiment that the politically astute Judge Therry could appreciate. For the conviction of Mickie did provoke complaint, and from an unexpected quarter, to which both Plunkett and Therry were called upon to reply.

Frederick Walker, the commandant of the Native Police, briefly stationed at Durundur, just 80 kilometers north of Brisbane and in the heart of the traditional lands from which many of the attacks on Europeans were supposed to have originated, sent 'a private account' to the colonial secretary, Edward Deas Thomson, expressing concern about events in the district. The Native Police had originally apprehended Mickie, but Walker intimated that Wickham's arrest warrants for the Gregor attack were so broad that they encompassed most of the young Aboriginal men of the district. He confided: 'I can give the Attorney General a half a dozen more [boys] under the same warrant. All I have to do is go round the different stations.' He wanted 'an amnesty for every one included in that warrant'. He objected to the fact that Mickie had been convicted of the murder of Mrs Shannon, which he presumed was 'as accessory after the fact', for 'he was a mere boy at the time and ... the murderers, made every boy woman and child carry away the property'.[76] Thomson forwarded Walker's communication to Plunkett and Therry for their opinions. Plunkett was as usual concise and legally focused. He made no comment on the police magistrate's warrants but pointed out that the correct conviction was for 'aiding and abetting' and that 'as the life of the Convict has been spared (in the humanity and expediency of which I entirely concur) I see nothing in the case of Mickie to call for further consideration at present'.[77]

Therry, on the other hand, wrote at length and with some indignation. He thought some of Walker's mode of expression 'very unsuitable'; he explained the law of aiding and abetting and its applicability to Mickie's case. He did concede that 'no doubt there are shades and degrees of guilt in the participation each had in the commission of the crime and it is for this reason that I recommended the commutation in Mickey's case'. In his concluding paragraph, he echoed the sentiments of the *Moreton Bay Courier*:

> Mr Walker's letter does not in the slightest degree alter my opinion as to the propriety of that commutation and I venture further to suggest that tho' Mr Walker's sympathy may be very commendable, it appears to me that the fate of Mr Gregor and his servant is not without some claim to sympathy too, and that it should not be too exclusively bestowed on those who breach the law.[78]

It was a harsh conclusion, given that Frederick Walker had been five years continuously in the field facing the day-to-day reality of frontier violence. Commandant Walker was officially reprimanded for his comments, made 'under feelings of excitement'.[79] Judge Therry had now been responsible for the commutation of two death sentences for the attack on Gregor's station at the Brisbane assize; he wanted to make it clear that he was not going 'soft' on Aboriginal defendants. There would be no amnesty on any of the Aboriginal men accused of involvement in the Gregor attack; it had become too great a symbol in the debate over the law's capacity to defend white lives on violent frontiers. The pressure on the legal system over the Gregor attack was not abating. It was about to come crashing on Dundalli's head the following year.

The arrests of Mickaloe, Tinkabed and Mickie, and the detention of Billy Barlow and Billy Quart Pot, must have been deeply disturbing for the Pine River people, the Ningy Ningy and the Joondaburri. Did they believe that their political foes—the Mianjin and Quandamooka—had given information to the police, as had happened in the Jackey Jackey, Oumulli and probably Tinkabed cases? There was much to discuss so it was perhaps not surprising that a Brisbane Valley settler claimed that in December 1852–January 1853 was the biggest Bunya council since 1846.[80]

Attendance was disrupted, however, by patrolling Native Police. At least, that was Commandant Walker's boast. Governor FitzRoy had approved the formation of a new corps of police in 1848. In 1847, following the disbandment of the Border Police at the end of 1846, he had had to face the dilemma of how to maintain order in pastoral districts. Humanitarians in the London Colonial Office and in New South Wales were not prepared to countenance a return to military incursions, and unmounted town police were useless in the bush. A Native Police force had been in operation in the Port Phillip district, (now the state of Victoria) since 1842 and FitzRoy authorised the formation of an additional force for the Clarence district of northern New South Wales and the western Darling Downs. Frederick Walker was appointed commandant and spent many months recruiting Aboriginal men from south-west New South Wales, so his detachment did not commence operations on the lower Condamine and Macintyre rivers until 1849. He was soon receiving requests for assistance from the Burnett and Wide Bay pastoral districts, and in 1850 undertook further recruitment.[81]

Walker was keenly aware of the policing reforms that were underway in New South Wales and understood official distaste for settler raids. He was always careful to maintain the outward forms of law and in his official reports complained of settlers who expected him to wage war, who did not provide him with warrants or who provided him with warrants that were nonsensical.[82] Consequently his force was the subject of constant complaints,[83] despite a number of arrests and many deaths of Aboriginal accused 'while evading capture', and Walker was removed from its command in January 1855.[84]

Even before the attacks on Cash's and McGrath's stations in 1852, the *Moreton Bay Courier* was complaining of the 'lawless conduct [of the natives] in the immediate vicinity of Brisbane'.[85] Official requests for the Native Police to patrol the Pine Rivers and Brisbane Valley resulted in Walker leading a detachment from November 1852 to mid-1853 to the north of Brisbane, where it was active in arresting Chinese station workers and young men such as Mickie and Billy Quart Pot and escorting them to Brisbane for questioning.[86] Commandant Walker claimed that his Native Police had succeeded in disrupting the Bunya gathering without firing a single shot, although they failed to prevent the killing of a servant on Balfour's station that season.[87]

It wasn't just the Native Police pressing in on the freedom of the Undambi and Joondaburri. As the city of Brisbane grew, increasing numbers of Europeans were coming onto coastal lands, and in November 1853 the government authorised land sales at Sandgate.[88] Diamond, a Bribie Island man, evicted two Europeans camped at Luggage Point in September 1853, pointedly destroying the barrels of their guns before returning them.[89] When Tom Dowse set up camp on his newly purchased block at Sandgate, he and his sons were similarly ejected by a large group of Aboriginal men at 2 a.m. one night in December 1853.[90]

With this Native Police and white settler activity on Ningy Ningy and Joondaburri lands, the tactics of the Mianjin and Quandamooka of using whites to their own ends in internal political struggles became all the more dangerous for Dundalli. Some leading men of the district were absent serving prison sentences in Sydney and, given police interest, Billy Barlow also needed to check his movements about the township. It was becoming dangerous fighting on two fronts. For the Joondaburri to concentrate their effort against further European incursions on their lands, they needed to reach agreement with their political opponents in order to end the constant payback.

Through all the police harassment of his friends and allies, Dundalli stayed clear of the vicinity of Brisbane, where there was still a reward posted for his involvement in the Gregor murders. According to Welsby he avoided the settlement, although we know he worked in a boat crew which took him all around Moreton Bay. Otherwise he confined himself to the Pine River district and Bribie

Island.⁹¹ His decision to come into Brisbane in May 1854, which led to his arrest, is thus extremely puzzling. What had changed between 19 May 1853—Mickaloe's release date—and May 1854 to lead him to believe that it was safe, when increasing activity by whites, including patrols around the Pine River by the Native Police, were threatening the northern peoples' security?

In other parts of Australia a great fight was a means to ending long-running disputes.⁹² Petrie claimed that the traditional owners of the Brisbane region 'always after any gathering, even a fight ... would in the end part well pleased with each other, and excellent friends'.⁹³ But the Brisbane regional fights of the previous fifteen years had not been able to resolve the longstanding divisions. The renowned elders of the late 1830s and early 1840s who may have had the authority to organise a final regional equivalent of a 'makaratta' (sometimes translated as a treaty) had now passed—Moppy in 1842 or '43, Ubie Ubie in December 1843, Mulrobbin in 1852.⁹⁴ Did Dundalli, who was still only in his thirties, have the standing to settle the grievances once and for all?

There is little evidence to explain this but we do know of one event that was of great significance to the Joondaburri. In late 1853, Harry from the Logan River 'stole' the daughter of one of the Bribie Island or Ningy Ningy families. Dundalli's people consequently demanded a pullen pullen with the Logan people to win her back. It was held on 22 December 1853 on the green flood plain of Norman Creek—today it is a recreational reserve not far from Stones Corner, overshadowed by the South East Freeway and extending either side of Juliette and Cornwall streets. The Logan River people were supported by their allies the Stradbroke Islanders as they lined up in battle formation to face their counterparts of the Ningy Ningy and Joondaburri. As the battle retreated and advanced, it seemed that the Quandamooka and Logan people were to be overcome, when a cry from the Joondaburri halted proceedings. A Bribie Island man had been speared in the chest and died within ten minutes. He was a warrior of some standing, the brother of Diamond. There had been no outright victory by the northerners and the Joondaburri now claimed the right to avenge Diamond's brother. A few days later the battle resumed at Logan. Frustratingly, neither the *Moreton Bay Free Press*—the *Courier*'s new rival in town—nor the *Illustrated London News* give us the outcome of this second battle, which might have helped to explain Dundalli's subsequent behaviour.[95]

Another large meeting was held near Brisbane in late May 1854, but all we have is a passing reference made by a correspondent to the *Moreton Bay Free Press* to almost eight hundred Aboriginal people being in and around Brisbane as well as some published recollections from 1933—seventy-nine years after the event—that claim there was a large gathering between Indooroopilly and Taringa that precipitated Dundalli's capture.[96] Something took place at these meetings to lead Dundalli to believe that his enemies would not act against him if he ventured into Brisbane. It is possible that the death of Diamond's brother was deemed by Dundalli to be restitution for many of the disputes in the region since at least December 1846.

Given the assistance of Mianjin and Quandamooka people in some of the arrests in the region, it is also probable that Dundalli interpreted colonial policing as a product of his people's feuding, and that once restitution had been paid by the Ningy Ningy and Joondaburri, they would be safe from further police action. No doubt he believed that the colonial legal system could not function when not being used by the peoples of south-east Queensland for their own ends; there is much corroborating evidence to support such a view. The Indigenous and European legal systems operated in parallel, and the leading participants of each assumed that their own system was the dominant one. It is as if in these early years neither the Indigenous nor European communities appreciated how effectively the other's set of laws functioned within its own sphere. Rather than being foolhardy in his decision to visit Brisbane in May 1854, Dundalli seemed to believe that his safety was assured now that any grievances borne against him had been settled by the Bribie Islander's death and the outcomes of these pullen pullens in December and May. However, his moderate approach, which had been evident in the measured responses to so many European incursions into northern lands in the years 1851–53 and in his reactions to the loss of warriors, including his own brother, was not necessarily shared by his Indigenous political rivals and certainly not by his settler enemies.

In May 1854, when he came into the township of Brisbane, his misjudgement cost him dearly. He was now within reach of the Brisbane constabulary.

7

THE FEUD CONTINUES: CAPTURE, TRIAL, AFTERMATH

Even within the township of Brisbane, the constables alone could not take Dundalli. The police had no idea what he looked like, so any arrest would depend on assistance from the Aboriginal community. They knew Dundalli only by reputation and what they did know filled them with dread. Chief Constable Sneyd was sceptical that his town constables were up to the task but on 25 May 1854 decided it was worth sending a couple of his town police in plain clothes, along with the Mianjin informers, to the end of Wickham Street, where Dundalli was working on a house block.

All of Dundalli's adult life had been proscribed by the three-way politics of the Brisbane Aborigines and their allies, the broad coalition of northern peoples, and the European settlers. His death would be no different. A couple of days after Supreme Court business was over for that circuit, Dundalli came into town and took work with a local brickmaker. A local man, Wumbungur, recognised him as he was clearing trees in Fortitude Valley. He and his Brisbane friends informed a settler, William Baker, and the usual system of deception using Aboriginal opponents, white reward seekers and rough policing was underway. The only exceptional characteristic of this police 'raid' was that it was carried out in daylight. Constables Tredenick and Downs, in plain clothes, hid near where Dundalli was working. He wore his hair long in the traditional style, and while he was in the midst of felling a tree Baker claims to have grabbed his long locks, pulling him backwards and enabling the constables to bind his legs and arms, despite an immense struggle. Like so many colonial stories, Baker's version omits the role of the Aboriginal men and it hardly seems believable that Baker would approach a tall, powerful man who was presumably wielding an axe. Petrie's account states that it was Wumbungur who wrestled with Dundalli until the police could apply handcuffs and halter, which seems more likely. Dundalli resisted so powerfully that it took several men to secure him. He was too big to carry so a dray was commandeered from the brickyard of his employer, a man named Massie, to convey him to the Brisbane watch-house where, despite being handcuffed and leg-ironed, he made one last struggle to free himself at the archway of the old convict barracks. After police questioning he was transferred to Brisbane Gaol on 25 May and held for a committal hearing on 3 June.[1] He denied he was Dundalli, using instead the name of 'Wilson', his blood brother's name and the man for whom he had been working the previous year.[2]

Since Dundalli's arrest came just three days after the conclusion to the May assize, he faced the maximum time of six months in gaol awaiting a trial, which could not be scheduled before the next circuit court in November. Confinement in a small crowded ward and yard for weeks on end was an agonising punishment for Indigenous men and women—of which judges of the New South Wales Supreme Court had been well aware for many years.[3] The timing meant that Dundalli also had to endure the Brisbane winter in the cold of the musty old female factory, in a committal ward measuring 6.6 × 6.9 metres.[4] Throughout these months he must have longed for the sociability and assurance of an Aboriginal hearth, as much as its warmth. He missed

Sippy, an Aboriginal man from the Darling Downs who in January had escaped the gaol and later been recaptured and tried, by just three days. Sippy could have told Dundalli how easy it was to scale the outer gaol wall.[5] Mickaloe's friend, the Gubbi Gubbi man Darryguree, whom Dundalli undoubtedly knew, had also been rearrested and successfully tried for wounding at the May circuit court, but he had been shipped off to Sydney with Sippy and the other prisoners destined to serve their longer sentences at Darlinghurst Gaol.[6] Davy, a Wakka Wakka man, was in the gaol from May to August but it is doubtful they had any chance to make contact—at the May circuit court Davy had been sentenced to death for the murder of a squatter in the Burnett district and so would probably have been held in either the Confine or Hard Labour ward or, more likely, the solitary cells, as there were no specific condemned cells provided at Brisbane. Dundalli must have known about Davy's hanging, however, which was carried out in front of the gaol entry gates on 22 August 1854 and would have been visible from the prison yards.[7] The contrast with the joyful life of freedom on the waters of Moreton Bay and the sands of Bribie Island could not have been starker.

So it is not surprising to find that Dundalli was an unhappy prisoner and disdainful of the former convicts who largely comprised his ward-mates. In his first fortnight of incarceration he was reported to have assaulted fellow prisoners and also to have seized the turnkey when he opened the ward door one morning; he had to be restrained with assistance from other warders.[8] Given that he was already being kept in irons—a punishment meted out to unruly prisoners—Gaoler Feeney probably held him in solitary confinement for a short period. The solitary cells were the original women's cells built by Commandant Logan and measured a stifling 85 centimetres wide by 220 centimetres long, so he would have only just managed to lie down. Although these cells were recognised by the authorities as inadequate, they were still in constant use in the 1850s.[9] Here the kipper trials of his youth, which had imposed several arduous disciplines on him, such as refraining from eating and speaking, and even looking upwards for days on end, must have steeled him, reminding him of his powers of endurance in the face of such deprivation.[10] Even when back in the ward, Dundalli's irons were not removed, as he was deemed a flight risk by the turnkeys. The *Moreton Bay Courier*, as inflammatory as ever, argued his behaviour was grounds for him to be tried immediately by special commission, but the idea was not taken up by the Crown Law officers. Dundalli was forced to endure the torture of many more months in chains in the claustrophobic old gaol.

Finally the days grew warmer and the time for the next sittings of the circuit court drew near. Outside the gaol young Billy Barlow had already begun organising payback operations for Dundalli's capture.[11] Perhaps a sympathetic white prisoner shared the news of Billy Barlow's activities with him, but the authorities had done their best to paint him as a blackguard to be feared and it is unlikely that the turnkeys gave him any news that might have raised his spirits. Dundalli was regarded as the most incorrigible of the prisoners awaiting trial, and his cases were scheduled for the last day of the criminal sittings. There was no legal preparation for him. His defence would rely on the generosity of any visiting barrister whom the judge would assign on the spot.

The Supreme Court sat in the Brisbane police court—it was the converted chapel on the top floor of the old convict barracks, which remained the town's most imposing building. It still dominated the southern end of Queen Street in the 1870s, its bleak history and age infusing its drabness alongside the new Victorian-era buildings of post-separation Queensland.[12] The judge and the law officers had to make do with former convict guard and military offices which adjoined the old chapel. The town lockup and the lockup keeper's quarters were uncomfortably close; they were on the ground floor immediately below the judge's room and court. The noise from the lockup keeper's nursery frequently disturbed the judges in the chambers above.[13]

The visiting legal officials did not have to endure the discomfort for too long that November. In 1851 there had been so many cases to try that the circuit had lasted six days but, in November 1854, five cases were deferred owing to the non-appearance of witnesses and bailed defendants. The court managed to process the remaining ten criminal cases in just two days—six trials on Monday, 20 November, and four on Tuesday, 21 November. The discomfort for legal officers would not be physical but emotional. Two of the trials on the Tuesday were Dundalli's.[14]

This was the tenth circuit court sitting in Brisbane so it fell again to Judge Therry to preside over yet another trial for the attack on Gregor's station. It was the most sensational case of the Brisbane circuit to date and coincided with Judge Therry's last appearance in Brisbane.[15] Neither Plunkett nor Moore Dillon from the Crown Law Office was available, so the crown employed the private barrister William Purefoy to prosecute. Judge Therry requested the visiting barrister Peter Faucett to take Dundalli's defence. There were five indictments against Dundalli: the four murders of Andrew Gregor, Mary Shannon, William Waller and William Boller, and wounding with intent to do some grievous bodily harm to Johan Hausmann from the German mission in 1845. In the end Purefoy decided to proceed with only two of the five: the murders of William Boller and of Andrew Gregor.

The tensions at the November 1854 assize for the trial of Dundalli were the most intense that Brisbane had experienced up to this time. Dundalli was brought in chains from the gaol up to the court on the second floor. Every town constable was on duty owing to Dundalli's fearsome reputation, his physical strength and the dire warnings from Gaoler Feeney. The crown's main witnesses were again the ex-convict James Smith and the much interrogated Ralph Barrow. Margaret Shannon was now thirteen but she had not been called by the crown since she had admitted at Mickaloe's committal hearing that she could not identify any of the Aboriginal men involved. Neither was her father, Thomas, since the attorney-general had concluded that his trauma rendered him ineffective as a witness. Among those at court was John Hausmann, who was expecting to be called to testify about Dundalli's involvement in the attack on him in 1845. His presence added to the pressures on Ralph Barrow, who was still living and working at the former German mission. Barrow would have been about eighteen years of age by now but the mood of the town made it next to impossible for him to behave in any independent manner; he knew the town was counting on him to recall Dundalli as a central player in the station attack, whatever his memory of the events eight years earlier.

The attack on the sawyers was dealt with first. At the time of the original inquest in September 1847, James Smith had claimed to recognise a Gubbi Gubbi man, although he could not name him and was unable to identify any of the other participants in the assault. Subsequently some Indigenous workers on nearby Whiteside Station were alleged to have stated that Dundalli was involved, and from that time on Smith confidently asserted Dundalli's presence.[16] Seven years later Smith's insistence that Dundalli was present left Faucett with little room to mount a defence. After a brief recounting of events by the witnesses for the crown, Faucett concluded with 'an eloquent and powerful appeal to the jury on behalf of the prisoner, and closed his address with some strong comments upon the insufficiency and the mockery of the protection said to be thrown around the blacks by the British Government'.

It was not a plea that could win favour with the presiding judge but Faucett, who had only arrived in Sydney in 1852, seemed unaware of Therry's noble record as assistant prosecutor at the Myall Creek trials in 1838. Therry, 'in charging the jury, expressed his emphatic dissent from these sentiments'[17] and invoked Myall Creek yet again. 'The law was equally careful of the life of a black as of a white, and within his own experience, he knew of no less than seven cases where white men had been executed for the murder of aboriginal natives', Therry stressed, before summarising the evidence 'at length'.[18]

Dundalli was found guilty of the murder of William Boller—the press reports vary as to whether the jury took fifteen minutes or an hour to reach their decision—and the court moved on to hear a case of wounding with intent and another of horse stealing before returning to Dundalli and his second indictment. His trial for the murder of the squatter Andrew Gregor was the last trial for the day and for this criminal session.[19]

Having provoked Therry's ire earlier in the day Faucett tried a new tactic to win some sympathy from the judge and jury. He objected to the fact that Dundalli remained in shackles even while in the dock. The prosecution conceded it was not normal procedure but argued that Dundalli was an exception, he 'being a savage of great strength and daring', and called the gaolkeeper to provide evidence of Dundalli's attempted escape.[20] Judge Therry, however, acknowledged the right of the defendant to be unfettered and was about to order the removal of the heavy irons when Faucett withdrew his objection, claiming that he was satisfied with 'the admission of the prisoner's right'.[21]

The trial proceeded with Dundalli in chains in the dock and Ralph Barrow in the witness stand. Despite the lack of time to prepare, Faucett was familiar with Barrow and the issues of the case, having taken the defence of Mickie before Judge Therry eighteen months previously. His cross-examination proved that Barrow 'had no idea of how long ago the event occurred. He also . . . did not know the names of any other blacks present'.[22] Knowing how this same weak evidence had failed to create doubt in the minds of Mickie's jurymen, Faucett addressed them on the discrepancies and called John Clements Wickham to the stand. This was high drama. Wickham was the most senior official in Brisbane, had only recently been promoted to the position of government resident, and was the magistrate who had conducted the Gregor inquest and heard Barrow's original testimony at the scene of the raid. Wickham made clear that Barrow had named 'several other blacks' as being present at the attack.[23]

Over the past eight years Barrow had given different evidence at each committal hearing and Supreme Court trial. Therry had presided at three of these trials, yet he undercut Faucett's argument, including Wickham's testimony, completely. The judge, in his summation of the issues for the jury, insisted that 'from first to last' Barrow 'had maintained that Dundalli had struck the blow which killed Mr Gregor'. It was an extraordinary statement. The clerk of petty sessions had merely to open the Brisbane Bench Book to show that the judge was wrong on the facts.[24] Furthermore, given the propensity of Brisbane juries in these interracial cases to affirm guilt, it was hardly necessary. At the end of a long day, the jury 'retired for a few minutes' before returning with a verdict of guilty.[25] Judge Therry 'with considerable emotion then passed sentence of death'.[26]

Between Purefoy's declamations that the courtroom would be 'unsafe' should Dundalli be unfettered, Faucett's apparent fear of his own client and Therry's interventions to undermine the defence arguments, the press reports of Dundalli's trials, despite their brevity, reverberate with tensions. The stress went beyond any sensitivities among members of the bar. Therry's memoirs provide the answer— the destabilising factor was the defiant personality facing his white accusers and defenders from the dock.

Dundalli's disdain for Supreme Court procedure and authority was one of the factors fuelling the judge's antipathy. The dignity of the court and of his professional behaviour weighed heavily on Therry and he guarded them both fiercely.[27] Other than the Myall Creek trials, Dundalli's is the only interracial case that Therry gives any attention to in his *Reminiscences of Thirty Years Residence in New South Wales*. His sense of intimidation in Dundalli's presence can still be felt even though he wrote this account nearly ten years after the trial. The gaolers had dressed Dundalli in a working man's smock and trousers and his dreadlock coils had been cut and styled in European fashion.[28] They were of little use in covering his warrior status; even without the display of his muscular build, his tribal scars, his body paint or weapons, Dundalli conveyed a sense of 'formidable ... ferocious strength', according to Therry. He towered over the judge, who described him as 'the largest man I ever looked upon' and recorded the presence of six constables in court to guarantee security during his trials.[29] So much of Therry's time in the colonial court system had been spent defending the liberal model of the law and its application across the racial divide. Here he was faced with an Indigenous defendant who refused to be grateful, refused to respect those who sought to help him and showed nothing but contempt for British law. Nor was Dundalli a man who could be readily patronised—he was neither young, nor weak, nor did he cower. According to Therry, despite evidence that Dundalli spoke English well, he disrupted the trial by beckoning to a settler he recognised in the court and asking him to offer the judge a bribe of sixpence. At another stage in the hearing he addressed the judge directly, in the pidgin English of the Moreton Bay region, apparently offering to row him back to Sydney. Disrespect for the solemnity of court ritual disturbed Therry deeply. He failed to recognise these incidents as a rejection of the court's authority; in his view they could only be 'distressing ... indications of marked inferiority of mind'.[30]

The formal processes of the British court had effectively rendered traditional law and authority invisible. Within its walls Dundalli, a traditional lawman, was recast as a criminal, and his enforcement of its customs as ferocious savagery. The political decision to deny Aboriginal sovereignty had created this inequality and now the formal procedures of British law reinforced it. As a criminal defendant he was required to stand passively in chains while others debated his actions in a language that was not his own. Dundalli—who had studied the southern skies so well that he knew the times when his ancestors wished him to organise a kipper ceremony—could not swear an oath on a Christian Bible. That made the admissibility of his evidence in a court of law, just as it did for all Aboriginal defendants until 1876, impossible.[31] He was not even allowed to speak in his own defence. Gentlemen who had never seen him or his country argued over his life while he, as an Indigenous defendant, was left mute. Naturally then the newspaper reports of the trial sideline Dundalli the defendant so that he is barely visible in the courtroom. Only Therry's memoirs and a few lines from the bar help us overcome the structural inequality of the courtroom scene so that Dundalli's remarkable physical presence and personal authority can be imagined. These, plus Dundalli's final actions on the scaffold, provide the counterbalance to the distortions of the legal narrative. Applying British law to Australian colonial frontiers undoubtedly saved lives by placing some limitations on settler violence but it also brought a greater injustice, with its ideological cloak that smothered and silenced Aboriginal legality.

As a colonial judge of the New South Wales Supreme Court, Therry was brought face to face with the limits of a Colonial Office policy that insisted that there could be no state of war on the Australian frontiers. An imperial policy that refused to see Indigenous Australians as a rival power could only criminalise their behaviour once they were defined as British subjects. The injustice of this policy as it applied to young men involved in group action was softened by legal procedure that required individual identity to be proven. In addition, the facility for judicious use of the power to commute the most severe penalty enabled Therry to ease his conscience in 1851 and 1853 by recommending the release of Mickaloe and the imprisonment of young Mickie, despite their respective death sentences. A man whose social networks included the Irish aristocracy and British prime ministers found it easy to look upon these young men not as enemies but as 'untutored savages' to be pitied and protected.[32] When confronted by a man whose opposition and disdain could not be silenced, however,

Therry responded with reciprocal contempt; he failed to recognise any integrity in Dundalli's position and in his memoirs decried Dundalli's lack of intelligence and his 'savage ferocity'.[33] Paternalism gave way to the colonial dehumanisation of Therry's political opponents, those settlers who had opposed any legal rights for Indigenous Australians.

Therry's portrayal of Dundalli is completely out of step with witnesses from Brisbane and even Dundalli's longstanding enemy, the *Moreton Bay Courier*, which begrudgingly acknowledged his intelligence and his leadership.[34] There were no appeals from the community over Therry's awarding of the death penalty. The *Moreton Bay Free Press* had opposed Davy's hanging in August but there was no one to speak up in Dundalli's case. Commandant Frederick Walker, who in 1853 had urged an amnesty on any further arrests over events on Gregor's station, was one of many northerners who had confidently asserted Dundalli's guilt in these attacks. (By December 1854 Walker was on his own downhill spiral toward alcoholism and dismissal.) Wickham seems to have had misgivings about the trial process but he made no official complaints about its outcome. There is no record of any concern from Duncan, who had taken such a strong stance to defend Mickaloe's rights in 1851, while his friend Father Hanly was unsympathetic after Dundalli decisively rebuffed him when he went to visit him in gaol.

As Dundalli was returned to the gaol, there was one last chance to save his life. Therry was required to provide advice to the Executive Council about any death sentences passed during the November criminal sessions. The judge's advice was the last and only avenue of review. On later reflection in Sydney, Therry must have reconsidered his instructions to the jury regarding the certainty of Ralph Barrow's testimony—reference to the murder of Andrew Gregor was removed from council papers. The Executive Council minute regarding Dundalli's execution referred only to his responsibility for the murder of William Boller. Therry was able to uphold the integrity of the legal process while suppressing the challenge to British law that Dundalli represented. There was no reprieve from the Executive Council.[35] Dundalli was to hang, based on the word of Smith, a former convict who could not sign his name.

Dundalli's disdain for the colonial court was consistent with his contempt for his gaolers and fellow prisoners. He spent the days following his trial insisting that they would not dare to hang someone of his standing but would merely send him to Sydney, as the authorities had done with so many of his countrymen. Only the noise of the gallows being erected, a couple of weeks after his trial, removed that hope. At that moment he lost the composure that he had maintained so steadfastly for the past six months and wailed piteously.

The next morning, Friday, 5 January 1855, Dundalli bravely mounted the gallows unaided. His arms and legs had been pinioned while in his cell. It says much about his self-possession that he noticed familiar faces among the white crowd and called on them to help him. Then, as he saw his people in the scrub opposite, he delivered a speech 'with much earnestness' in his own tongue.[36] He firstly called to his wife—it is the only insight the colonial sources give us about Dundalli's personal life and it is such an important one. However much gender politics fuelled the internal Aboriginal politics of south-east Queensland, Dundalli's own marriage was a companionate one, whether it had been arranged or self-chosen. Some of the sources also mention that Dundalli's son was present, while another old timer claimed Dundalli's wife had two piccaninnies with her.

Next he called to Billy Barlow and the Joondaburri, and their allies among the Gubbi Gubbi and Ningy Ningy, who had gathered in the scrub opposite the gaol gates. His message to them was simple: avenge my death in accord with the ancient law of south-east Queensland. He mentioned Wumbungur by name.[37] The town police, the other Aboriginal participants, the judge, jury and prosecution witnesses were secondary players. In Dundalli's view Wumbungur was the key performer—his capture had been a product of Aboriginal politics, not the farcical charade that passed for British justice. Many years later, realising the importance of this speech in the history of colonialism, amateur anthropologist and linguist Archibald Meston attempted a part reconstruction in Gubbi Gubbi language based on what he had gleaned from William Baker and his widow:

Gneen nurwarn billarr, balgina Bakerram, Woomboonggoroo, waera weerepple
You throw the spear, kill them both so they never come back.[38]

The Meston–Baker words don't do justice to what had happened: the town had just witnessed inspirational Aboriginal leadership. Caught up in a brutal and alien penal system, Dundalli had the presence of mind to rally his people and remind them of the struggle. His spontaneous use of the gallows to address his countrymen gives a glimpse of the charisma that had drawn men to him.

His address was cut short by the official executioner for New South Wales, Alexander Green, lowering the cap over his head. The undersheriff gave a signal and the bolt was withdrawn. A cry went up from Dundalli's people on the hill opposite that chilled the hearts of the settlers.[39] The British prided themselves on the mercifulness of their system of hanging, which was designed to lead to instant death by breaking the neck. But Dundalli didn't swing—Green had completely misjudged his height. Instead Dundalli's legs fell on his coffin, which had been placed beneath the drop. A turnkey quickly withdrew the coffin but owing to Dundalli's immense height his feet then reached the ground. As the Brisbane crowd looked on Green grabbed Dundalli's legs and tied them behind to his pinioned arms. The *Courier* tried to claim that Dundalli's death was instantaneous but the truth is that he must have been strangled to death as Green pulled on his legs. The paper had to concede that Green's bungling was 'a most sickening sight to behold'. The only thing more disgusting in its eyes was that women who had come with their children were present.[40]

Nonetheless the paper smugly defended his execution, despite its brutal execution, and claimed that 'his death will teach the blacks ... who look up to him, that our laws may overtake the guilty',[41] proving that it had completely failed to understand the significance of Dundalli's speech, which was the very opposite of an endorsement of British justice. Hostile sources such as J.J. Knight and the *Moreton Bay Courier*, and sympathetic ones such as Constance Petrie, all agree that the main message of his gallows speech was for his people to exact retribution against Wumbungur and others who had aided him.[42] They all concur that Dundalli was not the penitent sinner morally endorsing the justice of his execution whom white officials had hoped for. Instead he used his death to reaffirm the primacy of the laws and principles inherited from his Aboriginal ancestors: there must be balance in human affairs for peace and order to be re-established—balance in sharing blessings, balance in injury and harm, one death for another. Even in the face of death Dundalli called for the upholding and enforcement of traditional law. He had subverted the moral purpose of British law's most dreadful ritual.

The Bribie Islanders had been busily organising payback even while Dundalli languished in the claustrophobia of the old Brisbane Gaol. In these months large numbers of Aboriginal people 'from the northern coast of the bay' had gathered in Brisbane and at the Pine Rivers to debate retaliation for the Brisbane man who had engineered Dundalli's capture. The *Courier* objected to them assembling within the township and near white settlers for they 'cause[d] much loss and annoyance to the settlers in the suburbs of the town, and much anxiety to those on the Pine River'.[43] By October 1854, the *Sydney Morning Herald* correspondent was describing the continued ominous presence of these young Ningy Ningy and Joondaburri men as 'native infantry' and the 'scouts of Dundalli's tribe' as 'spies and rovers [who] ought to be frightened back to their own hunting grounds'.[44] There was little the chief constable could do to prevent these gatherings, given the small number of town police under his command and the fact that they were unmounted. He had eleven ordinary constables and one district constable, and only the district and chief constables were mounted. There simply weren't any police resources for the extensive territory that reached from the outskirts of Brisbane to Wide Bay.[45] If settlers in the northern suburbs or at the Pine River could not look to the Brisbane police for protection, neither could Wumbungur. Even in 1854, thirty years after the first arrival of the British at Redcliffe, it remained impossible for Sneyd to intervene in Aboriginal–Aboriginal conflict, even for someone who had been as useful to the authorities as Wumbungur.

By March 1855 Billy Barlow had organised agreement among tribal allies to avenge Dundalli. In that month, some eight weeks after Dundalli's execution, the Reverend William Ridley, a new missionary keen to evangelise among the Moreton Bay Aboriginal peoples, commenced a missionary tour to the stations north of Brisbane in company with John Hausmann. When they were 10 or 11 kilometres past Caboolture en route to Durundur Station, they suddenly came upon 'a party of full 60 blackfellows all armed'. While Ridley recorded that 'the display of their spears and clubs was formidable' they were nonetheless sociable and, recognising Hausmann, surrounded the two missionaries 'in a friendly manner ... asking us questions'. The armed party was on an operation to fulfil Dundalli's last instructions, for when Ridley arrived at Kilcoy he recorded with disappointment that 'most of the Aborigines from here were away with the armed gathering to avenge the death of Dundalli on the Brisbane black who gave information of him'.[46]

Wumbungur did not survive the confrontation. In a newspaper article published seventy-three years later, Archibald Meston claims 'Woomboonggoroo' was killed near Spring Hill. Aboriginal people subsequently renamed the area Woomboonggoroo.[47] Whatever happened, the Bribie Islanders remained as compelling a force as ever, their confidence undiminished by the horrific spectacle on the scaffold of 5 January.

Their fulfilment of Dundalli's final wishes went beyond payback on Wumbungur. Dundalli's great legacy was the strength of Bribie Island's political life in the years that followed and their strong alliance with the Pine River, Durundur and Sunshine Coast peoples, which was frequently referred to in the local press.

Even while Dundalli awaited trial, the Joondaburri were enforcing local law in northern Moreton Bay waters. In October 1854 Joseph Goold and Thomas Anderson, two European members among an Aboriginal crew of the Harbour Master, went missing; when their boat eventually washed up on the beach at Sandgate it showed signs of violent struggle. What actually happened remains a mystery; however, Goold had a criminal record, so it is not out of the question that the white man provoked the Bribie Islander crew. The incident aggravated European anxieties. It proved whites did not control the bay or Brisbane's coastal lands, despite the large and growing sea traffic to and from Brisbane, and despite the show of strength that Dundalli's capture seemed to represent. The *Courier* bemoaned the weakness of European authority in the face of continued Aboriginal control of bayside land:

> Within thirteen miles of North Brisbane is the surveyed village of Sandgate at Cabbage Tree Creek. At this spot large quantities of land have been sold at high prices by the Government, and some thousands of pounds have been invested by persons anxious to build upon and improve the place forthwith. Yet . . . no person dares to attempt to improve his land within an hour's ride of the capital because his life would be in danger from the attacks of the natives . . . All along the northern shore of the bay is one dreary waste of bush, entirely abandoned to the blacks . . .

At this very spot we learn that the blacks landed on the late melancholy occasion, and perhaps it was here—where but for the grossest neglect a thriving village population might now be established—that the murderous assault was made ... the coolness that succeeds such events is astonishing. All hope of arresting the murderers seems to be abandoned.[48]

Dundalli was in custody yet Aboriginal men continued to defy white officialdom in the northern and bayside areas of Brisbane.

The township of Brisbane remained a confined frontier. On the north side the urban limit did not stretch beyond Fortitude Valley. Spring Hollow and York's Hollow remained Aboriginal camping grounds. Between the valley and Captain Wickham's Newstead House was scrub. A number of farms had been established across the creek from Wickham at Breakfast Creek, which also continued to be an important Aboriginal campsite and fishery. New settlers had joined the German community at Nundah and at Eagle Farm. Between these suburbs and Darby McGrath's station, established in 1852 at The Gap, was bushland. The troubles at Cash's and at McGrath's had been attributed to Dundalli's daring opposition, but as settlers sought to move onto purchased lands in suburbs such as Sandgate, or to take up new cattle leases on the Pine River in the years following Dundalli's execution, they encountered fierce resistance. The Gap today is a suburb of Brisbane, while the eastern reaches of the South Pine form the most northerly boundary of the city of Brisbane, but in the years 1855 to 1859 they were still not under effective British control.

There was little the Brisbane authorities could do. There had been incessant demands for the Native Police to be used in Brisbane but that force had faced endless logistical problems. After patrolling the Pine and Brisbane river valleys in 1852–53, Commandant Walker was forced to return his detachment to Wide Bay, where squatters repeatedly demanded police protection. Even the security of the small coastal town of Maryborough was not assured. The white population of Maryborough numbered perhaps five hundred, and their numbers were declining as the southern gold rushes drew men away from frontier districts. Both Commissioner Bidwell and his successor as commissioner of crown lands for Wide Bay, Arthur Halloran, estimated the Aboriginal population of Wide Bay as about five thousand strong. The northern Gubbi Gubbi had terrorised Bidwell over many months and now the new commissioner, Arthur Halloran, felt their power. They stole from the commissioner's gardens, even while he was home, as well as provisions and weaponry from his orderlies.[49] Walker was scathing when he was ordered to provide Native Police protection for the Wide Bay commissioner's establishment just south of the township. He pointed out that the commissioner 'knows that the lives and the property of the Settlers must be secured before the Native Police can attend to sweet potatoes and have to protect a *police station*'. Nonetheless he assured the colonial secretary that the local officer would do what he could.[50]

The situation at Maryborough reached crisis point when young Darryguree was arrested for the second time in February 1854. The Badtjala men from Fraser Island had surrounded the township of Maryborough, ordering the whites to release him and threatening to destroy the town. With two constables absent on escort duty, there had been only two town police and two of the commissioner's orderlies available to confront the Badtjala, who were around Maryborough in 'such formidable numbers', armed with spears and nulla nullas, that Halloran ordered his men to 'disperse them'.[51] By the end of 1854 the Native Police Force was overextended on northern and western frontiers and mired in controversy. The successful arrest of Darryguree, like Dundalli's which followed, belied the weakness of white control and Aboriginal strength. There was simply no detachment permanently available for the Moreton Bay district and that at Wide Bay was overstretched.

This was made clear in the months following Dundalli's execution. The Whiteside and Samsonvale stations had suffered from intermittent Aboriginal hostilities since their foundations in the 1840s, but in September 1855 the organised nature of the Pine River people's resistance to incursions on their land was apparent. In that month, in the bed of a creek on Whiteside Station, George Griffin's widow, Jane Griffin, discovered bush barricades which had been constructed by Aboriginal people in order to muster and spear cattle systematically. During Dundalli's lifetime the Pine River Valley had been an important meeting place for the northern tribes, so the systematic harvesting of beef to feed large meetings was an interesting adaptation to this unwanted European presence. It is further proof of the strength of the northern alliance.[52]

Although Police Magistrate Wickham and his successor William Brown had at various times organised mounted police patrols of two constables to the Pine River and Sandgate, this had not been sustainable on any regular basis. There had also been proposals for a police station to be constructed at the mouth of the Brisbane River that could have readily accessed the coasts and islands of the bay, but they appear to have come to nought.[53] A small detachment of six troopers under the command of a sub-lieutenant of Native Police briefly patrolled the northern and coastal districts from June to September 1855, but it had not succeeded in limiting attacks on cattle at Whiteside nor in executing any arrests. Then in 1855–56 the government reduced the force, cutting the number of detachments to four and the number of troopers by forty-eight, guaranteeing no detachment for Moreton Bay.[54] These cutbacks provoked another flowery *Courier* editorial, which described the force's retraction as evil and emphasised the ongoing impediment to the development of Sandgate.[55]

The government had raised more than £1957 from the sale of land at Sandgate in 1853 and its Brisbane purchasers included influential local pastoralists and businessmen.[56] They were growing increasingly disgruntled in the face of this policing stalemate and subsequently formed a committee to lobby the New South Wales government for protection for the coastal suburbs. The committee prepared a 'memorial' from concerned citizens—today it would be called a 'petition'—and also took out paid advertising to promote its views. It published its 'Notice to Government' as a newspaper advertisement, which ran from 22 March to the end of April 1856. The purchasers were naturally aggrieved that the government had made a considerable profit on the land when it clearly did not have effective control over the district. Their notice made clear that it was the Aboriginal tribes who controlled and occupied these lands and that the government had granted them deeds that could not be enforced:

> Know ye that the Marine Township of Sandgate, situated on the shore of Moreton Bay, only 12 miles from the Township of North Brisbane, and which township of Sandgate has all been sold by the Government, at prices averaging from 2 to 400 per cent. above the upset price; and know ye, by this notice, that all parties that have attempted to sit down on the said township, to erect dwellings, have been driven away by the blacks; and I now solemnly declare by this notice, that no person can attempt to make improvements on their purchased township allotments at Sandgate except at the risk to their lives; and which township to this day remains a wilderness. And we by this notice pray ye for protection to enable us to build our houses thereon.
> Richard J. Coley. Chairman of Committee.[57]

With the granting of full self-government to New South Wales in 1856 and the election of new representatives from the northern districts to parliament, the *Courier* pressed its priorities to the new members for the County and Boroughs of Stanley: third on its list was 'that dreaded and dangerous spot Sandgate'. It argued that these lands had been sold 'on the implied if not express understanding that the buyers would be protected, in making improvements, from the assaults of the hostile tribes of aboriginals ... in this would-be Government township'. Its editorial ignored the immense organisational difficulties that any administration faced in providing the intensive on-the-ground 'policing' required to claim lands that had never been ceded by the coastal tribes. It described government inaction as 'listlessly apathetic and evidently careless'.[58]

Not surprisingly the new government replied favourably to the Sandgate memorialists. In his new role of government resident, Captain Wickham was advised that there was no means for supplying a Native Police Force for the district but that the current commandant, Lieutenant Morrisset, had been instructed to patrol the 'disturbed portion of the Moreton Bay district' whenever possible.[59] The *Courier* responded facetiously that it was 'rather a roving commission for the gallant officer' whose force now had responsibility for pacifying a district that extended from the Clarence and Macleay rivers of northern New South Wales in the south to the Upper Dawson in the north, some 700 kilometres north to south and a similar distance east to west, with just eighty-five men.[60] 'And also for the valiant sons of the soil who roam about Cabbage Tree Creek', it added.[61] The fighting spirit of the Bribie Islanders had strengthened the resolve of the traditional owners across the northern parts of what today is greater Brisbane. Neither the colonial government under the authority of the London Colonial Office, nor the local administration under self-government, had the capacity to wrest their lands from them in 1856.

Despite the insecurity of property, new settlers continued to take up cattle leases close to the older existing stations at the North and South Pine rivers and north to Caboolture. And the traditional owners of the Pine Rivers continued to evict them. Today the lands of James Cash's cattle station fall within the northern boundaries of Brisbane at Bridgeman Downs. He had first set up his run in 1851, but like his Whiteside and Samsonvale neighbours, his cattle suffered from unremitting harassment from the Aboriginal owners. His efforts to defend his station from Aboriginal attack were preserved in Brisbane oral history by a member of the Zillmann family, who in 1926 recalled how

> Cash on the South Pine had trouble with the blacks—he bored large auger holes through the slabs of his house so as to take the muzzle of a gun through and could then keep the blacks away. The blacks then tied fire sticks to their spears, and tried throwing the spears onto the bark roof of the house, but the gun kept them away, and they did not gain their end, burning him out.[62]

In the mid-1850s there were fresh attempts at establishing cattle stations in the Pine Rivers district. A Mr Young tried to do so but in September 1856, while he was absent in Brisbane, two hundred Aboriginal men descended on the station, taking whatever they wanted and spearing several cattle.[63] Just three weeks later, between three hundred and four hundred men were waiting in ambush at a Mr Westaway's new station on the North Pine. Becoming aware of the men's intentions, Westaway and his servant, both of whom were mounted, attempted to charge the gathering but the warriors simply urged the two white men on. Realising that they were soon to be surrounded, Westaway led a retreat back to their hut. From there the servant fired blank shot, which triggered a shower of waddies. Now Westaway grasped that they were at even greater risk; as the northern men prepared to storm the hut he and his man fled. When they returned two days later on Monday morning the hut had been robbed of all his goods and provisions. Westaway, who spoke the local dialect, reported that the local people had been joined by Durundur and Wide Bay peoples and claimed that the leader was one of the latter, who called several times to him to go, 'as plenty more blacks were coming, and pointed the direction that he was to take'. Once again this alliance of northern peoples proved that they were in the ascendant on these, their own lands. The *Courier* complained of 'official incapacity and gross neglect in withholding protection to life and property'.[64]

In the twelve months that followed, farmland was purchased at Bald Hills, which would eventually come to define the city of Brisbane's north-east boundary. The hills abutted fine wetlands, tidal flats and mangroves of the South Pine River, which flowed to the bay. The new settlers had been anxious about purchasing so close to Ningy Ningy heartlands, and they and their families and friends added to the lobbying of the government resident for police protection. By October 1857 the government had agreed to an expansion of the Native Police and a new detachment was to be raised for the Moreton Bay district commencing January 1858.[65] Until then Chief Constable Sneyd and a mounted district constable undertook a weekly patrol of these northern districts. As the police patrolled on Wednesdays, local Aboriginal people sent smoke signals which floated into the air for miles along the bay, warning the Ningy Ningy and their allies to stay clear.[66]

The Bribie Islanders' continued rejection of white authority—especially its expression through the Native Police—was brought home forcefully in the last weeks of 1857. A native trooper was sent to go among the northern tribes as far as Caboolture, which would have taken him through the country of Pine River Valley, Dalla and Ningy Ningy peoples, to seek recruits for the expansion of the Native Police. His trip was cut short when he was confronted by a leading Joondaburri man, who assaulted him with a butcher's knife, cutting the trooper's arm 'clean off by the shoulder'. Aboriginal women hastily applied clay, their traditional method for treating wounds, but could not stem the blood flow and the man died the next day. It was a stern expression of Bribie Islander rejection of colonial policing.[67]

Despite the risk to security, the government conducted further Sandgate land sales in 1855 and again in 1858.[68] As the amount of invested money increased, a group of Brisbane shareholders boldly planned the development of a boarding house or hotel at this pretty bay.[69] They met in August 1857 and by October a publican by the name of Loudon had commenced operations there. He seems to have survived, unlike Dowse and others, by simply agreeing to Aboriginal demands for provisions. When the town police patrol visited they reported that 'the blacks ... have proved troublesome to Mr. Loudon, getting almost everything they wanted by shear [sic] boldness in demanding it'. Police Magistrate Brown, himself a Sandgate landholder, promised to visit Loudon and do all he could until the Native Police detachment arrived.[70]

A detachment of eight troopers under Lieutenant Williams promptly arrived in January 1858, but no sooner had it commenced patrols around Sandgate than an attack on a station on the Logan River to the south of Brisbane resulted in it being called away. An attack by Aborigines on the Logan? In official correspondence in 1856 residents such as Henry Buckley had confidently described the Stradbroke Islanders, with whom the Logan people were allies, as 'peacable'.[71] It is further proof that white settlers simply did not understand the Aboriginal politics of this region, in which cooperation with whites was 'peacable' only as long as it suited particular Aboriginal aims. Still, the withdrawal of the detachment to the Logan is also proof that settler authorities did not have the capacity for more intensive paramilitary operations. This was the context for a confident gathering of three hundred Aboriginal men on Whiteside Station in April 1858.

While responding to a complaint from Jane Griffin, Lieutenant Williams's detachment came under sudden and unexpected attack on 15 April 1858 while on patrol on her station. They had stumbled upon a large Aboriginal camp in scrubs along the river that ran through the property. The Aboriginal trooper to the left of Lieutenant Williams, Trooper John, was speared in the throat and fell instantly, eight or nine spears piercing his body. Lieutenant Williams promptly regrouped his men and ordered them to return fire. He estimated ten minutes of firing by the remaining members of the detachment before the northern men dispersed. At the end of the encounter, as well as the death of Trooper John, Troopers Charlie and Mark were injured while six warriors had fallen and two others were injured.[72]

Lieutenant Williams had unwittingly ridden into the midst of a large Aboriginal meeting. Here on these lands, where Dundalli had also frequently met with friends and allies, impressive preparation had been underway to feed a large assembly of five hundred or more men, women and children—Williams recounted how the trees surrounding the camp had been hung with fresh carcasses of beef. Wickham's official report blamed 'the Natives occupying the sea coast between the Brisbane River, and Wide Bay [who] have been for a length of time ... an absolute terror to the Settlers in the more immediate vicinity of Sandgate and the Pine Rivers'.[73] European authorities were anxiously aware of the hostility of the tribal nations from this 200-kilometre stretch of coastline. These warriors were contemptuous of white authority. Despite fighting back against men who were armed and mounted, the warriors had shouted in English 'kill the white fellow' and 'you bloody coward'.[74] To traditional fighting men the lack of an open challenge and the uneven match of weaponry and horses all made this style of conflict an affront to their code of martial chivalry. Their reference points remained their own political and legal values, which had not been surrendered in the face of the firepower of the Native Police.

This attack reduced the Native Police detachment to five active men, and although its patrols of the district resumed in the weeks that followed, the security of the coastal parts of the Whiteside run was never satisfactorily resolved. Mrs Griffin had had enough. Tom Petrie recalled a conversation with her son, whom he met at the North Pine in about 1859. John Griffin told him that

We can't keep a beast down there for the blacks, they run them into the swamps and spear them, then have great feasts. If any of us go down in that direction, we have always to be on our guard—that is the reason I am armed like this (touching his weapons [of two horse pistols and a carbine hanging at his side]).[75]

A few months later his mother sold the ten coastal portions of the Whiteside run, amounting to almost half the total area of the station that her family had held since 1843, to Tom Petrie.[76] It was a victory for the Pine Rivers elder Dalaipi. Petrie had been friends with Dalaipi's son Dal-ngang since childhood so the two men had known one another for some twenty-two years and trusted one another. When Petrie decided to look for land for a station he had first approached Dalaipi who, unaware of colonial property or pastoral lease laws, had urged him to take up Whiteside. Now Petrie legally owned a large portion of it as a result of the Pine River people's sustained harassment. They had succeeded in removing an unsympathetic and uncompromising owner and installing a European whom they trusted and who was prepared to respect their sacred sites and allow their continued enjoyment of them. Tom Petrie was known among the Gubbi Gubbi as 'belonging to Dalaipi' and he named his run Murrumba Downs, the local word for 'good'.[77] He remained in occupation until the end of the nineteenth century. Now Dalaipi, like Paddy, the Dalla elder at Durundur, could guarantee his people's movement across this portion of their lands.

Although Paddy no longer featured in accounts of life at Durundur in the 1860s, his people's lifestyle continued there. In 1848 the Archer brothers had sold Durundur to the McConnel brothers. Compared with David Archer, John McConnel—who later went into partnership with Harry Wood, the man after whom the town of Woodford is named—was less sympathetic to Aboriginal interests and rights. Nonetheless, the Aboriginal community at Durundur remained sizeable. The station was dependent on Aboriginal labour and so John McConnel had accepted the Archers' arrangements and tolerated continuous Aboriginal occupation. John's son Arthur McConnel recalled their ceremonies and gatherings as a child growing up on the station:

> The Durundur and Upper Mary river blacks were a fine lot of people. The boys first rate stock hands and some of the gins good workers about the homestead—and while my father owned Durundur gave no trouble. They were very frightened of the coast and Bribie blacks whom they termed 'Saucy fellows' and any who were camped away from the head station came in whenever they heard that the Bribie people were on the walk about.[78]

So by 1859, the year Queensland was granted status as a self-governing colony separate from New South Wales, the northern Aboriginal alliance had guaranteed access to important Bora grounds, meeting places and sacred sites as a result of European recognition of their communities at Durundur and Murrumba Downs, and the inability of whites to successfully occupy coastal areas from the north bank of the Brisbane River mouth all the way to Wide Bay. The lawmen and elders who followed in Dundalli's footsteps had protected their special places, which allowed their community, law and politics to survive across the region and even within the boundaries of the new colonial capital.

The coastal peoples were also dominant in the battle for Sandgate until 1859, but in that year the local Native Police detachment was not only reinforced but also given a new officer: the most notorious officer in the force's brutal history, Lieutenant Frederick Wheeler.[79] Despite the detachment's activities over more than twelve months, conditions at Sandgate were still described as 'in a rough state' in 1859, although more houses were being constructed and pleasure visits to the seaside began to be advertised in the local press.[80] Wheeler's hand was strengthened by the erection of Native Police barracks and horse paddocks right in the village of Sandgate in the course of 1859.[81]

Wheeler ranged over a wide territory of south-east Queensland, including the Sunshine Coast and Caboolture, in an effort to break the alliance of the Ningy Ningy, Joondaburri, Pine River and Dalla peoples. He sought to terrorise all Aboriginal people, including those living peaceably at Murrumba Downs and Durundur, as accounts from both Petrie and Arthur McConnel prove.[82] Despite Wheeler's ruthless rampages when he came across Aboriginal gatherings, Aboriginal people continued to evade his dispersals and to persist with their traditional meetings.[83] In December 1862 four of his troopers deserted and he struggled to replace them.[84] Then in 1865, one of his sergeants ordered the shooting of a 'friendly' Aboriginal boat crew on the beach at Sandgate. This was not necessarily unusual police behaviour in the field, but now it was deemed an atrocity by the local press. The decision was made to close the Sandgate Native Police camp.[85]

Ten years after the execution of Dundalli, the man who had been presumed to be the source of all resistance to settler occupation, the Europeans finally felt confident in their control and settlement of this northern seaside suburb of Brisbane. The occupation of Sandgate had taken eight years of episodic paramilitary operations from 1857 to 1865. It required conquest to achieve a hold over the northern suburbs of Brisbane, which was not effective until six years after Queensland was made a separate colony.

Nor did authorities have an uncontested hold over the Brisbane coastline. In January 1859 two Bribie Island men took swift and lethal action against three white dugong fishermen on St Helena Island, reinvigorating settler anguish. The decomposing body of one of them, Bob Collins, was found near Luggage Point a fortnight after he had set out with an American and a Dutchman to go dugong hunting.[86] Collins had misled two Bribie Island men as to his aims; after promising to sail them north so they could join that summer's Bunya gathering, he instead took them, their wives and children south to St Helena. Collins and his men were armed and while on the island they 'took possession' of the wives. This appears to be Petrie's euphemism for rape. Billy Dingy, the husband of one of the women, waited until he found each of the white men alone and killed them. The two Aboriginal men then took their wives and children north to Caloundra, where they left Collins's boat with all its gear, including armaments and provisions, intact.[87] In February, Bribie Islanders returning from that year's Bunya assembly told Petrie what had happened and he in turn reported it to authorities in Brisbane.[88]

Why did the Bribie Islanders even bother to inform whites about what had taken place? The Bribie Islanders were happy to be partially incorporated into the economy of Moreton Bay but this did not mean they ceded their basic human rights, their dignity or their own laws. Instead they made an effort to introduce the Europeans to their ways. Just as when Dundalli had stepped from behind a tree during the attack at the Pine River in September 1847 and explained to James Smith what was happening in his own language, they consistently explained their actions to the white community. Now the Joondaburri used Petrie for the same ends. Equally consistently the whites either failed, or wilfully refused, to comprehend the message.

In response to this episode the *Moreton Bay Courier* editorialised on the rights of Europeans to use lynch law if Billy Dingy and his accomplice could not be arrested; at the very least, it argued, they should be shunned and refused entry to the township. Whites understood the powerful lure of modern technology and commodities to the Aboriginal community—just not that the Joondaburri did not want them at any price. The editorial is also yet another admission that the inner suburbs of Brisbane were the limit of white authority: 'Those who reside in the more settled portion of Australia, may not feel so strongly as we do on the subject in our isolated position; yet Englishmen, all over the world, will understand the necessity of teaching the natives to respect the life of a white man.'[89] It did not want negotiation with the Bribie Islanders; it wanted a show of imperial strength, which a township of only just over five thousand European souls could hardly muster when surrounded by an Indigenous community of similar numbers.

So it was that in the early months of 1859, as British parliamentary officials were preparing the legislation that would decree the northern districts a separate self-governing colony, the lawmen of the northern alliance still effectively controlled much of the lands and waterways of what is now the state capital. White officials believed that they could crush all local resistance with Dundalli's hanging, but the Joondaburri were unimpressed by the 'majesty' of British law. They had not been persuaded of the justice of the colonisers' legal system, nor had the firepower of its Native Police Force convinced them of the morality of colonisation. It had not just been Dundalli's fighting power, nor his oratory as a tribal lawman, which had swayed them; rather, like him, they preferred the honour and chivalry of their martial code and the dignity of their law to a system that did not allow a man to stand up and fight in defence of his honour, in defence of his brothers, in defence of his wife and children and in defence of his lands. Dundalli's death had reinforced their beliefs in the 'proper way'—the ancient laws of their ancestors. Whatever claims were being made at Westminster about the ownership and governance of the lands that were about to become known as Queensland, outside the confined spaces of white suburbs and homesteads, ancestral law remained the law of the land.

Epilogue

REMEMBERING DUNDALLI

'Here is their spirit, in the heart of the land they loved...'[1]

Sixty-four years after Dundalli's execution, a settler by the name of Robert Lane spoke to the *Brisbane Courier* about the tensions in the town. 'I was ordered to get out of the city,' he recalled, 'as the blacks might be hostile. I was going up Eagle St when the drop fell, and the yells of the Blacks in the bushes where our railway now runs could be heard distinctly.'[2]

It was the fourth time since 1842 that colonists had believed that white settlement in the north might come under attack. In August 1843 Multuggerah of the Yaggera had sent a warning to his 'brother', the squatter John Campbell, that he should not travel to the Darling Downs, for 'it was to be war now in earnest ... their intention was to spear all the commandants, then to fence up the roads and stop the drays from travelling, and to starve the "jackaroos" (strangers)'.[3] Campbell had laughed at the notion but later recalled that 'within three weeks ... the blacks had carried out their programme'.[4]

Three years later, in the aftermath of Dundalli's attack on Gregor's station, the explorer Ludwig Leichhardt, who had spent several months in the field with Aboriginal guides and enjoying the hospitality of northern pastoral stations, wrote anxiously to his good friend David Archer, 'the time of hostility and war is approaching fast'.[5]

The third occasion was the night of 28 November 1849 when it seemed that most of the township of Brisbane believed that the Mianjin were about to attack, and convinced the officer in command to call out the local military detachment to defend them. It was a sign of how in awe Europeans were of Aboriginal physical fitness and fighting power. When the much-travelled attorney-general arrived in town to prosecute the soldiers for their illegal action, he did not ridicule the locals as northern hicks with vivid imaginations. On the contrary, he admitted that 'since his arrival in Brisbane [he] had seen sufficient numbers of natives about the town to make him believe that if they had really formed themselves into a body for an united attack on the inhabitants, there might be good grounds for alarm'.[6] It was not just the numbers of Aboriginal people in the north that worried the Europeans, it was also their martial skills. When Constable Conroy followed the regiment out to Mianjin homes, he carefully kept ten paces behind them. When cross-examined in court about this he explained that even with the soldiers armed and ready to fire, he 'would not have gone into the camp; a black might have knocked out his brains before anyone could interfere'.[7]

The northern settlers knew Aboriginal people were capable of waging war. As Arthur Halloran, commissioner of crown lands for Wide Bay, had written to his superiors in 1854, 'if they knew their own strength, this place would very soon be abandoned'.[8]

The Brisbane frontier was one of Australia's longest, lasting more than forty years, commencing in 1824 at Redcliffe and continuing until 1865 and later around the northern part of Moreton Bay. It was also an urban frontier, as Europeans called upon the paramilitary force of the Native Police to wrest control over their suburbs. These events were central to the foundation of another Australian colony yet they are not remembered in any official way.

Until we recognise how much blood was spilt securing Australian lands will we really have reconciliation? Dundalli was one of many Aboriginal men who died to protect his country, who passed the test of character that war demands, who drew on mateship, courage and endurance to survive. It seems extraordinary that none of Australia's war memorials recognise their extraordinary bravery. There could be no better embodiment of heroism than fighting against armed and mounted men as they invaded your lands, as Dundalli's people had to do on so many occasions over more than four decades.

Dundalli's was a special kind of valour in the midst of colonial violence. This violence wasn't only out there on the pastoral plains; it was also present in the urban spaces, in the courtrooms and on the beaches. In death and in life, Dundalli was an exemplar of traditional law. His actions help to illuminate the complex nature of Australia's geographical and cultural frontier. Exploring his life sheds light on the local Aboriginal peoples' systems of law and government and their means of law enforcement; in other words, their political sovereignty and how that inhibited the spread of colonial society across the landscape.

If the Australian legend can be applied to Australians fighting overseas wars, then it can equally be applied to men like Dundalli who fought for this country against foreign invaders.

ACKNOWLEDGEMENTS

This book has developed in conversation with many people. It benefited from colleagues who tolerantly lent me books not returned for many months and Murri friends who did their best to explain the complexities of Aboriginal relationships. I am indebted to Rod Fensham of the Queensland Museum who kindly gave me access to the translations of Ludwig Leichhardt's German diaries before publication; to Marion Diamond, now retired from the University of Queensland, who collected material in the Bodleian Library for me while she was on holidays; to Bryce Barker of the University of Southern Queensland, some of whose books are still sitting on my shelves; to Rod Fisher who directed me to an important source on the 1850s; and to other dear history and archaeology colleagues who kindly read drafts or gave practical advice, especially when times were tough, in particular Trevor McClaughlin, Bernadette Turner, Noeline Hall, Ray Kerhove and Michael Strong. Michael Aird's knowledge of Aboriginal portraits is unsurpassed and I am most grateful for his assistance with acquiring images of Paddy and Dundalli. I must also thank Neil Ennis for allowing me to use his photographs, which beautifully reflect his love of place and of history.

Other materials were happily gathered over many years at too many research institutions to itemise. However, I want to express my appreciation of librarians at John Oxley, Mitchell and Sunshine Coast libraries, Queensland Museum and the Queensland Art Gallery for permission to reproduce many of the photographs. Elizabeth Weiss at Allen & Unwin is inspiring in her willingness to bring histories of conflict such as this one to new audiences, but it only came to fruition as a result of Clare James and Sarah Baker's patience and skill in making it all readable.

The book would never have been written without Sam Watson's initial encouragement or Stephen Hagan's continued support. I am also indebted to Gubbi Gubbi historian Alex Bond, who tried to set me straight on cultural history on many occasions. Needless to say, any errors or misunderstandings that remain are mine. Lastly I thank my husband, Drew Hutton, who understands how a sense of injustice can energise a project over many years, and how important stories are to our individual and community identities.

BIBLIOGRAPHY

Abbreviations

Australian Institute of Aboriginal and Torres Strait Islander Studies	AIATSIS
Colonial Secretary	CS
John Oxley Library	JOL
Mitchell Library	ML
National Library of Australia	NLA
Public Record Office, UK	PRO
Queensland State Archives	QSA
Society for the Propagation of the Gospel	SPG
State Library of New South Wales	SLNSW
State Records of New South Wales	SRNSW
University of Queensland Press	UQP

Manuscripts and archival material

Archer, David. Durundur Diary, 1843–1844, OM79–17/1, JOL.
Archer, David. Letters from Leichhardt, A1383–1, CY 3058, ML.
Archer Family: General & Business Correspondence, A3882, CY3690, ML.
Archer Family: Letters, M1742, Box 5169, JOL.
Archer Family: Letters and Papers, 1841–1913, A3874, CY3929, ML.
Archer Family: Papers, Personal & Business, A3875, CY3897, ML.
Archer Family Correspondence: Some letters from Australia written home between 1833 & 1855 by the brothers, London, 1933, 4783, OM80–10, JOL.
Archer, John. Letters 1833–1855, Ms F1665, Fryer Library.
Brisbane Gaol, Prison Register, PRI 1/25, QSA.
Broughton, W. G. Bishop Broughton's Letters to the Society for the Propagation of the Gospel, 1843 to 1849, MIC 7933, Fryer Library.
Certificates of Freedom 1823–69, 4/4409, SRNSW.
Clerk of Works Moreton Bay Correspondence: 1856–59, WOK/1, QSA.
Colliver, F.S. Papers, Queensland Museum.
Copy of an unfinished letter by Andrew Petrie to an unnamed Brisbane paper regarding a trip to Bribie Island in 1837, Brisbane, 20 May 1861, Ts 683, JOL.
Coroners' Inquests 1834–94: Years 1838–1852, vol. 2–3, NRS 343, SRNSW.
Court of Petty Sessions, Brisbane—Depositions and Minutes Book 07/12/1850–30/12/1854, Series 753, QSA.

CS Commissioners of Crown Lands 1844–1849, 4/2640–4/2843, SRNSW.
CS In Letters: 1850 4/2887, SRNSW.
CS In Letters: 1854 4/3256, SRNSW.
CS In Letters: Misc Persons: 1843, 4/4559.2, SRNSW.
CS Letters Received Main Series: 1852, 4/3075, SRNSW.
CS Letters Received re Moreton Bay: 1858, A2/39, QSA.
CS Moreton Bay 1839–1850, 4/2460.3–4/2913, SRNSW.
CS Special Bundles: Monthly reports of visiting magistrates: Brisbane Gaol
    1850–1858, 4/7192, SRNSW.
CS Special Bundles: Moreton Bay, CCL 1843–47, 4/1141.1, SRNSW.
CS Special Bundles: Native Police: Moreton Bay, 1855–1858, 4/719.2, SRNSW.
CS Special Bundles: Returns of the State of the Gaols, 1850–1856, 4/7341, SRNSW.
CS Special Bundles: Wide Bay, 1849–57, 4/7173, SRNSW.
Deposition and Minute Books, 06/02/1846–31/10/1846, Series 753, Item 518884,
    p. 36, QSA.
Deposition Book, Brisbane 8 February 1850, QSA Item ID 518885.
Dowse, Thomas. 'Recollections of old times in Moreton Bay', a transcript of the
    original manuscript (OM79–68/16) online, JOL.
Dowse, Thomas. 'Thomas Dowse Diary' (OM84–31) online, JOL.
Duncan, William Augustine. 'Autobigraphy', ML.
Durundur station, Caboolture, Q'land. Extracts from a diary, 17 Oct 1842 –
    14 May 1843 made on Durundur station by the wife of an employee of the
    Archers during a visit by Dr Ludwig Leichhardt. Document 1825, ML.
Early Brisbane Clippings, 1894–1947, OM91–36, JOL.
Eipper, Christopher. 'Statement of the Origin, Condition and Prospects of the
    German Mission to the Aborigines at Moreton Bay', Sydney: 1841, JOL.
Gaiarbau's story of the Jinibara tribe of south-east Queensland (and its
    neighbours), collected by L.P. Winterbotham, MS 45 / MS 429, AIATSIS.
Government Resident Moreton Bay IL: 1851 RES/A3, QSA.
Government Resident Moreton Bay IL: 1856 Res/A7, QSA.
Governors' Despatches, 1844, A1233, ML.
Griffin, George. Diary Kept by Captain G. Griffin at Whiteside via Petrie
    'Moreton Bay', 1st January 1847 – 16th May 1849, OM72–42/1, JOL.
Griffin, George. Remarks and Transactions at the Whiteside Station 1 Jan 1851 –
    25 Dec 1851, OM 72-42/2, JOL.
Index to Orphan Schools Records, SRNSW.
Inspection Returns and Confidential Reports, Eleventh Regiment of Foot,
    1st Period 1850: General Observations, WO 27/399, PRO.
Inspection Returns and Confidential Reports, 1st–25th Regiments, 1st Period
    1851, WO 27/409, PRO.
Inspection Returns and Confidential Reports, 11th Regiment, 1st Period 1852,
    WO 27/419, PRO.
Knight, J.J. 'John Dunmore Lang: Preacher, Politician, and Patrist', 1899, JOL.
Lang, Rev. John Dunmore. Papers A2240, vol. 20, CY579, ML.
List of 15 Male Convicts per the Ship *Layton*, SRNSW.

McConnel, A.J. Diary, OM79–13/18/1, JOL.
McConnel, A.J. Diary, transcription by Margaret Chittick, OM79–13/18/2, JOL.
McConnel, David Cannon. Papers, M3271 Box 5621, JOL.
McConnel Family, Papers, OM78–72, JOL.
McConnel Family, Papers, 1844–1977, UQFL89, Fryer Library.
McConnel, Frederic. Stories of Australian Bush Life, 1844: Experiences of the late Frederic McConnel, typescript, <http://nla.gov.au/nla.aus-f7689> NLA.
McConnel, Mary. Papers relating to the McConnel family of Cressbrook, F3107, Fryer Library.
McConnel, Mary. 'Memories of Days Long Gone By', Brisbane, M. McConnel, 1905, <http://nla.gov.au/nla.aus-f7689> NLA.
Meston Cutting Book No. 3 (1 & 3), Queensland Museum.
Moreton Bay: Book of Trials, Item 869682, Series ID 5646, QSA.
Muehling, E., extracts from 'Fuhrer durch Queensland', 1898, translated by Anita Stapleton, JOL.
Ninth Annual Report Apsley Aboriginal Mission, Wellington, 31 December 1849 in Documents Relating to Aboriginal Australians, 1816–1853: Mission Reports, DL Add 81, SLNSW.
Official Papers: Archival Estrays: Commissioner of Crown Lands, Report on State of the Aborigines of the District of Moreton for the year 1849. Add 79, ML.
Official Papers: Archival Estrays: Inquiry into affrays with Aborigines CSIL Add 82, ML.
Official Papers: Archival Estrays: Wickham to Deas Thomson and sworn statements for inquiry into affrays with Aborigines CSIL Add 10, ML.
Papers of Phyllis Gregor, Bodleian Library, Oxford University, UK.
Questionnaire from the Society for the Propagation of the Gospel in Foreign Parts, 22 May 1846, typescript, Anglican Church Archives, Brisbane.
Returns of the Colony (Blue Books), 1850.
Ridley, Rev. William, Narrative of labour among the Aborigines of Australia, Ms Q165, CY3386, ML.
Schmidt, Karl W. Report of an expedition to the Bunya Mountains in search of a suitable site for a mission station, translated by Dr L. Grope and edited and notated by P.D. Wilson, F.S. Colliver & F.P. Woolston, Acc. 3522/1 & 3522/2, Box 7072, JOL.
Supreme Court, Criminal Jurisdiction: Clerk of the Peace, Brisbane 1846, 9/6337, SRNSW.
Supreme Court, Criminal Jurisdiction: Clerk of the Peace, Brisbane 1850, 9/6359, SRNSW.
Supreme Court, Criminal Jurisdiction: Clerk of the Peace, Brisbane 1851, 9/6366, SRNSW.
Supreme Court, Criminal Jurisdiction: Clerk of the Peace, Brisbane 1853, 9/6378, SRNSW.
Supreme Court, Criminal Jurisdiction: Clerk of the Peace, Brisbane 1854, 9/6386, SRNSW.

Supreme Court, Criminal Jurisdiction: Judgment Books, Brisbane Circuit Court, 1850–1856, 4/5745–5753, SRNSW.
Supreme Court, Register of Depositions received from Benches, 1837-49, 7/6055, SRNSW.
Wagner, Claire. Papers, OM92–152, JOL.
Walker, George E. Diary, OM64–9/86, JOL.
Walker Papers, OM64–9/123, JOL.
Zillmann Family Papers, OM74–28, Box 8889, JOL.

Books and articles

Aird, Michael. *Brisbane Blacks*, Southport, Qld: Keeaira Press, 2001.
Anderson, Ian. 'Re-claiming TRU-GER-NAN-NER: Decolonising the symbol' in Penny Van Toorn & David English (eds), *Speaking Positions: Aboriginality, gender and ethnicity in Australian cultural studies*, Melbourne: Victoria University of Technology Department of Humanities, 1995.
Anderson, Peter John, MA LLB (ed). *Officers and Graduates of King's College Aberdeen*, Aberdeen: New Spalding Club, 1893.
Annual Report of the Australian Diocesan Committee of the Societies for the Propagation of the Gospel in Foreign parts . . . for the Year 1847, Sydney: Society for the Propagation of the Gospel, 1848.
Archer, T. *Recollections of a Rambling Life*, Brisbane: Boolarong, 1988 [facs of 1897 edn].
Atkinson, Alan. *Camden: Farm and village life in early New South Wales*, Melbourne: Oxford University Press, 1988.
Backhouse, James. *A Narrative of a Visit to the Australian Colonies*, London: Hamilton, Adams, 1843.
Baker, D.W.A. 'Lang, John Dunmore (1799–1878)', *Australian Dictionary of Biography*, vol. 2, Melbourne: Melbourne University Press, 1967, pp. 76–83.
Banivanua Mar, Tracey & Edmonds, Penelope (eds). *Making Settler Colonial Space: Perspectives on race, place and identity*, London: Palgrave UK, 2010.
Banks, Mary Macleod. *Memories of Pioneer Days in Queensland*, London: Heath Cranton, 1931.
Beckett, Ray & Beckett, Richard. *Hangman: The life and times of Alexander Green, public executioner to the colony of New South Wales*, West Melbourne: Nelson, 1980.
Bennett, J.M. (ed). *A History of the New South Wales Bar*, Sydney: Law Book, 1969.
Bennett, J.M. *A History of the Supreme Court of New South Wales*, Sydney: Law Book, 1974.
Bennett, J.M. *Callaghan's Diary*, Sydney: Francis Forbes Society for Australian Legal History, 2005.
Bond, Alex. *The Statesman, the Warrior and the Songman*, Nambour, Qld: Interactive Community Planning Australia, 2009.
Bond, June. 'The other Tribe of Cherbourg (Kabi-Kabi)', *Social Alternatives*, vol. 7, no. 1, 1988, pp. 44–6.

Bottoms, Timothy. *Djabugay Country: An Aboriginal history of tropical North Queensland*, St Leonards, NSW: Allen & Unwin, 1999.
Bridges, Barry. 'The Aborigines and the law: New South Wales 1788–1855', *Teaching History*, vol. 4, part 3, 1970.
Brisbane River Valley 1841–50: Pioneer observations and reminiscences, Brisbane History Group Sources No. 5, Brisbane: Brisbane History Group, 1991.
Callaghan, Thomas. *Callaghan's Diary*, Sydney: Francis Forbes Society, 2005.
Campbell, John. 'The early settlement of Queensland' and other articles with which is also printed 'The raid of the Aborigines', Ipswich, Qld: Ipswich Observer, 1875.
The Church in Australia Part II: Two journals of missionary tours in the districts of Maneroo and Moreton Bay, New South Wales, in 1843, London: Society for the Propagation of the Gospel, 1846, 3rd edn.
Cilento, Sir Raphael. *Captain Walker's Marathon*, Toowong: Boolarong, 1986.
Clendinnen, Inga. *Dancing with Strangers*, Melbourne: Text, 2003.
Clendinnen, Inga. 'Spearing the governor', *Australian Historical Studies*, vol. 33, no. 118, 2002, pp. 157–74.
Cochrane, Peter. *Colonial Ambition: Foundations of Australian democracy*, Melbourne: Melbourne University Press, 2006.
Coleman, Julia. 'A new look at the north coast: Fish traps and "villages"' in Sandra Bowdler (ed), *Coastal Archaeology in Eastern Australia*, Canberra: Research School of Pacific Studies, ANU Department of Prehistory, 1982, pp. 1–10.
Connors, Libby. 'Distant and disinterested: Oversight of northern policing as Colonial Office policy in the 1840s and 1850s', *Australia and New Zealand Law and History E-Journal*, 2012, Refereed, pp. 78–95.
Connors, Libby. 'A house divided: the Griffin family of Whiteside and frontier conflict in the 1840s', *Queensland History Journal*, vol. 20, no. 11, 2009, pp. 578–92.
Connors, Libby. 'Sentencing on a colonial frontier: Judge Therry's decisions at Moreton Bay', *Legal History*, vol. 12, no. 1, 2008, pp. 81–97.
Connors, Libby. 'The theatre of justice: Race relations and capital punishment at Moreton Bay 1841–59' in Rod Fisher (ed), *Brisbane: The Aboriginal presence 1824–1860*, Brisbane: BHG, 1992, pp. 48–57.
Connors, Libby. 'A Wiradjuri child at Moreton Bay', *Queensland History Journal*, vol. 20, no. 13, 2010, pp. 775–87.
Connors, Libby. 'Witness to frontier violence: An Aboriginal boy before the Supreme Court', *Australian Historical Studies*, vol. 42, no. 2, 2011, pp. 230–43.
Connors, Libby. 'Women, children and violence in Aboriginal law: Some perspectives from the southeast Queensland frontier' in Diane Kirkby (ed), *Past Law, Present Histories*, Canberra: Australia and New Zealand School of Government & ANU Press, 2012, pp. 125–36.
Cooke, Simon. 'Arguments for the survival of Aboriginal customary law in Victoria: A case note on *R v Peter* (1860) and *R v Jemmy* (1860)', *Australian Journal of Legal History*, vol. 5, no. 2, 1995, pp. 201–41.

Coote, William. *History of the Colony of Queensland: From 1770 to close of the year 1881*, Brisbane: William Thorne, 1882.

Craig, W.W. *Moreton Bay Settlement or Queensland before Separation Together with a Brief Account of the Rise of the Colonies of Australasia*, Brisbane: Watson Ferguson, 1925.

Cryle, Denis. *The Press in Colonial Queensland: A social and political history 1845–1875*, St Lucia: UQP, 1989.

Cryle, Mark. 'Introduction' in Constance Campbell Petrie, *Tom Petrie's Reminiscences of Early Queensland*, St Lucia: UQP, 1992, pp. iv–xliv.

Currey, C.H. 'Sir Roger Therry (1800–1874)', *Australian Dictionary of Biography*, vol. 2, 1967, pp. 512–13.

Demarr, James. *Adventures in Australia Fifty Years Ago: Being a record of an emigrant's wanderings through the colonies of New South Wales, Victoria and Queensland during the years 1839–1844*, London: Swan Sonnenschein, 1893.

De Winton, G.J. *Soldiering Fifty Years Ago: Australia in 'The Forties'*, Ludgate Circus, UK: European Mail, 1898.

Dornan, Dimity & Cryle, Denis, *The Petrie Family: Building colonial Brisbane*, St Lucia: UQP, 1992.

Earls, Tony. *Plunkett's Legacy: An Irishman's contribution to the rule of law in New South Wales*, North Melbourne: Australian Scholarly Publishing, 2009.

Edmonds, Penelope. 'Unpacking settler colonialism's urban strategies: Indigenous peoples in Victoria, British Columbia, and the transition to a settler-colonial city', *Urban History Review*, vol. 39, no. 2, 2010, pp. 4–20.

Edwards, W.H. *An Introduction to Aboriginal Societies*, South Melbourne: Cengage, 1998, 2nd edn.

Elkin, A.P. *Aboriginal Men of High Degree: Initiation and sorcery in the world's oldest tradition*, Rochester, Vermont: Inner Traditions, 1994.

Evans, Ray. *A History of Queensland*, Cambridge: Cambridge University Press, 2007.

Evans, Ray. 'The Mogwi take Mi-an-jin: Race relations and the Moreton Bay penal settlement 1824–42' in Rod Fisher (ed), *Brisbane: The Aboriginal presence 1824–1860*, Brisbane: BHG, 1992, pp. 7–30.

Fairhall, Patricia (ed). *Ningi Ningi: Our first inhabitants*, Redcliffe: Redcliffe Historical Society, 1989.

Fisher, Rod. *Boosting Brisbane*, Salisbury: Boolarong & Brisbane History Group, 2009.

Fitzgerald, Ross. *A History of Queensland: From the Dreaming to 1915*, St Lucia: UQP, 1982.

Ford, Roger & Blake, Thom. *Indigenous Peoples in Southeast Queensland: An annotated guide to ethno-historical sources*, Woolloongabba: Foundation for Aboriginal and Islander Research Action, 1998.

Foreman, Edgar. *The History and Adventures of a Queensland Pioneer*, Lewes, UK: EMR Publications, 1996 [revised edn, first published 1928].

Fyans, Foster. *Memoirs Recorded at Geelong, Victoria, Australia by Captain Foster Fyans (1790–1870): Transcribed from his holograph manuscript given by descendants to the State Library, Melbourne 1962*, Geelong: Geelong Advertiser, 1986.

Goodman, Jordan. *The Rattlesnake: A voyage of discovery to the Coral Sea*, London: Faber & Faber, 2005.

Gregory, Helen. *The Brisbane River Story: Meanders through time*, Yeronga: Australian Marine Conservation Society, 1996.

Gunson, Niel, 'Eipper, Christopher (1813–1894)', *Australian Dictionary of Biography*, vol. 1, Melbourne: Melbourne University Press, 1966, pp. 351–53.

Gunson, Niel, 'Schmidt, Karl Wilhelm Edward (–1864)', *Australian Dictionary of Biography*, vol. 2, Melbourne: Melbourne University Press, 1967, pp. 421–3.

Gunson, Niel (ed), *Australian Reminiscences & Papers of L.E. Threkeld: Missionary to the Aborigines, 1824–1859*, Canberra: Australian Institute of Aboriginal Studies, 1974.

Gunson, W.N. 'The Nundah missionaries', *Journal of the Royal Historical Society of Queensland*, vol. 6, no. 3, 1960–61, pp. 511–39.

Hall, J. 'Sitting on the crop of the bay: An historical and archaeological sketch of Aboriginal settlement and subsistence in Moreton Bay, southeast Queensland' in Sandra Bowdler (ed), *Coastal Archaeology in Eastern Australia*, Canberra: Research School of Pacific Studies, ANU Department of Prehistory, 1982, pp. 79–95.

Harrison, Colin. *Birds of Australia*, London: Bison, 1988.

Hart's Army List, London: John Murray, 1852.

Hiatt, L.R. *Arguments about Aborigines: Australia and the evolution of social anthropology*, Cambridge: Cambridge University Press, 1996.

Historical Records of Australia, series I, vol. 21 (Oct 1840–Mar 1842), Library Committee of the Commonwealth Parliament, 1924.

Johnston, W. Ross. *Brisbane: The first thirty years*, Bowen Hills, Qld: Boolarong, 1988.

Keen, Ian. *Aboriginal Economy and Society: Australia at the threshold of colonisation*, South Melbourne: Oxford University Press, 2003.

Kerkhove, R. 'Aboriginal Trade in Fish and Seafoods in Nineteenth Century South-East Queensland: A Vibrant Industry?' *Queensland Review*, vol. 20, no. 2, 2013, pp. 144–56.

Knight, J.J. *In the Early Days: History and incident of pioneer Queensland*, Brisbane: Sapsford, 1898 [2nd edn].

Lang, John Dunmore. *Cooksland in North-Eastern Australia; the Future Cotton-Field of Great Britain: Its characteristics and capabilities for European colonization*, London: Longman, Brown, Green & Longmans, 1847.

Lang, John Dunmore. *Queensland, Australia; a Highly Eligible Field for Emigration and the Future Cotton-Field of Great Britain: With a disquisition on the origin, manners, and customs of the Aborigines*, London: Edward Stanford, 1861.

Leichhardt, Ludwig. *Leichhardt Diary No 3: 30 July 1843 to 18 November 1843 with additions to 3 December 1843*, translated by Thomas Darragh, Brisbane: Queensland Museum, 2013.

Leichhardt, Ludwig. *Leichhardt Diary No 4: 23 November 1843–March 1844*, translated by Thomas Darragh, Brisbane: Queensland Museum, 2013.
Long, Erica. 'Early white settlement on the Pine River', *Journal of the Royal Historical Society of Queensland*, vol. 16, no. 5, 1997, pp. 189–209.
Long, Erica. 'A History of the Timber Industry in the Pine Rivers District,' *Access History*, vol. 2, no. 1, 1998, pp. 55–73.
Love, W.R.F. *Bribie Dreaming: The original island inhabitants*, Bribie Island, Qld: L. Love, 1994.
MacGillivray, John. *Narrative of the Voyage of HMS Rattlesnake, Commanded by the Late Captain Owen Stanley, RN, FRS, during the Years 1846–1850*, vol. 1, Adelaide: Libraries Board of South Australia, 1967 [facs of 1852 edn].
Mackenzie-Smith, John. *Brisbane's Forgotten Founder: Sir Evan Mackenzie of Kilcoy 1816–1883*, Brisbane: BHG, 1992.
Mackenzie-Smith, John. *The Scottish Presence at Moreton Bay 1837–59*, Brisbane: BHG, 2005.
Mathew, John. *Two Representative Tribes of Queensland: With an inquiry concerning the origin of the Australian race*, London: T. Fisher Unwin, 1910.
McDonald, Lorna. *Over Earth and Ocean: The Archers of Tolderodden and Gracemere, a Norse–Australian saga 1819–1965*, St Lucia: UQP & Central Queensland University Press, 1999.
McKinnon, Firmin. 'Early pioneers of the Wide Bay and Burnett', *Journal of the Royal Historical Society of Queensland*, vol. 3, no. 2, October 1940, pp. 90–9.
McNiven, Ian J. 'Cooloola Aborigines: Ethnohistorical reconstructions of Aboriginal lifeways along the Cooloola coast', *Proceedings of the Royal Society of Queensland*, vol. 102, 1992, pp. 5–24.
Molony, John. *An Architect of Freedom: John Hubert Plunkett in New South Wales 1832–1869*, Canberra: ANU Press, 1973.
Moorehead, Alan. *Darwin and the Beagle*, Ringwood, Vic.: Penguin, 1971.
Moreton-Robinson, Aileen. 'Unmasking whiteness: A Goori Jondal's look at some Duggai business', *Queensland Review*, vol. 6, no. 1, 1999, pp. 1–7.
Moreton-Robinson, Aileen (ed). *Whitening Race: Essays in social and cultural criticism*, Canberra: Aboriginal Studies Press, 2004.
Mozley, Ann. 'Huxley, Thomas Henry (1825–1895)', *Australian Dictionary of Biography*, vol. 1, Melbourne: Melbourne University Press, 1966, pp. 577–8.
Nicoll, Fiona. 'Reconciliation in and out of perspective: White knowing, seeing, curating and being at home in and against Indigenous sovereignty' in Aileen Moreton-Robinson (ed), *Whitening Race: Essays in social and cultural criticism*, Canberra: Aboriginal Studies Press, 2004.
Perrignon, W.B. 'Faucett, Peter (1813–1894)', *Australian Dictionary of Biography*, vol. 4, Melbourne: Melbourne University Press, 1972, pp. 157–8.
Petrie, Constance Campbell. *Tom Petrie's Reminiscences of Early Queensland*, Hawthorn, Vic.: Lloyd O'Neil, 1975 [facs of 1904 edn].
Rayner, K. 'Handt, Johann Christian Simon (1794–1863)', *Australian Dictionary of Biography*, vol. 1, Melbourne: Melbourne University Press, 1966, pp. 509–10.

Rayner, K. 'Gregor, John (1808–1848)', *Australian Dictionary of Biography*, vol. 1, Melbourne: Melbourne University Press, 1966, pp. 472–3.

Reynolds, Henry. *Aboriginal Sovereignty: Reflections on race, state and nation*, Sydney: Allen & Unwin, 1996.

Reynolds, Henry. *The Forgotten War*, Sydney: New South, 2013.

Reynolds, Henry. *The Other Side of the Frontier*, Townsville: James Cook University History Department, 1981.

Richards, Jonathan. 'Frederick Wheeler and the Sandgate Native Police Camp', *Journal of the Royal Historical Society of Queensland*, vol. 20, no. 3, 2007, pp. 107–22.

Ridley, Rev. William. *Kamilaroi, and Other Australian Languages, and Songs, Traditions, Laws and Customs of the Australian Race*, NSW Government Printer, 1875 [2nd edn].

Roe, Michael. 'Duncan, William Augustine (1811–1885)', *Australian Dictionary of Biography*, vol. 1, Melbourne: Melbourne University Press, 1966, p. 337.

Russell, Henry Stuart. *Genesis of Queensland*, Toowoomba: Vintage, 1989 [facs of 1888 edn].

Select Committee on the Condition of the Aborigines, *Votes & Proceedings of the Legislative Council of New South Wales*, 1845.

Select Committee on the Condition of the Aborigines: Replies to circular, *Votes & Proceedings of the Legislative Council of New South Wales*, 3rd session, 1846.

Select Committee on the Native Police, Queensland Parliament, *Votes & Proceedings*, 1861.

Simpson, Stephen. *The Simpson Letterbook*, transcribed by Gerry Langevad, St Lucia: Anthropology Museum, 1979.

Skinner, L.E. *Police of the Pastoral Frontier*, St Lucia: UQP, 1975.

Some Original Views around Kilcoy, Brisbane: Department of Aboriginal & Islander Advancement, 1982.

Steele, J.G. *Aboriginal Pathways in Southeast Queensland and the Richmond River*, St Lucia: UQP, 1984.

Steele, J.G. *Brisbane Town in Convict Days, 1824–1842*, St Lucia: UQP, 1975.

Stokes, John Lort. *Discoveries in Australia with an Account of the Coasts and Rivers Explored and Surveyed during the Voyage of HMS Beagle in the Years 1837–38–39–40–41–42–43*, vol. 1 & 2, Adelaide: Libraries Board of South Australia, 1969 [facs of 1846 edn].

Therry, Roger. *Reminiscences of Thirty Years Residence in New South Wales*, Sydney: Sydney University Press for Royal Australian Historical Society, 1974 [facs of 1863 edn].

Thorpe, Osmund. *First Catholic Mission to the Aborigines*, Sydney: Pellegrini, 1950.

Tindale, Norman B. *Aboriginal Tribes of Australia: Their terrain, environmental controls, distribution, limits and proper names*, Canberra: Australian National University Press, 1974.

Tynan, Patrick J. *Duramboi*, Virginia, Qld: Church Archivists' Press, 1997.

Tynan, Patrick J. *Johnny Cassim: Coolie-convict-catechumen-colonial entrepreneur*, Toowoomba: Church Archivists' Press, 2005.

Walker, J.H. *The Wreck, the Rescue and the Massacre: An account of the loss of the barque, Thomas King, on Cato's Reef, New Holland, in April 1853*, London: Wesleyan Conference Office, 1875.

Welsby, Thomas. *The Collected Works of Thomas Welsby*, vol. 1 & 2, ed by A.K. Thomson, Brisbane: Jacaranda Press, 1967–68.

Woods, G.D. *A History of Criminal Law in New South Wales: The colonial period, 1788–1900*, Sydney: Federation Press, 2002.

Zillmann, J.H.L. *Career of a Cornstalk: Including fifty years of Australian history, with sketches of leading statesmen, politicians & public men, also personal reminiscences of pioneer settlers and old families, interspersed with some extracts of original poetry*, Sydney: Duncan & Macindoe, 1914.

Zillmann, J.H.L. *Past and Present Australian Life: Being for the most part personal reminiscences with stories of the first explorers, convicts, blacks and bush-rangers of Australia, and a short historical sketch of the colonies, their progress and present condition*, London: Sampson Low, Marston, Searle & Rivington, 1889.

Theses

Connors, Libby. The 'birth of the prison' and the death of convictism: The operation of the law in pre-separation Queensland 1839 to 1859, PhD (History) University of Queensland, 1990.

Nolan, Janette. Pastor J.G. Haussmann: A Queensland pioneer 1838–1901, PhD (History) University of Queensland, 1964.

Rayner, K. History of the Church of England in Queensland, PhD (History) University of Queensland, 1963.

Sullivan, Hilary, Aboriginal gatherings in south-east Queensland, BA Hons (Prehistory and Anthropology), ANU, 1977.

Whalley, Peter, An introduction to the Aboriginal social history of Moreton Bay, south-east Queensland from 1799 to 1830, BA Hons (Anthropology and Sociology) University of Queensland, 1987.

Newspapers

Aberdeen Journal, 1830–1831.
Australian, 1838, 1844–1848.
Belfast Newsletter, 9 June 1837.
Bell's Life in Sydney and Sporting Reviewer, 3 April 1847.
Brisbane Courier, 1876, 1919–1933.
Brisbane Town News from the Sydney Morning Herald 1842–46: Brisbane History Group Sources No. 3, Brisbane: BHG, 1989.
Caledonian Mercury, 22 July 1837.
Colonial Observer, 1841–1843.
Colonial Times, 1850.
Daily Mail, 1923–1924.

Government Gazette, 16 November 1846
Illustrated London News, 1854
Illustrated Sydney News, 1854.
Maitland Mercury & Hunter River General Advertiser, 1843–1859.
Manchester Guardian, 1 May 1847.
Moreton Bay Courier, 1846–1859.
Moreton Bay Free Press, 1852–1858.
North Australian, Ipswich & General Advertiser, 1858–1859.
Sydney Chronicle, 1846–1847.
Sydney Morning Herald, 1842–1859.

Websites

First Report of the Aboriginal Mission Murrunggallang, Wellington in Documents Relating to Aboriginal Australians, 1816–1853: Mission Reports, DL Add 81, SLNSW, available at <http://acms.sl.nsw.gov.au/album/ItemViewer.aspx?itemid=862003&suppress=N&imgindex=6>. Accessed 12 February 2010.

'Maroochy Barambah', Daki Budtcha Records, Artists page, available at <www.dakibudtcha.com.au/index.php/maroochy-barambah.htm>. Accessed 7 April 2014.

Queensland Places, Centre for the Government of Queensland, University of Queensland, 2011, available at <http://queenslandplaces.com.au/node/1132>. Accessed 10 September 2012.

South Australian Museum: Tindale's Catalogue of Australian Aboriginal Tribes, available at <http://archives.samuseum.sa.gov.au/tindaletribes/>. Accessed 23 July 2009.

NOTES

PREFACE
1. See for example *Brisbane Courier*, 18 January 1919, p. 12; *Daily Mail*, 21 January 1924, p. 9.
2. Rod Fisher, *Boosting Brisbane: Imprinting the colonial capital of Queensland*, Brisbane: Boolarong & Brisbane History Group, 2009, pp. 171–2; 187–90.
3. *Illustrated Sydney News*, 16 December 1854, p. 440.

PROLOGUE
1. Ray Beckett & Richard Beckett, *Hangman: The life and times of Alexander Green, public executioner to the colony of New South Wales*, West Melbourne: Nelson, 1980, p. 97.
2. *Brisbane Courier*, 18 January 1919, p. 12.
3. *Moreton Bay Courier*, 26 August 1854, p. 2.

1 GROWING UP IN THE BLACKALL RANGE
1. The discussion about food is drawn from Gaiarbau's story of the Jinibara tribe of south-east Queensland (and its neighbours), collected by L.P. Winterbotham, MS 45 AIATSIS, pp. 81–92; Diary of A.J. McConnel, transcription by Margaret Chittick, OM79–13/18/2, JOL, pp. 12–15.
2. Gaiarbau's story, p. 42.
3. Karl Schmidt, Report of an expedition to the Bunya Mountains in search of a suitable site for a mission station, translated by Dr L. Grope and edited and notated by P.D. Wilson, F.S. Colliver & F.P. Woolston, Acc. 3522/1, Box 7072, JOL, p. 12.
4. Fyans in 1836 cited in Helen Gregory, *The Brisbane River Story: Meanders through time*, Yeronga: Australian Marine Conservation Society, 1996, p. 8; Gaiarbau's story, pp. 98–9.
5. Based on Norman B. Tindale, *Aboriginal Tribes of Australia: Their terrain, environmental controls, distribution, limits and proper names*, Canberra: Australian National University Press, 1974; J.G. Steele, *Aboriginal Pathways in Southeast Queensland and the Richmond River*, St Lucia: UQP, 1984; Roger Ford & Thom Blake, *Indigenous Peoples in Southeast Queensland: An annotated guide to ethno-historical sources*, Woolloongabba: Foundation for Aboriginal and Islander Research Action, 1998. The Ningy Ningy name is disputed by Aboriginal linguist Dr Eve Fesl but it is used in this account

NOTES

because it was often the only identity given in colonial records. There is disagreement among the peoples of south-east Queensland regarding traditional boundaries. I have been guided by Foundation for Aboriginal and Islander Research Action in the spelling and use of names.

6   European records document that he had at least one brother.
7   The discussion of childbirth is drawn from Gaiarbau's story, pp. 72–7 and *Colonial Observer*, 4 November 1841, p. 35.
8   Gaiarbau's story, pp. 16–26; John Mathew, *Two Representative Tribes of Queensland: With an inquiry concerning the origin of the Australian race*, London: T. Fisher Unwin, 1910, pp. 132–7.
9   Constance Campbell Petrie, *Tom Petrie's Reminiscences of Early Queensland*, Hawthorn, Vic.: Lloyd O'Neil, 1975 [facs of 1904 edn], pp. 175, 319; Colin Harrison, *Birds of Australia*, London: Bison, 1988, pp. 91–3. His name is spelt here according to court records; Petrie spelt his name as Ommuli.
10 Gaiarbau's story, pp. 107–9.
11 Gaiarbau's story, pp. 78–80.
12 John Dunmore Lang, *Cooksland in North-Eastern Australia; the Future Cotton-Field of Great Britain: Its characteristics and capabilities for European colonization*, London: Longman, Brown, Green & Longmans, 1847, p. 394.
13 See Journal of the brethren Eipper & Hausmann during their residence at Umpie boang from 22nd of Nov to the 3rd Dec 1842 in Lang Papers A2240, vol. 20, CY579, ML, in which Eipper notes the emotional meetings between a father and uncle and their daughter and niece and a grandfather and grandson after lengthy separations. For a husband's concern for his wife see the missionaries' report in *Colonial Observer*, 21 October 1841, p. 23.
14 Charles Archer to Jamie & Simon, Durundur, August 1844, Archer Family: Letters and Papers, 1841–1913, A3874, CY3929, ML.
15 Gaiarbau's story, p. 71.
16 Gaiarbau's story, pp. 140–4; Petrie, *Reminiscences*, pp. 109–14.
17 Gubbi Gubbi historian Alex Bond gives this word for a head man and 'mudjimba' for the femal counterpart. Gaiarbau gives the name 'muning-burum'. Gaiarbau's story, p. 74.
18 Gaiarbau's story, p. 33.
19 Schmidt, Report of an expedition, p. 9; also *Colonial Observer*, 7 December 1842, p. 662.
20 *Colonial Observer*, 23 July 1842, p. 347. 'Bail' or 'bal' was a local pidgin rendering of the negative.
21 Gaiarbau's story, pp. 42–6; Ian Keen discusses the phenomenon of 'big men' in North Queensland and 'boss men' in central Australia in Ian Keen, *Aboriginal Economy and Society: Australia at the threshold of colonisation*, South Melbourne: Oxford University Press, 2003, pp. 253, 260.
22 Gaiarbau's story, pp. 140–1.
23 Gaiarbau's story, pp. 14–15; *Some Original Views around Kilcoy*, Brisbane: Department of Aboriginal & Islander Advancement, 1982, pp. 64–5; Leichhardt cited in Lang, *Cooksland*, p. 375.

24 Gaiarbau's story, pp. 114–20.
25 Gaiarbau's story, p. 139.
26 Gaiarbau's story, pp. 42–3.
27 Petrie, *Reminiscences*, p. 22.
28 Gaiarbau's story, p. 127.
29 Gaiarbau's story, p. 129; for description of a challenge and camp's silence see *Colonial Observer*, 14 October 1841, p. 10.
30 *Colonial Observer*, 4 November 1841, p. 35.
31 This was the missionaries' estimate of the assembly at Toorbul, 22 August 1841. *Colonial Observer*, 28 October 1841, p. 27.
32 *Colonial Observer*, 21 October 1841, p. 23.
33 Gaiarbau's story, p. 45.
34 Charles Archer, Durundur, to his father 29 April 1845, Archer Family Correspondence: Some letters from Australia written home between 1833 & 1855 by the brothers, London, 1933, OM80–10, JOL.
35 'Account of a Fight . . . by Thomas Pamphlet' & 'Account of a Fight . . . by John Finnegan' in Lang, *Cooksland*, pp. 410–15.
36 Petrie, *Reminiscences*, p. 47; Gaiarbau's story, pp. 65, 127.
37 Finnegan in Lang, *Cooksland*, p. 413.
38 In colonial times 'Moreton Bay' referred not only to the bay but also to the pastoral district of Moreton Bay which stretched from the Logan River district in the south to the Caboolture River in the north and west to the Great Divide.
39 Petrie, *Reminiscences*, p. 22.
40 See the description for Peak Crossing in Queensland Places, Centre for the Government of Queensland, University of Queensland, 2011, available at <http://queenslandplaces.com.au/node/1132>.
41 *Colonial Times*, 24 May 1850, p. 4. This article is signed 'JW of the Leicester Building' which allows him to be identified as John Watts, who taught French, Italian and Spanish as well as 'mercantile' subjects at the Classical and Commercial Academy in Murray Street, Hobart. See *Colonial Times*, 12 April 1850, p. 3. It has proven impossible to confirm that he was ever at Moreton Bay during its penal station days but his names of European and Aboriginal men and other details are accurate.
42 *Australian*, 22 December 1838, p. 3. Although published twelve years apart this article and the *Colonial Times* article by John Watts have a very similar structure and employ their own distinct phonetic spelling of Aboriginal names. In the *Colonial Times* article published in 1850, Watts compared the Stradbroke Island warriors to the Light Company of the 39th; this regiment was stationed at Moreton Bay in 1827—see J.G. Steele, *Brisbane Town in Convict Days 1824–1842*, St Lucia: UQP, 1975, p. 81.
43 W.H. Edwards, *An Introduction to Aboriginal Societies*, South Melbourne: Cengage, 1998 [2nd edn], p. 58.
44 Rod Fisher, *Boosting Brisbane*, Salisbury, Qld: Boolarong & Brisbane History Group, 2009, p. 97.
45 Petrie, *Reminiscences*, p. 162.

46 Gaiarbau's story, pp. 139–40.
47 Gaiarbau's story, p. 15.
48 Gaiarbau's story, pp. 44–7; Petrie, *Reminiscences*, pp. 38–46.
49 Gaiarbau's story, pp. 20, 47–8.
50 T. Archer, *Recollections of a Rambling Life*, Brisbane: Boolarong, 1988 [facs of 1897 edn], pp. 46–60; John Mackenzie-Smith, *Brisbane's Forgotten Founder: Sir Evan Mackenzie of Kilcoy 1816–1883*, Brisbane: BHG, 1992, p. 54.

2 THE YOUNG NEGOTIATOR

1 Rod Fisher, *Boosting Brisbane*, Salisbury: Boolarong & Brisbane History Group, 2009, p. 97.
2 Based on W. Ross Johnston, *Brisbane: The first thirty years*, Bowen Hills, Qld: Boolarong, 1988, p. 55; Ray Evans, 'The Mogwi take Mi-an-jin: Race relations and the Moreton Bay penal settlement 1824–42' in Rod Fisher (ed), *Brisbane: The Aboriginal presence 1824–1860*, Brisbane: BHG, 1992, pp. 15–17.
3 James Backhouse, *A Narrative of a Visit to the Australian Colonies*, London: Hamilton, Adams, 1843, pp. 363–4.
4 Backhouse, *Narrative of a Visit*, p. 367.
5 Foster Fyans, *Memoirs Recorded at Geelong, Victoria, Australia by Captain Foster Fyans (1790–1870): Transcribed from his holograph manuscript given by descendants to the State Library, Melbourne 1962*, Geelong: Geelong Advertiser, 1986, pp. 146–7.
6 Fyans, *Memoirs*, p. 163.
7 Evans, 'The Mogwi', pp. 19–21; Peter Whalley, An introduction to the Aboriginal social history of Moreton Bay, south-east Queensland from 1799 to 1830, BA Hons thesis (Anthropology and Sociology), University of Queensland, 1987, pp. 71–7.
8 Whalley, 'Aboriginal social history of Moreton Bay', p. 90.
9 Cotton cited in Evans, 'The Mogwi', p. 22; see also Johnston, *Brisbane*, p. 57.
10 Ticket-of-leave men were convicts who had been issued with a permit for a prescribed district that allowed them to find their own employment. They had to report regularly to authorities and were not allowed to leave the district for which the ticket had been issued.
11 Eipper, Statement of the Origin, Condition and Prospects of the German Mission to the Aborigines at Moreton Bay, cited in J.G. Steele, *Brisbane Town in Convict Days 1824–1842*, St Lucia: UQP, 1975, p. 282.
12 W.N. Gunson, 'The Nundah missionaries', *Journal of the Royal Historical Society of Queensland*, vol. 6, no. 3, 1960–61, p. 520; Janette Nolan, 'Pastor J.G. Haussmann: A Queensland pioneer 1838–1901', PhD (History) thesis, University of Queensland, 1964, p. 19.
13 Gunson, 'The Nundah missionaries', p. 519.
14 *Colonial Observer*, 14 October 1841, p. 10; 18 November 1841, p. 51; & 27 July 1842, p. 355.
15 Mission diaries are available for January 1840; 30 July–17 September, 1 October–8 November, 10–24 November, 25–31 December 1841;

1 January–13 May, 27 September–31 December 1842; 1–17 January, 23 January–18 July 1843. 'Journeys with the Natives' took place November 1839, 2–13 August 1841, 17–30 August 1841, 14 October–19 November 1841, 11–18 February 1842, 22–25 February 1842, ?–5 March 1842, 12–31 March 1842, 4–19 April 1842, 5 April–19 May 1842, 1–18 June 1842, 28 September–18 October 1842, 4–11 November 1842, 22 November–3 December 1842, 28 December 1842–6 January 1843, 6 March–28 April 1843. Rev. John Dunmore Lang, Papers A2240, vol. 20, CY579, ML; *Colonial Observer*, 1841–1842. The record of the final expedition of 1843 was published by the Gossner Missionary Society in Berlin in *Die Biene auf dem Missionfelde* (no. 3 of 1843); a translation by Dr L. Grope is held by the John Oxley Library; Karl Schmidt, Report of an expedition to the Bunya Mountains in search of a suitable site for a mission station, translated by Dr L. Grope and edited and notated by P.D. Wilson, F.S. Colliver & F.P. Woolston, Acc. 3522/1, Box 7072, JOL.

16 Johnston, *Brisbane*, pp. 62–3.
17 Nolan, 'Pastor Haussmann', p. 24.
18 Entry for 13 January 1840, Mission Diary in Lang Papers.
19 Henry Stuart Russell, *Genesis of Queensland*, Toowoomba: Vintage, 1989 [facs of 1888 edn], pp. 262–3. Russell's names for the moieties or skin groups are not quite correct. See Gaiarbau's story of the Jinibara tribe of south-east Queensland (and its neighbours), collected by L.P. Winterbotham, MS 45 AIATSIS, pp. 16–19; John Mathew, *Two Representative Tribes of Queensland: With an inquiry concerning the origin of the Australian race*, London: T. Fisher Unwin, 1910, pp. 153–60.
20 John Dunmore Lang, *Cooksland in North-Eastern Australia; the Future Cotton-Field of Great Britain: Its characteristics and capabilities for European colonization*, London: Longman, Brown, Green & Longmans, 1847, pp. 398–9.
21 Nicker appears in a group photo taken at Durundur in 1867 and reproduced in Michael Aird, *Brisbane Blacks*, Southport, Qld: Keeaira Press, 2001, p. 18.
22 In 1853 Dundalli 'exchanged names' and became 'brother' to William Wilson, a European who then owned the ketch *Aurora*. R v Dundalli Assault and Robbery, 2 June 1854, Court of Petty Sessions, Brisbane – Depositions and Minutes book 07/12/1850 – 30/12/1854, Series 753, QSA.
23 See list in Roger Ford & Thom Blake, *Indigenous Peoples in Southeast Queensland: An annotated guide to ethno-historical sources*, Woolloongabba: Foundation for Aboriginal and Islander Research Action, 1998, p. 15, & the index to *Brisbane Town News from the Sydney Morning Herald*, 1842–46: Brisbane History Group Sources No. 3, Brisbane: BHG, 1989.
24 Mullan and Ningavil from the Mt Lindsay region were found guilty of the murder of Assistant Surveyor Stapleton and one of his workmen, William Tuck, on 31 May 1840. Libby Connors, 'The theatre of justice: Race relations and capital punishment at Moreton Bay 1841–59', in Rod Fisher (ed), *Brisbane: The Aboriginal presence 1824–1860*, Brisbane: BHG, 1992,

pp. 50–2; Raymond Evans, *A History of Queensland*, Melbourne: Cambridge University Press, 2007, p. 54.
25 *Colonial Observer*, 11 November 1841, p. 42.
26 Lang, *Cooksland*, p. 398.
27 *Colonial Observer*, 21 October 1841, p. 23.
28 *Colonial Observer*, 21 October 1841, p. 23.
29 The details of Niqué and Hartenstein's journey to Toorbul, 17–30 August 1841, are taken from *Colonial Observer*, 28 October 1841, p. 27 & 4 November 1841, p.35.
30 Dates are derived from Tom Archer's account in *Recollections of a Rambling Life*, Brisbane: Boolarong, 1988 [facs of 1897 edn], pp. 50–6; see also John Mackenzie-Smith, *Brisbane's Forgotten Founder: Sir Evan Mackenzie of Kilcoy 1816–1883*, Brisbane: BHG, 1992, p. 54. The purchase by the McConnels is covered in McConnel Family, Papers, Box 4, UQFL89, Fryer Library.
31 Lorna McDonald, *Over Earth and Ocean: The Archers of Tolderodden and Gracemere, a Norse–Australian saga 1819–1965*, St Lucia: UQP & Central Queensland University Press, 1999, p. 115.
32 Archer, *Recollections*, pp. 53, 59–60.
33 Tom to his father, 3 May 1846, Archer Family Correspondence: Some letters from Australia written home between 1833 & 1855 by the brothers, London, 1933, 4783, OM80–10, JOL; Charles to his father, Durundur, 10 April 1847, Archer Family Correspondence, OM80–10, JOL; David to his father, Waroongundie, 16 February 1846, Archer Family Correspondence, OM80–10, JOL.
34 Jack to David, Sydney, 13 March 1845, in Archer Family: Letters, M1742, Box 5169, JOL. This is a transcript of one of Jack's letters; I have corrected the typing errors.
35 Cited in McDonald, *Over Earth and Ocean*, pp. 81–2.
36 John Archer to his father, head of River Brisbane, 8 November 1841, John Archer Letters: 1833–1855, MS F1665, Fryer Library.
37 Archer, *Recollections*, p. 69.
38 Thomas Archer to his father, Waroongundie, 22 March 1846, John Archer Letters.
39 Thomas Archer to his father, Durundur, 10 September 1843, John Archer Letters.
40 Archer, *Recollections*, pp. 71–5.
41 See the account of Petrie among 'strange blacks', Constance Campbell Petrie, *Tom Petrie's Reminiscences of Early Queensland*, Hawthorn, Vic.: Lloyd O'Neil, 1975 [facs of 1904 edn], p. 193; and Lang's account of Davis's response when he fell out with his adopted father, Lang, *Cooksland*, pp. 420–1.
42 Charles to his father, Durundur, 29 April 1845, John Archer Letters.
43 Gaiarbau's story, pp. 1–5; see also J.G. Steele, *Aboriginal Pathways in Southeast Queensland and the Richmond River*, St Lucia: UQP, 1984, pp. 208–9.
44 Charles Archer to his father, Durundur, 29 April 1845, John Archer Letters; Archer, *Recollections*, p. 70.

45 Archer, *Recollections*, p. 70.
46 Thomas Archer to his father, 6 January 1842, Archer Family Correspondence, OM80–10, JOL.
47 Gaiarbau's story, pp. 46, 49–50; see also Steele, *Aboriginal Pathways*, pp. 206–9, who argues that Durundur people were probably Dallambara; Tindale, 'Dalla' in South Australian Museum: Tindale Biography & Tribal Boundaries, available at <http://www.samuseum.australia.sa.com/aa338/tindaletribes/dalla.htm>.
48 John Archer to his father, head of River Brisbane, 8 November 1841, John Archer Letters; Thomas Archer to his mother, 10 April 1842, Archer Family Correspondence, OM80–10, JOL.
49 Charles Archer to his father, Durundur, 29 April 1845, John Archer Letters.
50 A.J. McConnel, Diary, transcription by Margaret Chittick, OM79–13/18/2, JOL, p. 9.
51 Mrs Campbell, 'Durundur—Early Woodford', Item 310 in McConnel Family, Papers, 1844–1977, Box 4, UQFL89, Fryer Library.
52 *Colonial Observer*, 13 January 1842, p. 116.
53 Although Gavanmary appears to be a Dalla man, he was close to Deciby. They could have shared a totem or moiety connection, or there could have been some other personal reason for his attachment.
54 *Colonial Observer*, 13 January 1842, p. 116.
55 Gaiarbau's story, p. 129.
56 Petrie, *Reminiscences*, p. 60.
57 Diary entry for Saturday 13 November 1841, incomplete diary extract, Lang Papers, ML.
58 *Colonial Observer*, 13 January 1842, p. 116. Gorman placed a 1-mile limit on soldiers' movements around the penal station and banned their grog ration for a period; see entry for 8 November 1842 in Journal of the brethren Eipper & Hartenstein who resided among the Natives on the Pine River from Nov 4–11 1842, Lang Papers, ML.
59 Entries for 5–25 January 1842, Extracts from the Diary of the German Mission to the Aborigines at Moreton Bay from the 25th December 1841 to the 13th of May 1842, Lang Papers, ML.
60 Petrie translates it as 'one eye'; see Petrie, *Reminiscences*, p. 139.
61 Yilbung was found guilty of theft of corn from the Windmill and assault of a constable in 1839; see Moreton Bay: Book of Trials, Item 869682, Series ID 5646, QSA, 8 July 1839, pp. 136–7. He presumably tried this a second time in March 1842 but the entries in the Book of Trials end 28 February 1842. The mission diary entry for Tuesday, 8 March 1842, records that Millbong Jemmy was punished 'very slightly' by the commandant for assaulting a constable while Petrie narrates his theft from the Windmill, entrapment by the miller, assault of a constable followed by a punishment of flogging and twenty-four hours solitary. Extracts from the Diary, Lang Papers, ML; Petrie, *Reminiscences*, pp. 168–9.

62 Parenthesis in the original, entry for Wednesday, 9 March 1842, Extracts from the Diary, Lang Papers, ML.
63 The south-east Queensland people had a spear thrower, known elsewhere as a woomera, but the missionaries did not give a description of the 'womeran' so it is not clear what this weapon was.
64 Journal of the brethren Niqué & Rodé who were itinerating among the Natives at Umpie boang from the 12th of March to the 31st 1842, Lang Papers, ML.
65 Entry for 20 March 1842, Extracts from the Diary, Lang Papers, ML.
66 Emphasis and parenthesis in the original. Entry for 17 February 1842, Extracts from the Diary, Lang Papers, ML; entry for 16 March 1842, Journal of the brethren Niqué & Rodé, Lang Papers, ML.

3   THE GREAT TOORS OF 1842–43

1 The coastal peoples' name for the inlanders. See entry for the Dalla in Norman Tindale's Catalogue of Australian Aboriginal Tribes, South Australian Museum, 2014, available at <http://www.samuseum.sa.gov.au/tindaletribes/dalla.htm>.
2 Lorna McDonald, *Over Earth and Ocean: The Archers of Tolderodden and Gracemere, a Norse–Australian saga 1819–1965*, St Lucia: UQP & Central Queensland University Press, 1999, pp. 100–1; *Brisbane River Valley 1841–50: Pioneer observations and reminiscences*, Brisbane History Group Sources No. 5, Brisbane: Brisbane History Group, 1991, p. 3.
3 Tom Archer to his mother, Durundur, 10 April 1842, Archer Family Correspondence: Some letters from Australia written home between 1833 & 1855 by the brothers, London, 1933, 4783, OM80–10, JOL.
4 Tom Archer, *Recollections of a Rambling Life*, Brisbane: Boolarong, 1988 [facs of 1897 edn], pp. 47–8.
5 Archer, *Recollections*, p. 54.
6 John Campbell, 'The early settlement of Queensland' and other articles with which is also printed 'The raid of the Aborigines', Ipswich, Qld: Ipswich Observer, 1875, p. 10.
7 Balfour's sworn statement before Commandant Gorman, 11 October 1841, reproduced in *Brisbane River Valley*, pp. 66–7.
8 Commandant Gorman's letter to colonial secretary, 26 October 1841, reproduced in *Brisbane River Valley*, p. 67.
9 Campbell, 'Early settlement', pp. 9–10.
10 Entry for 15 November 1841, General Diary of the German Mission at Moreton Bay, Rev. John Dunmore Lang, Papers A2240, vol. 20, CY579, ML; Extract from the General Diary of the German Mission at Moreton Bay for the months of October and November 1841, *Colonial Observer*, 13 January 1842.
11 Archer, *Recollections*, pp. 70–1.
12 John Mackenzie-Smith, *Brisbane's Forgotten Founder: Sir Evan Mackenzie of Kilcoy 1816–1883*, Brisbane: BHG, 1992, pp. 71–2, 75–6.

13　Entry for 16 March, Journal of the brethren Niqué & Rodé, who were itinerating among the Natives at Umpie boang from the 12th of March to the 31st 1842, Lang Papers, ML; Mackenzie-Smith, *Brisbane's Forgotten Founder*, p. 75.

14　Entry for 16 March, Journal of the brethren Niqué & Rodé, Lang Papers, ML; Reports Kilcoy Poisoning, New South Wales Governors' Despatches, January–April 1844, A1233, ML.

15　John Dunmore Lang, *Cooksland in North-Eastern Australia; the Future Cotton-Field of Great Britain: Its characteristics and capabilities for European colonization*, London: Longman, Brown, Green & Longmans, 1847, p. 276. This detail is not included in Schmidt's report of July 1842. Karl W. Schmidt, Report of an expedition to the Bunya Mountains in search of a suitable site for a mission station, translated by Dr L. Grope and edited and notated by P.D. Wilson, F.S. Colliver & F.P. Woolston, Acc. 3522/1 & 3522/2, Box 7072, JOL.

16　Commissioner Simpson gave Bracewell's full name as David Bracewell; Henry Stuart Russell gave it as Bracefell and Andrew Petrie as Bracefield. This account uses the *Australian Dictionary of Biography* and Simpson's spelling.

17　Official accounts by the runaway convicts were given to the Commissioner of Crown Lands on their return to Brisbane, while the pastoralist Henry Stuart Russell kept notes of the sea journey to Wide Bay which rescued the runaways and included the runaways' earliest details of the Kilcoy events in his published colonial history. Commissioner Simpson, 30 May 1842, l/no. 42/4284 in CS Moreton Bay 1842 4/2581.2, SRNSW; Henry Stuart Russell, *Genesis of Queensland*, Toowoomba: Vintage, 1989 [facs of 1888 edn], pp. 279–80.

18　The deaths of the shepherds were reported at the German mission on 17 February 1842, see entry for 17 February 1842, Extracts from the Diary of the German Mission, Lang Papers, ML.

19　David Cannon McConnel to his brother Henry, Stanley Creek, 3 July 1842, Item 24, David Cannon McConnel Papers, M3271 Box 5621, JOL.

20　Russell, *Genesis*, p. 281. The shepherd was a man by the name of Murray. Commissioner Simpson, 30 May 1842, l/no. 42/4284 in CS Moreton Bay, 1842, 4/2581.2, SRNSW.

21　Constance Campbell Petrie, *Tom Petrie's Reminiscences of Early Queensland*, Hawthorn, Vic: Lloyd O'Neil, 1975 [facs of 1904 edn], p. 32.

22　Lang, *Cooksland*, pp. 427–8; John Mathew, *Two Representative Tribes of Queensland: With an inquiry concerning the origin of the Australian race*, London: T. Fisher Unwin, 1990, pp. 114, 177.

23　A.P. Elkin, *Aboriginal Men of High Degree: Initiation and sorcery in the world's oldest tradition*, Rochester, Vermont: Inner Traditions, 1994, p. 51; Ian Keen, *Aboriginal Economy and Society: Australia at the threshold of colonisation*, South Melbourne: Oxford University Press, 2003, p. 257. See also Rev. William Ridley, *Kamilaroi, and Other Australian Languages, and Songs*,

Traditions, Laws and Customs of the Australian Race, Sydney: NSW Government Printer, 1875 [2nd edn], p. 159.
24 Petrie, *Reminiscences*, pp. 32–3.
25 Statements of Bracewell & Davis as to the supposed administration of Poison to some Blacks by White Men enclosure in Commissioner Simpson, 30 May 1842, l/no. 42/4284 in CS Moreton Bay, 1842, 4/2581.2, SRNSW.
26 *Colonial Observer*, 23 July 1842, p. 347.
27 *Colonial Observer*, 23 July 1842, p. 347; *Colonial Observer*, 3 December 1842, p. 651.
28 Eipper reports that they had been fighting 'Mountain Natives'. Entry for 25 April, *Colonial Observer*, 23 July 1842, p. 347.
29 Narrative of James Davis, enclosure in Commissioner Simpson, 30 May 1842, l/no. 42/4284 in CS Moreton Bay, 1842, 4/2581.2, SRNSW.
30 Tindale's Catalogue, available at <http://www.samuseum.sa.gov.au/tindaletribes/taribelang.htm>. Gubbi Gubbi historian Alex Bond believes Davis's estimates of distance are wrong and that Ginginburrah is a poor rendering of Jinibara.
31 Russell, *Genesis*, pp. 278, 282; Patrick J. Tynan, *Duramboi*, Virginia, Qld: Church Archivists' Press, 1997, p. 30; Narrative of James Davis, enclosure in Commissioner Simpson, 30 May 1842, l/no. 42/4284 in CS Moreton Bay, 1842, 4/2581.2, SRNSW.
32 Statement of Bracewell & Davis, enclosure in Commissioner Simpson, 30 May 1842, l/no. 42/4284 in CS Moreton Bay, 1842, 4/2581.2, SRNSW.
33 Petrie, *Reminiscences*, pp. 270–1.
34 Russell, *Genesis*, p. 291.
35 David Cannon McConnel to his brother Henry, Stanley Creek, 3 July 1842, Item 24, David Cannon McConnel Papers, M3271, Box 5621, JOL.
36 Entry for 23 November, Journal of the brethren Eipper & Hausmann during their residence at Umpie boang from 22nd of Nov to the 3rd Dec 1842, Lang Papers, ML.
37 Entry for 11 November 1843, p. 79, Ludwig Leichhardt, *Leichhardt Diary No 3*, translated by Thomas Darragh, Brisbane: Queensland Museum, 2013. Leichhardt's reaction appears to have shamed Mort, who wrote home to his mother and sister of his disagreement with the McConnel brothers about taking Aboriginal lands by force. Henry Mort to his mother and sister, Cressbrook, 28 January 1844, Mary McConnel: Papers relating to the McConnel family of Cressbrook, F3107, Fryer Library.
38 Simpson to Colonial Secretary, Brisbane 13 July 1842, l/no. 42/5265, CS Moreton Bay 1842, 4/2581.2, SRNSW. There is no entry for Commandant in the Index for Coroner Inquests May 1838–Nov 1844, vol. 2, NRS 343, SRNSW.
39 David Cannon McConnel to his brother Henry, Stanley Creek, 3 July 1842.
40 Entry for 15 November, Extracts from the General Diary of the German Mission 27th September 1842 to 17th January 1843, Lang Papers, ML.
41 *Colonial Observer*, 28 October 1841, p. 27.

42 Entry for 3 December, Journal of the brethren Eipper & Hausmann, Lang Papers, ML.
43 Entries for 28 and 30 December, Journal of W Schmidt during a journey to Toorbal made with A Rodé from the 28th December 1842 to the 6th January 1843, Lang Papers, ML.
44 Entries for 28–31 December, 1, 3 January, Journal of W Schmidt, Lang Papers, ML.
45 Entry for 16 March, Journal of the brethren Niqué & Rodé, Lang Papers, ML.
46 Entries for 4–5 January 1843, Journal of W Schmidt, Lang Papers, ML.
47 Durundur station, Extracts from a diary, 17 Oct 1842–14 May 1843 made on Durundur station by the wife of an employee of the Archers during a visit by Dr Ludwig Leichhardt. Typescript with MS additions, Document 1825, ML.
48 Extracts from the General Diary of the German Mission from Jan 23rd to July 18th 1843, Lang Papers, ML.
49 Both Rev. Eipper and Commissioner Simpson recorded this intelligence from Worumillo. See entry for 30 March 1843, Observations March–Ap 1843, Lang Papers, ML; entry for 26 March in Journal of an excursion to the Bunya Country situated in the north of the Moreton Bay District NSW, New South Wales Governors' Despatches: 1844, A1233, ML. This comment is not included in Simpson's report in Stephen Simpson, *The Simpson Letterbook*, transcribed by Gerry Langevad, St Lucia: Anthropology Museum, 1979; see p. 8.
50 Return of the number of White men Killed and wounded by the Aborigines in the District of Moreton Bay from the Year 1841 to 1844 inclusive, enclosure in l/no. 44/7954 Police Magistrate Moreton Bay, 19 October 1844, in CS Moreton Bay, 1844, 4/2656.2, SRNSW.
51 Return of the number of White men Killed and wounded ... in CS Moreton Bay, 1844, 4/2656.2, SRNSW.
52 David Archer, Durundur Diary, April 1843–start 1844, OM79-17/1, JOL; Archer, *Recollections*, p. 76; Last pages of Observations March–Ap 1843, Lang Papers, ML; *Maitland Mercury & Hunter River General Advertiser*, 16 September 1843, p. 2.
53 Archer, *Recollections*, pp. 77–9.
54 *Maitland Mercury*, 16 September 1843, p. 2.
55 Christopher Eipper, Sydney, 20 September 1843, l/no. 43/6881, CSIL: Misc Persons: 1843, 4/4559.2, SRNSW.
56 Police Mag Wickham, Moreton Bay, 19 October 1844, l/no. 44/7954 in CS Moreton Bay, 1844, 4/2656.2, SRNSW. In the enclosed return accompanying this letter Wickham listed Mickey Mickey's sentence as 'transportation to Norfolk Island'.
57 Uniacke cited in Lang, *Cooksland*, p. 410.
58 Copy of an unfinished letter by Andrew Petrie to an unnamed Brisbane paper regarding a trip to Bribie Island in 1837, Brisbane, 20 May 1861, TS 683, JOL.

59 Report of the present state of the Aborigines in the District of Moreton Bay for the 1st January 1844, Governors' Despatches Jan–Apr 1844, A1233, ML.
60 Petrie, *Reminiscences*, p. 173.
61 Archer, *Recollections*, pp. 56–7.
62 *Moreton Bay Courier*, 17 June 1848, p. 3 [*MBC*]; this was a report by a gentleman who recently visited the island 'in search of natural curiosities'. Huxley and MacGillivray were the naturalists on board HMS *Rattlesnake*, which visited Moreton Bay in October–November 1847, January 1848 and again in May 1849. During the visit of October 1847 the ship moored in the northern part of the bay and MacGillivray took the opportunity to spend a fortnight on Moreton Island making natural history notes and recording his encounters with the Ngugi and their visitors. John MacGillivray, *Narrative of the Voyage of HMS Rattlesnake, Commanded by the Late Captain Owen Stanley, RN, FRS, during the Years 1846–1850*, vol. 1, Adelaide: Libraries Board of South Australia, 1967 [facs of 1852 edn], pp. 45–50, 166–8. See also Thomas Welsby, *The Collected Works of Thomas Welsby*, vol. 1, ed by A.K. Thomson, Brisbane: Jacaranda, 1967, p. 40; Ann Mozley, 'Huxley, Thomas Henry (1825–1895)', *Australian Dictionary of Biography*, vol. 1, Melbourne: Melbourne University Press, 1966, pp. 577–8.
63 Pamphlett cited in Lang, *Cooksland*, p. 415.
64 E.g. Lieutenant Otter to Captain Fyans, 27 August 1836, in J.G. Steele, *Brisbane Town in Convict Days, 1824–42*, St Lucia: UQP, 1975, p. 232; Petrie, *Reminiscences*, p. 237; Copy of an unfinished letter by Andrew Petrie, TS 683, JOL.
65 Report on the present state of the Aborigines . . . for the 1st January 1844, Governors' Despatches.
66 Petrie, *Reminiscences*, pp. 10, 148, 170–5.
67 *Simpson Letterbook*, p. 27.
68 *MBC*, 17 June 1848, p. 3.
69 *MBC*, 17 June 1848, p. 3.
70 *Brisbane Courier*, 28 December 1912, p. 10. Moppy's death was not reported by Commissioner Simpson who only noted it as part of his Annual Report on the State of the Aborigines for 1844.
71 Commissioner Simpson to Colonial Secretary, 3 October 1843, enclosure in l/no 46/4122 in CS Moreton Bay, 1846, 4/2735.2, SRNSW.
72 Return of the number of White men Killed and wounded . . . in CS Moreton Bay, 1844, 4/2656.2, SRNSW. There were six deaths on the Darling Downs in the same period; see the return compiled by Commissioner Rolleston in the same letter.
73 Brigade Office to Colonial Secretary, 18 October 1843, enclosure in l/no 46/4122 in CS Moreton Bay, 1846, 4/2735.2, SRNSW.
74 Entry for 28 October 1843, p. 74 of *Leichhardt Diary No 3*.
75 Schmidt, Report of an expedition, p. 5.
76 Commissioner Simpson to Colonial Secretary, 3 October 1843, enclosure in l/no 46/4122 in CS Moreton Bay, 1846, 4/2735.2, SRNSW.

77 Commissioner Simpson, 3 October 1843, *Simpson Letterbook*, p. 12; David Cannon McConnel to his brother Frederic, 27 October 1844, Item 40, David Cannon McConnel Papers, M3271, Box 5621, JOL.
78 Entries for 26 January, 15, 22, 30 May, Extracts from the General Diary of the German Mission from 23 January to 18 July 1843, Lang Papers, ML.
79 Letter of 6 May 1844 & Report on the State of the Aborigines for the year ending 1844 in *Simpson Letterbook*, pp. 15–16; W.N. Gunson, 'The Nundah missionaries', *Journal of the Royal Historical Society of Queensland*, vol. 6, no. 3, 1960–61, pp. 527–8; *Early Brisbane Clippings, 1894–1947*, p. 213, OM91–36, Box 9256, JOL.
80 *Sydney Morning Herald*, 13 March 1845, p. 2 & 22 March 1845, p. 2. [*SMH*]
81 Compare extracts from E. Muehling, *Fuhrer durch Queensland*, 1898, translated by Anita Stapleton, JOL, p. 4 & deponent Hausmann in *Queen v Dundalli*, 2 June 1854, Court of Petty Sessions, Brisbane—Depositions and Minutes book, 07/12/1850–30/12/1854, Series 753, QSA.
82 Petrie, *Reminiscences*, p. 193.
83 J.H.L. Zillmann, *Past and Present Australian Life: Being for the most part personal reminiscences with stories of the first explorers, convicts, blacks and bush-rangers of Australia, and a short historical sketch of the colonies, their progress and present condition*, London: Sampson Low, Marston, Searle & Rivington, 1889, p. 114.
84 *Queen v Dundalli*, 2 June 1854, Court of Petty Sessions, Brisbane—Depositions and Minutes book, 07/12/1850–30/12/1854, Series 753, QSA; Muehling, *Fuhrer durch Queensland*, pp. 4–5; *SMH*, 21 March 1845, p. 2.
85 E.g. Zillmann, *Past and Present Australian Life*, pp. 114–15; *Early Brisbane Clippings*, p. 208.
86 *Simpson Letterbook*, p. 15.
87 *SMH*, 21 March 1845, p. 2.
88 David McConnel to his brother William, 22 May 1844, David McConnel to his brother Fred, 27 October 1844, in David Cannon McConnel Papers, Item 36 in M3271, Box 5621, JOL.
89 Letter to colonial secretary, 8 January 1846, *Simpson Letterbook*, p. 19.

4   THE ATTACK ON GREGOR'S STATION

1 Letter from Richard MacGregor to Phyllis Gregor, 15 August 1987, re Keith Parish Register: baptisms 1772–1820. Papers of Phyllis Gregor, Bodleian Library, Oxford University, UK.
2 Moreton Bay officials sometimes spelt the station name as 'Forguie'.
3 Tom Archer in a letter home to his father, 24 March 1844, cited in Lorna McDonald, *Over Earth and Ocean: The Archers of Tolderodden and Gracemere, a Norse–Australian saga 1819–1965*, St Lucia: UQP & Central Queensland University Press, 1999, p. 100; Itinerary of Stephen Simpson Esqr, County of Stanley Moreton Bay, Special Bundles: Moreton Bay, CCL 1843–47, 4/1141.1, SRNSW. John Gregor graduated with an MA in March 1831, his brother William in March 1848 and youngest brother Walter in

March 1849. The brothers are all listed with the spelling 'Grigor'. See Peter John Anderson, MA LLB (ed), *Officers and Graduates of King's College Aberdeen*, Aberdeen: New Spalding Club, 1893, pp. 286, 300–1.

4   Cited in McDonald, *Over Earth and Ocean*, p. 100.

5   Lang and his new parish ministers travelled on the *Portland* and arrived in Sydney in December 1837. *Belfast Newsletter*, 9 June 1837; *Caledonian Mercury*, 22 July 1837; K. Rayner, 'Gregor, John (1808–1848)', *Australian Dictionary of Biography*, vol.1, Melbourne: Melbourne University Press, 1966, pp. 472–3.

6   *Sydney Morning Herald*, 19 December 1842, p. 2; 6 & 9 January 1843, p. 1; 6 April 1844, p. 2 [*SMH*]; D.W.A. Baker, 'Lang, John Dunmore (1799–1878)', *Australian Dictionary of Biography*, vol. 2, Melbourne: Melbourne University Press, 1967, pp. 76–83.

7   Broughton to SPG, 3 February 1843, Bishop Broughton's Letters to the Society for the Propagation of the Gospel, 1843 to 1849, MIC 7933, Fryer Library.

8   Ninth Annual Report Apsley Aboriginal Mission, Wellington, 31 December 1849, in Documents relating to Aboriginal Australians, 1816–1853: Mission Reports, DL Add 81, SLNSW; Annual Report of the Australian Diocesan Committee of the Societies for the Propagation of the Gospel in Foreign Parts ... for the year 1847. Sydney, SPG, 1848, p. 13; First Report of the Aboriginal Mission Murrunggallang, Wellington, in Documents relating to Aboriginal Australians, 1816–1853: Mission Reports, DL Add 81, SLNSW, available at <http://acms.sl.nsw.gov.au/album/ItemViewer.aspx?itemid=862003&suppress=N&imgindex=6>.

9   Ralph's name is proof that he was associated with William Watson's self-funded Apsley Mission. He gave his full name as Ralph William Barrow, which suggests that he was named after the local Wellington police magistrate, William Barrow, who assisted Watson in October 1840 when he decamped with a large group of Aboriginal people from the official Church Missionary Society Mission at Wellington. In his first official report for his new Apsley mission in 1841, Watson provided a list of Aboriginal people but did not name them. Ralph was probably included among the notation 'Seven native boys – from 6 to 9 years'. There is a possibility though that he was one of 'two half-caste boys – 4 years' on Watson's list although none of the Brisbane sources ever refer to him as a half-caste. First Report of the Aboriginal Mission, available at <http://acms.sl.nsw.gov.au/album/ItemViewer.aspx?itemid=862003&suppress=N&imgindex=6>.

10 James Demarr, *Adventures in Australia Fifty Years Ago: Being a record of an emigrant's wanderings through the colonies of New South Wales, Victoria and Queensland during the years 1839–1844*, London: Swan Sonnenschein, 1893, p. 219.

11 *The Church in Australia Part II: Two journals of missionary tours in the districts of Maneroo and Moreton Bay, New South Wales, in 1843*, London: Society for the Propagation of the Gospel, 1846 [3rd edn], entry for 16 August 1843.

12   Tom Archer, *Recollections of a Rambling Life*, Brisbane: Boolarong, 1988 [facs of 1897 edn], pp. 105–6. 'Vox populi, Vox Dei' means 'The voice of the people [is] the voice of God' while 'Vox populis, vox Diaboli' means 'The voice of the people [is] the voice of the Devil'.
13   None of the very limited documentary evidence of Rev. John Gregor's life mentions Ralph Barrow so it is not known when precisely, or how, young Ralph was sent to Brisbane. He was not listed among the first-class passengers on board the *Shamrock* in January 1843, so he may have been in steerage or sent north at a later time.
14   Itinerary of Stephen Simpson, Special Bundles: Moreton Bay, CCL 1843–47, 4/1141.1, SRNSW.
15   See Diary Kept by Captain G. Griffin at Whiteside via Petrie 'Moreton Bay', 1 January 1847 – 16 May 1849, Griffin Diary, 6 & 7 September 1847, and *Moreton Bay Courier*, 8 April 1848 & 14 May 1859 [*MBC*].
16   Itinerary of Stephen Simpson, Special Bundles: Moreton Bay, CCL 1843–47, 4/1141.1, SRNSW.
17   Erica Long, 'Early white settlement on the Pine River,' *Journal of the Royal Historical Society of Queensland*, vol. 16, no. 5, 1997, p. 192.
18   William Joyner was listed as among the gentlemen invited to the Governor's Levee for Queen Victoria's birthday in May 1842. He married Isabella Penson 18 July 1845 in Sydney. *SMH*, 26 May 1842 & 18 July 1845. The spelling of Joyner and Mason's station varies in official records. Some accounts list it as Samson Vale and others Sampson Vale.
19   He gave his address as Park Street, Sydney, in January 1847; arrived in Brisbane on 31 January 1847 (possibly to attend a meeting called by local pastoralists for the introduction of cheap labour held in February) and departed on the *Sovereign* on 3 March 1847. *SMH*, 18 January 1847, p. 3; *MBC*, 6 February 1847, p. 2, & 6 March 1847, p. 2. His death in the shipwreck of the *Sovereign* was reported in several newspapers; *Bell's Life in Sydney and Sporting Reviewer*, 3 April 1847, p. 1, & *Australian*, 13 April 1847, p. 2.
20   Libby Connors, 'A house divided: the Griffin Family of Whiteside and frontier conflict in the 1840s', *Queensland History Journal*, vol. 20, no. 11, 2009, p. 583. The original lease for Whiteside Station was taken out by Captain Francis Griffin; his father George Griffin was also known as Captain Griffin. Francis went into debt and his parents George and Jane later became co-owners of Whiteside. When George died in 1851, his widow became owner of the lease.
21   Stephen Simpson, *The Simpson Letterbook*, transcribed by Gerry Langevad, St Lucia: Anthropology Museum, 1979, p. 19.
22   *Simpson Letterbook*, p. 24; Index to Orphan Schools Records, SRNSW; Depositions taken on the inspection of the bodies of Mr Andrew Gregor and Mary Shannon murdered by Native Blacks on the morning of 18 October 1846, Deposition and Minute Books, 06/02/1846–31/10/1846, Series 753, Item 518884, p. 36, QSA; *R v Constable* in Supreme Court, Criminal Jurisdiction: Clerk of the Peace, Brisbane, 1846, 9/6337, SRNSW; *R v Dundalli*

(Murder of Gregor & Shannon) in Supreme Court, Criminal Jurisdiction: Clerk of the Peace, Brisbane, 1854, 9/6386, SRNSW.
23. Connors, 'A house divided', p. 585; evidence of Thomas Shannon in *R v Constable*, Supreme Court, Criminal Jurisdiction: Clerk of the Peace, Brisbane 1846, 9/6337, SRNSW.
24. Depositions taken on the inspection of the bodies of Mr Andrew Gregor and Mary Shannon murdered by Native Blacks on the morning of 18 October 1846, Deposition and Minute Books, 06/02/1846–31/10/1846, Series 753, Item 518884, p. 36, QSA.
25. Commissioner Simpson, Report of the State of the Aborigines for the District of Moreton Bay for the year 1844, 10 January 1845, l/no. 45/669 in CS Commissioners of Crown Lands, 1845, 4/2680, SRNSW.
26. 'Cambell' is Simpson's spelling. He was sometimes also referred to as Cambela. The local newspaper spelt his name 'Campbell'. *MBC*, 5 September 1846, pp. 2–3; Coutts to Simpson, 4 September 1846, enclosed in Simpson to Colonial Secretary, 12 September 1846, l/no. 46/7120, CS CCL (3), 1846, 4/2720.1, SRNSW. The colonial secretary was concerned about the failure to conduct an inquest but Simpson reported that Aboriginal people had carried the fallen to the scrubs.
27. Frederic McConnel, 'Stories of Australian Bush Life, 1844: Experiences of the late Frederic McConnel', TS available at <http://nla.gov.au/nla.aus-f7689>.
28. Commissioner Simpson to Colonial Secretary, 3 October 1843, enclosure in l/no 46/4122 in CSIL: Moreton Bay, 1846, 4/2735.2, SRNSW.
29. 'The Aborigines have been as troublesome as ever this Winter, always choosing the time of heavy rain for there [sic] depredations, when it is almost impossible for the Squatters to defend themselves.' Simpson to E Deas Thomson, 1 August 1844, l/no 44/6594 in CS CCL (1), 1844, 4/2640, SRNSW.
30. John Campbell, 'The early settlement of Queensland' and other articles with which is also printed 'The raid of the Aborigines', Ipswich, Qld: Ipswich Observer, 1875, p. 18. Campbell's memoirs were written more than thiry years after events and he confuses the order and dates of incidents. Other than the dates, his details are confirmed by Stephen Simpson's reports.
31. Campbell, 'Early settlement', p. 10; *MBC*, 5 September 1846, p. 2.
32. Campbell claims that Multuggerah's brother had also been killed by whites but Simpson reported on three brothers in January 1845. Campbell, 'Early settlement', p. 10; Simpson, State of the Aborigines, 1844.
33. Based on William Fraser's and Jemmy Perowa's depositions in *R v Constable*, 9/6337, SRNSW.
34. Attorney-General Plunkett used Shannon's confusion and trauma after the attack as an example of why Aboriginal people should be allowed as witnesses in courts of law as part of his speech when introducing his Aboriginal Natives' Evidence Bill to the Legislative Council. *SMH*, 29 June 1849, p. 2.
35. Commandant Native Police to E. Deas Thomson, 11 July 1853, L/no. 53/6063 in bundle beginning 52/3069, CS Letters Received Main Series: 1852, 4/3075, SRNSW.

36 Ralph's testimony in *R v Constable*, 9/6337, SRNSW.
37 Ralph's testimony in *R v Constable*, 9/6337, SRNSW.
38 Margaret's unsworn testimony in *R v Constable*, 9/6337, SRNSW.
39 Moggy Moggy is the man whose identity is most difficult to confirm. Young Gubbi Gubbi man Mickaloe was subsequently arrested as Moggy Moggy and found guilty but white witnesses disputed his identity and all up he was given eight different names by different witnesses & the courts. See accounts of his committal hearings reported in *MBC* 16 & 23 August 1851. Jacky had been employed by Rev. John Gregor, then residing at the former German Mission, so I have assumed he is Ningy Ningy; Jemmy Parsons' identity is based on his employment at Forgie by Andrew Gregor; his surname indicates he had also already had an association with Rev. John Gregor. Beddy appears to be the German missionaries' Biddur. The others are based on police and court reports.
40 Thomas Archer to Davie, Blazes, Thursday 12 November, Archer Family Correspondence: Some letters from Australia written home between 1833 & 1855 by the brothers, London, 1933, 4783, Box 11261, OM80–10/76–109, JOL. This letter has been wrongly marked in red as 12/11/1845 when it clearly discusses the killing of Gregor so must be from November 1846.
41 Perowa's unsworn testimony in *R v Constable*, 9/6337, SRNSW.
42 The young Gubbi Gubbi man insisted his name was Mickaloe. See the account of his committal hearings in *MBC*, 16 August 1851, pp. 2–3 & 23 August 1851, p. 3.
43 Campbell, 'Early settlement', p. 10; note also the warning given to a visitor to Bribie Island in 1848 in *MBC*, 17 June 1848; Depositions ... on the bodies ... Gregor ... Shannon.
44 Clerk's emphasis and spelling. A ha'porth is colloquial for half pennyworth so she is explaining that even the smallest things were broken. She also said her mother was picking up a 'besom'—a traditionally made broom of straw and twigs—rather than a broom. Margaret Shannon's unsworn testimony in *R v Constable*, 9/6337, SRNSW.
45 The children and the Aboriginal elder at Durundur variously gave the names of Millbong Jemmy, Moggy Moggy and Jemmy as Mary Shannon's assailants with only Jemmy's name agreed upon by all three. The two children both named Millbong Jemmy as an active participant but Ralph said he struck Mary Shannon while Margaret said he assaulted Gregor. Paddy of Durundur did not name Millbong Jemmy as involved in the killings at all. Thomas Shannon said he was one of the men who was sent to collect bark for Gregor that morning. Depositions ... on the bodies ... Gregor ... Shannon & *R v Constable*, 9/6337, SRNSW.
46 Ian Keen, *Aboriginal Economy and Society: Australia at the threshold of colonisation*, South Melbourne: Oxford University Press, 2003, p. 246.
47 W.H. Edwards, *An Introduction to Aboriginal Societies*, South Melbourne: Cengage, 1998 [2nd edn], p. 73.
48 Keen, *Aboriginal Economy*, p. 244.

49 Constance Campbell Petrie, *Tom Petrie's Reminiscences of Early Queensland*, Hawthorn, Vic: Lloyd O'Neil, 1975 [facs of 1904 edn], p. 184.
50 *R v Dundalli* (Assault & theft Hausmann), 9/6386, SRNSW.
51 Commissioner Simpson to Colonial Secretary, Moreton Bay, 25 October 1846, enclosure in L/no. 54/10741 in CS In Letters: 1854, 4/3256, SRNSW.
52 The girls were admitted on 14 January 1847. Index to Orphan Schools Records, NRS12266, SRNSW. Margaret and Mary Ann were later adopted by Mr and Mrs Peattie of Brisbane and so returned to the district, but without their baby sister Eliza. The paper misnames Margaret as Mary; see *MBC*, 16 August 1851, p. 3.
53 Wickham to Attorney-General, 7 December 1846, enclosed in *R v Constable* 9/6337, SRNSW; John Gregor was among Leichhardt's keen supporters and was on the Darling Downs to offer Divine Service on the last Sunday prior to Leichhardt's departure from the eastern Darling Downs, 29 November 1846; *MBC*, 12 December 1846, pp. 2–3; *SMH*, 26 December 1846, p. 2.
54 John Gregor's replies to Questionnaire from the Society for the Propagation of the Gospel in Foreign Parts, 22 May 1846, TS, Anglican Church Archives, Brisbane; John Mackenzie-Smith, *The Scottish Presence at Moreton Bay 1837–59*, Brisbane: BHG, 2005, p. 149.
55 *MBC*, 10 October 1846, pp. 2–3.
56 Ludwig Leichhardt to David Archer, Hughes & Isaacs Station, 19 November 1846, Archer Family: General & Business Correspondence, A3882, CY3690, ML.

5 WHITE POLITICS AND BLACK POLITICS

1 Thomas Archer to Davie, Blazes, Thursday 12 Nov [wrongly annotated by archivist as 1845; should be 1846], Archer Family Correspondence: Some letters from Australia written home between 1833 & 1855 by the brothers, London, 1933, 4783, Box 11261, OM80–10/76–109, JOL.
2 *Moreton Bay Courier*, 21 November 1846, p. 2 [*MBC*].
3 Rev. J. Gregor to E. Deas Thomson, Brisbane, 2 November 1846, l/no. 46/8294, enclosure in l/no. 54/10741 in CS In Letters: 1854 4/3256, SRNSW.
4 Enclosure in l/no. 54/10741 10741 in CS In Letters: 1854 4/3256, SRNSW. It was published in the *Government Gazette*, 16 November 1846.
5 *MBC*, 21 November 1846, p. 2.
6 Thomas Archer to Davie, Blazes, Thursday 12 Nov 1846, Archer Family Correspondence.
7 See request for subscribers and advertisement in following issues of *MBC*: 14, 21, 28 November & 5 December 1846, p. 1, and commentary 28 November 1846, p. 3. The private reward had begun at £20 and grown to £30 so it must have been well subscribed to get to £40 to cover the four accused men named in their advertisement, although there were complaints in the press about slow payment by subscribers.
8 The annual salary of Brisbane's chief constable in 1845 and 1846 was £70 and that of the clerk to the bench of magistrates was £150. See enclosure in

Wickham to colonial secretary, Brisbane, 16 December 1845, l/no. 45/9221 in CS Moreton Bay, 1845, 4/2696.2, SRNSW.
9   W. Ross Johnston, *Brisbane: The first thirty years*, Bowen Hills, Qld: Boolarong, 1988, p. 106; *Sydney Morning Herald*, 2 December 1846, p. 2 [*SMH*].
10 John Kent to T.W. Ramsay, Commissariat Office Moreton Bay, 20 December 1844, l/no. 45/365 in CS Moreton Bay, 1845, 4/2696.2, SRNSW.
11 Gregor to Thomson and enclosures.
12 Inquest papers from this period have not survived but the inquest index records Wickham's coronial inquest and its conclusion 'Shot by Richard Bickerton'. Drawn from Coroners' Inquests, 1834–94: Years 1845–1852, vol. 3, no. 3564, 4/6613, SRNSW; *MBC*, 7 November 1846, p. 3; *SMH*, 30 November 1846, p. 2; Constance Campbell Petrie, *Tom Petrie's Reminiscences of Early Queensland*, Hawthorn, Vic: Lloyd O'Neil, 1975 [facs of 1904 edn], pp. 169–70; *R v Moggy Moggy*, Supreme Court, Criminal Jurisdiction: Clerk of the Peace, Brisbane, 1851, 9/6366, SRNSW.
13 *MBC*, 6 February 1847, p. 3.
14 Entry 3179, Coroners' Inquests.
15 *MBC*, 6, 21, 28 November 1846, 5 December 1846 & 6 February 1847, p. 3.
16 Doyle was sent to Moreton Bay on 31 October 1839; Lindon on 29 August 1844 and Reynolds on 28 February 1845. See their police histories enclosed in John Kent to colonial secretary, Moreton Bay, 10 November 1845, l/no. 46/5619 in CS Moreton Bay, 1846, 4/2735.2, SRNSW; *MBC*, 6 February 1847, p. 3.
17 Entry 3587, Coroners' Inquests; *MBC*, 12 December 1846, p. 2; *SMH*, 28 December 1846, p. 2. Since the inquests papers have not survived it is difficult to assess the claim about personal items from Uhr and Shannon. There was a pattern of convicts and police rifling through Aboriginal camps, stealing and breaking Aboriginal weapons and appropriating other goods after Aboriginal people had fled from the shooting. So personal items from Uhr, Gregor or Shannon could have been traded and come into the possession of any individual at the Rosewood wallaby hunt camp which Doyle, Lindon and Reynolds then confiscated and could claim had been found on Waakoon.
18 *Sydney Chronicle*, 2 December 1846, p. 2; *Sydney Chronicle*, 16 December 1846, p. 3.
19 Sworn statements taken 25 January 1847—Inquiry into affrays with Aborigines, Official Papers: Archival Estrays: CSIL Add 82, ML; *MBC*, 13 February 1847, p. 2.
20 William Augustine Duncan, *Autobiography*, p. 70, ML; Libby Connors, 'Sentencing on a colonial frontier: Judge Therry's decisions at Moreton Bay', *Legal History*, vol. 12, no. 1, 2008, pp. 86–8; John Mackenzie-Smith, *The Scottish Presence at Moreton Bay 1837–59*, Brisbane: BHG, 2005, pp. 181–2.
21 *MBC*, 16 January 1847, p. 3.
22 *Sydney Chronicle*, 2 January 1847, p. 3; *MBC*, 2 January 1847, p. 2.

23 J.C. Wickham to E. Deas Thomson, 3 November 1846, Official Papers: Archival Estrays: CSIL Add 10, ML.
24 Inquiry into affrays with Aborigines; Duncan, *Autobiography*, p. 70.
25 The *MBC* claimed 'upwards of fifty white people have been killed in this district, and in no one instance have the Sydney authorities ordered an investigation'. In fact the numbers of deaths had been raised with the Colonial Office and Captain Wickham had been required to write a report regarding the number of deaths at the end of 1844. It revealed that 16 had been killed and nine wounded in 1841–44. If we go back to 1839 to cover seven years the tally becomes 22 deaths and 10 wounded. For these assaults, three Aboriginal men had died and three had been wounded as authorities tried to make arrests; two had been publicly hanged, one died in custody, two more sentenced to death but commuted to terms of hard labour, two allowed to escape from custody when it was clear that the crown could not make a case but did not want to formally exonerate, and another was in custody awaiting trial. Another 13 deaths from the Darling Downs could be added to the *Courier*'s list but still do not make the 50 claimed in the editorial. *MBC*, 6 February 1847, p. 2; Wickham to Colonial Secretary, Moreton Bay, 19 October 1844, enclosures in l/no. 44/7954 in CS Moreton Bay, 1844, 4/2656.2, SRNSW; Libby Connors, 'The theatre of justice: Race relations and capital punishment at Moreton Bay 1841–59', in Rod Fisher (ed), *Brisbane: The Aboriginal presence 1824–1860*, BHG Papers, no. 11, 1992, pp. 48–57.
26 Select Committee on the Condition of the Aborigines, *Votes & Proceedings of the Legislative Council of New South Wales*, 1845, p. 948.
27 Select Committee on the Condition of the Aborigines: Replies to circular, *Votes & Proceedings of the Legislative Council of New South Wales*, 3rd session, 1846, p. 568.
28 *Aberdeen Journal*, 31 March 1830, p. 2.
29 Günther cited in *MBC*, 6 February 1847, p. 2.
30 Connors, Libby. 'A Wiradjuri child at Moreton Bay', *Queensland History Journal*, vol. 20, no. 13, 2010, p. 781.
31 *MBC*, 6 February 1847, p. 2.
32 *MBC*, 13 February 1847, p. 2; *SMH*, 23 February 1847, pp. 2–3; *Sydney Chronicle*, 24 February 1847, p. 2.
33 *MBC*, 21 November 1847, p. 2; *MBC*, 30 January 1847, p. 2.
34 *Australian*, 13 April 1847, p. 3.
35 *MBC*, 24 April 1847, pp. 2–3.
36 Petrie, *Reminiscences*, pp. 148–9. See also entries for 2, 12 & 22 March 1847 re staff and court visits in Griffin Diary. It is highly likely that the man the Aborigines referred to as 'John Master', who according to Petrie committed a number of atrocities against the Pine River peoples, was John Griffin, the youngest son of the Griffin family of Whiteside Station. He subsequently married the widowed Isabella Joyner, co-owner of Samsonvale Station, a little further to the west of Whiteside. Petrie, *Reminiscences*, pp. 6–8.

There is partial corroboration of this mistreatment in the station diaries; see entries for 6 February, 8 March, 25 & 29 September 1849 in Diary and in Remarks and Transactions at the Whiteside Station, 1 Jan 1851–25 Dec 1851, OM72–42/2, JOL.

37 *MBC*, 23 October 1847, p. 3.
38 Oumulli's name was variously listed in the colonial sources as Marmoulli, Omalee, Omilly and Oumulli. The last was the one used by Foundation for Aboriginal and Islander Research Action.
39 Constance Petrie described this area as Green Hills. Petrie, *Reminiscences*, p. 160.
40 Petrie, *Reminiscences*, pp. 176–7.
41 *MBC*, 3 June 1848, p. 3.
42 Police Office Brisbane, 30 May 1848, l/no. 48/7004 enclosed in l/no. 54/10741 in CS In Letters: 1854, 4/3256, SRNSW.
43 Attorney-General's Office, 12 July 1848, l/no. 48/8074, enclosed in l/no. 54/10741 in CS In Letters: 1854, 4/3256, SRNSW.
44 Yilbung was recorded as 'Ilboo', Moreton Bay: Book of Trials, Item 869682, Series ID 5646, QSA, 8 July 1839, pp. 136–7; Petrie, *Reminiscences*, p. 167.
45 See letter from Anti-Humbug, *MBC*, 2 January 1847, p. 2. On Stradbroke conflict see Ray Evans, 'The Mogwi take Mi-an-jin: Race relations and the Moreton Bay penal settlement 1824–42', in Rod Fisher (ed), *Brisbane: The Aboriginal presence 1824–1860*, Brisbane: BHG, 1992, pp. 19–21.
46 Yilbung's ready mixing with other groups and working with elders is drawn from Mission Diary 5 January 1842, 12 March 1842 & 23 January 1843, Extracts from the Diary of the German Mission to the Aborigines at Moreton Bay, Rev. John Dunmore Lang, Papers A2240, vol. 20, CY579, ML, and from *Colonial Observer*, 21 October 1841, p. 23. Petrie, *Reminiscences*, pp. 166–70.
47 *MBC*, 14 November 1846, p. 3.
48 No. 7991, Register of Depositions received from Benches, 7/6055, SRNSW; *MBC*, 9 October 1847, p. 2.
49 *R v Paul Paul* in Supreme Court, Criminal Jurisdiction: Clerk of the Peace, Brisbane 1850, 9/6359, SRNSW. Intriguingly, among the group was Nundhappy, against whom the clerk recorded 'known as Jackey'. Paul Paul insisted in his defence that Jackey Jackey was responsible for the deed; since it was in the police interest to continue to believe that Jackey Jackey was still alive it was a smart answer. Duncan's evidence that Aboriginal people were singing the 'Cry for the Dead' near the Windmill in the days after the York's Hollow police raid, however, are the strongest indication that Jackey Jackey was killed the night of 20 December. Judgment Book: Brisbane Circuit Court, November 1850, SRNSW; Prison no. 89, Brisbane Gaol, Prison Register, PRI 1/25, QSA, 1850.
50 *SMH*, 19 April 1843, p. 3; Entry for 25 January 1843, General Diary of the German Mission from 23 January to 18 July 1843, Rev. John Dunmore Lang, Papers A2240, vol. 20, CY579, ML.

51 *MBC*, 16 January 1847, p. 2. This explains Peattie's extreme nervousness when he heard that Yilbung and his supporters were crossing the river on 5 November 1846. Peattie accidentally discharged his gun, killing a crewman. See *MBC*, 7 November 1846, 'Distressing and Fatal Accident', p. 3; Petrie, *Reminiscences*, p. 169.
52 Select Committee on the Condition of the Aborigines, *Votes & Proceedings of the Legislative Council of New South Wales,* 1845, p. 952. Three children were returned after the mission was threatened in 1843 but Polding also says in his evidence that he had two boys, half-caste sons of a man called Smith, sent to Sydney because their Aboriginal mother struggled to support them as a result of Smith's neglect; they were still with him in September 1845 (p. 949).
53 Osmund Thorpe, *First Catholic Mission to the Aborigines*, Sydney: Pellegrini, 1950, pp. 116–18; *MBC*, 24 April 1847, p. 3; *SMH*, 23 February 1847, pp. 2–3; Inquiry into affrays with Aborigines; Entries from 13 May to July 1843, Extracts from the General Diary of the German Mission from 23rd January to 18th July 1843, Lang Papers, ML.
54 A depot consisting of a brick store and barracks had been built at Dunwich in 1827–28 during convict times but subsequently abandoned. Johnston, *Brisbane*, p. 31. The Catholic mission restored some of these buildings; Thorpe, *First Catholic Mission*, pp. 100–1.
55 Erica Long, 'A history of the timber industry in the Pine Rivers district,' *Access History*, vol. 2, no. 1, 1998, p. 58.
56 Griffin Diary, entries for 1–2 September 1847.
57 Griffin Diary, entries for 23 June, 21 August & 22 August 1847.
58 Griffin Diary, 10 September 1847.
59 Griffin Diary, 11 September 1847; *MBC*, 15 November 1851; *R v Moggy Moggy* in Supreme Court, Criminal Jurisdiction: Clerk of the Peace, Brisbane, 1851, 9/6366, SRNSW; *Moreton Bay Free Press*, 28 November 1854 [*MBFP*].
60 The most detailed was Smith's testimony in *R v Moggy Moggy* in Supreme Court, Criminal Jurisdiction: Clerk of the Peace, Brisbane, 1851, 9/6366, SRNSW.
61 Annual Report on the State of the Aborigines in the District of Moreton Bay for the Year ending the 31st December 1847, Commissioner of Crown Lands Moreton Bay in CS Commissioners of Crown Lands, 1848, 4/2811, SRNSW.
62 Smith's testimony in *R v Moggy Moggy* in Supreme Court, 1851.
63 *MBC*, 15 November 1851; Smith's testimony in *R v Dundalli* (2) in Supreme Court, Criminal Jurisdiction: Clerk of the Peace, Brisbane, 1854, 9/6386, SRNSW.
64 Thomas Welsby, *The Collected Works of Thomas Welsby*, vol. 1 & 2, ed by A.K. Thomson, Brisbane: Jacaranda, 1967–68, p. 374; P. Niqué, 'The Aborigines: Diary of Messrs Niqué and Hartenstein of the German Mission to the Aborigines at Moreton Bay', *Colonial Observer*, vol. 1, no. 4, 1841, entry for Saturday 21 August; Petrie, *Reminiscences*, p. 160.
65 T/L 46/646, Certificates of Freedom, 1823–69, 4/4409, SRNSW; Petrie, *Reminiscences*, p. 176 names him as 'Isam'. The newspaper used the name

'Lucette' but other Moreton Bay and official convict records list him as 'Doucette'.
66 List of 15 Male Convicts per the Ship *Layton*, SRNSW. Another of the Mauritius convicts was Cassim who was originally from India; for details of his life see Patrick J. Tynan, *Johnny Cassim: Coolie-convict-catechumen-colonial entrepreneur*, Toowoomba: Church Archivists' Press, 2005.
67 *MBC*, 13 February 1847, pp. 2–3.
68 Deposition Book, Brisbane 8 February 1850 (formerly Fryer MS F1987 now Item ID 518885, QSA), pp. 39–41. District Constable Murphy testified that Doucette had an Aboriginal wife but it is not clear if she was the woman involved in Oumulli's capture.
69 *MBC*, 3 June 1848, pp. 2–3.
70 Ian Keen, *Aboriginal Economy and Society: Australia at the threshold of colonisation*, South Melbourne: Oxford University Press, 2003, p. 252.
71 Petrie, *Reminiscences*, pp. 32–3.
72 Petrie, *Reminiscences*, pp. 24–5. Petrie refers to Bobby Winter as 'Bobbiwinta'.
73 Deposition Book, Brisbane, 8 February 1850, QSA Item ID 518885, pp. 39–41; Prison no. 19, Brisbane Gaol, Prison Register, PRI 1/25, QSA.
74 The barracks stood on the site of the Treasury building, now the Treasury Casino.
75 *MBC*, 8 December 1849, pp. 2–3.
76 *R v Richard Bambrick, William Kearns & James Tredenick*, Supreme Court, Criminal Jurisdiction: Clerk of the Peace, Brisbane, 1850, 9/6359, SRNSW.
77 Libby Connors, The 'birth of the prison' and the death of convictism: The operation of the law in pre-separation Queensland 1839 to 1859, PhD (History) thesis, University of Queensland, 1990, pp. 313–58.
78 *MBC*, 20 May 1850, p. 1.
79 *MBC*, 20 May 1850, p. 2.
80 Major General Wynyard, 13 June 1850, Inspection Returns and Confidential Reports, 1st Period 1850: General Observations, WO 27/399, PRO.
81 On recall of the detachment he was posted as guard to Cockatoo Island, which was probably a demotion. By 1852 he was no longer listed in the Inspection Returns. Major General Wynyard, 19 June 1851, Inspection Returns and Confidential Reports, 1st–25th Regiments, 1st Period 1851, WO 27/409, PRO; Major General Wynyard, 1 July 1852, Inspection Returns and Confidential Reports, 11th Regiment, 1st Period 1852, WO 27/419, PRO. *Hart's Army List* records George J. Arnold Cameron appointed lieutenant 11 April 1851 in the 10th Regiment of Foot and serving at Wuzeerabad in 1852. *Hart's Army List*, London: John Murray, 1852, p. 161.
82 See editorial, *MBC*, 8 December 1849, p. 2.
83 *MBC*, 8 December 1849, pp. 2–3; The Blue Books listed Fitzpatrick as discontinued as of 24 December 1849; see Returns of the Colony (Blue Books), 1850, p. 340. Appointments notified 27 December 1849 included Samuel Sneyd as new chief constable for Brisbane, no l/no. CS In Letters: 1850 4/2887, SRNSW.

84 *MBC*, 15 December 1849, p. 2.
85 Plunkett was one of those involved in drafting the 1856 constitution, which provided for an appointed Legislative Council. He argued in favour of tempering democracy and two of the grounds he gave were the treatment of Native Americans and the existence of slavery in the democratic US. John Molony, *An Architect of Freedom: John Hubert Plunkett in New South Wales 1832–1869*, Canberra: Australian National University Press, 1973, p. 82; Tony Earls, *Plunkett's Legacy: An Irishman's contribution to the rule of law in New South Wales*, North Melbourne: Australian Scholarly Publishing, 2009, p. 172; Michael Roe, 'Duncan, William Augustine (1811–1885)', *Australian Dictionary of Biography*, vol. 1, Melbourne: Melbourne University Press, 1966, p. 337.
86 Noting attached to Government Resident Moreton Bay forwarding report Commandant Native Police, 5 March 1858, CS Special Bundles: Native Police: Moreton Bay, 1855–1858, 4/719.2, SRNSW.
87 *MBC*, 8 December 1849, pp. 2–3; *MBC*, 20 May 1850, p. 1; Petrie, *Reminiscences*, pp. 144–5.
88 Entry for 1 January 1844, p. 20 of Ludwig Leichhardt, *Leichhardt Diary No 4: 23 November 1843–March 1844*, translated by Thomas Darragh, Brisbane: Queensland Museum, 2013.

6 ATTEMPTS AT CONCILIATION

1 Alex Bond, *The Statesman, the Warrior and the Songman*, Nambour, Qld: Interactive Community Planning Australia, 2009, p. 9.
2 John Mathew, *Two Representative Tribes of Queensland: With an inquiry concerning the origin of the Australian race*, London: T. Fisher Unwin, 1910, p. 129.
3 Thomas Welsby's account of Dundalli was drawn from the Stradbroke Islanders. It has a number of errors but consistently paints him as a murderer to be feared. Thomas Welsby, *The Collected Works of Thomas Welsby*, vol. 1 & 2, ed by A.K. Thomson, Brisbane: Jacaranda, 1967–68, p. 383.
4 Gaiarbau's story of the Jinibara tribe of south-east Queensland (and its neighbours), collected by L.P. Winterbotham, MS 45, AIATSIS, p. 45.
5 *Sydney Morning Herald*, 27 July 1849, p. 3 [*SMH*]. The *Moreton Bay Courier* [*MBC*] had reported the attack and Boddin's flight to the mainland on 14 July with much exaggeration and several errors. Unfortunately its issue for 21 July, which probably covered Gray's inquest, is missing.
6 Wilson's testimony in *R v Dundalli Assault and Robbery*, 2 June 1854, Court of Petty Sessions, Brisbane—Depositions and Minutes Book, 07/12/1850–30/12/1854, Series 753, QSA. On Aboriginal commerce in early Brisbane see Ray Kerkhove, 'Aboriginal trade in fish and seafoods in nineteenth century South-East Queensland: A vibrant industry?' *Queensland Review*, vol. 20, no. 2, 2013, pp. 144–56.
7 Constance Campbell Petrie, *Tom Petrie's Reminiscences of Early Queensland*, Hawthorn, Vic.: Lloyd O'Neil, 1975 [facs of 1904 edn], p. 10.

8   Stephen Simpson, Commissioner of Crown Lands, Report on State of the Aborigines of the District of Moreton for the year 1849, Official Papers: Archival Estrays: CSIL Add 79.
9   *SMH*, 27 July 1849, p. 3.
10 Welsby, *Collected Works*, pp. 374–6.
11 See Ian Keen, *Aboriginal Economy and Society: Australia at the threshold of colonisation*, South Melbourne: Oxford University Press, 2003, p. 246.
12 *MBC*, 2 August 1851, p. 3.
13 He was later killed by traditional owners much further north along the Queensland coast in the Percy Isles east of Mackay. *MBC*, 18 November 1854, p. 2.
14 Keen, *Aboriginal Economy*, p. 266.
15 Petrie, *Reminiscences*, p. 162; John Dunmore Lang, *Cooksland in North-Eastern Australia; the Future Cotton-Field of Great Britain: Its characteristics and capabilities for European colonization*, London: Longman, Brown, Green & Longmans, 1847, pp. 410–13.
16 *MBC*, 2 August 1851, p. 3.
17 *MBC*, 28 June 1851, p. 3.
18 *MBC*, 11 August 1851, p. 1.
19 Stephen Simpson, *The Simpson Letterbook*, transcribed by Gerry Langevad, St Lucia: Anthropology Museum, 1979, p. 30; *MBC*, 14 June 1851, p. 3.
20 Reverend Gregor was an ally of the pastoralists and bitterly disliked by some of his Brisbane congregation who out-bade him for the old penal station chaplain's house when the old government buildings were put up for auction. See John Gregor's replies to Questionnaire from the Society for the Propagation of the Gospel in Foreign Parts, 22 May 1846. TS, Anglican Church Archives, Brisbane; John Mackenzie-Smith, *Scottish Presence at Moreton Bay 1837–59*, Brisbane: BHG, 2005, p. 149.
21 *MBC*, 29 January 1848, pp. 2–3.
22 *R v Mickie*, Supreme Court, Criminal Jurisdiction: Clerk of the Peace, Brisbane, 1853, 9/6378, SRNSW.
23 *MBC*, 16 August 1851, p. 3.
24 *MBC*, 16 August 1851, p. 2.
25 Libby Connors, The 'birth of the prison' and the death of convictism: The operation of the law in pre-separation Queensland 1839 to 1859, PhD (History) thesis, University of Queensland, 1990, p. 53.
26 See Prison nos 347 to 360, Brisbane Gaol, Prison Register: 1851, PRI 1/25, QSA. On the history of the old Brisbane Gaol see Connors, Birth of the prison, pp. 64–7.
27 Prison Register, 1851, Prison no. 357.
28 *MBC*, 16 August 1851, p. 3.
29 *MBC*, 23 August 1851, p. 2.
30 *MBC*, 23 August 1851, p. 3.
31 *MBC*, 30 August 1851, p. 2.

32 This should have been Boller but Smith was illiterate and had told the clerk that that was how he said his name, so it is incorrectly spelt in many official records and newspaper reports. See *MBC*, 6 September 1851, p. 2; *R v Moggy Moggy*, Supreme Court, Criminal Jurisdiction: Clerk of the Peace, Brisbane, 1851 9/6366, SRNSW.
33 *MBC*, 6 September 1851, p. 2; J.S. Ferriter to Attorney-General, 1 September 1851, in *R v Moggy Moggy*, 9/6366.
34 The gaol clerk discharged Paddy alias Jemmy Parsons alias Mickaloe on 23 September and re-confined him as Moggy Moggy on the same day. See Prison Register, 1851, Prison nos 343 & 369.
35 See, e.g., *MBC*, 19 May 1852, p. 2.
36 Mary McConnel, *Memories of Days Long Gone By*, Brisbane: M. McConnel, 1905, p. 10, available at <http://nla.gov.au/nla.aus-f7689>.
37 Prison inmates numbered 96 in two wards in the lead up to one of the circuit court sittings in this era. Connors, Birth of the prison, p. 67.
38 Based on newspaper reports of the sittings. *MBC*, 18 May 1850, p. 2; 16 November 1850, p. 2; 24 May 1851, Supplement, p. 2; 15 November 1851, p. 2; 19 May 1852, p. 2; 26 November 1853, p. 2; 27 May 1854, p. 2; 25 November 1854, p. 2; 2 June 1855, p. 2 and 24 November 1855, p. 2; *Moreton Bay Free Press*, 23 November 1852; 17 May 1853 [*MBFP*].
39 J.M. Bennett, *Callaghan's Diary*, Sydney, Francis Forbes Society for Australian Legal History, 2005, p. xvi; J.M. Bennett (ed), *A History of the New South Wales Bar*, Sydney: Law Book, 1969, p. 54.
40 W.B. Perrignon, 'Faucett, Peter (1813–1894)', *Australian Dictionary of Biography*, vol. 4, Melbourne: Melbourne University Press, 1972, pp. 157–8.
41 *MBC*, 15 November 1851, p. 3.
42 J.G. Steele, *Aboriginal Pathways in Southeast Queensland and the Richmond River*, St Lucia: UQP, 1984, p. 181.
43 *MBC*, 28 June 1851, p. 3.
44 J.H. Walker, *The Wreck, the Rescue and the Massacre: An account of the loss of the barque, Thomas King, on Cato's Reef, New Holland, in April 1853*, London: Wesleyan Conference Office, 1875, p. 59.
45 Walker, *The Wreck*, pp. 17–37.
46 Walker, *The Wreck*, pp. 37–57.
47 *MBC*, 5 June 1852, p. 2.
48 One of the Indigenous guides was Nicker. *MBC*, 19 June 1852, p. 2.
49 *MBC*, 19 June 1852, p. 2.
50 Letter no. 51/90, Colonial Secretary's Office to Police Magistrate, Brisbane, 22 December 1851, in Letters addressed to the Government Resident, Moreton Bay by the Colonial Secretary, Sydney, 1851, Government Resident, Moreton Bay, IL: 1851, RES/A3, QSA.
51 Francis Bigge to Colonial Secretary, 30 January 1852, enclosure in L/no. 52/3069, CS Letters Received Main Series: 1852, 4/3075, SRNSW.
52 Police Magistrate Brisbane to Colonial Secretary, 10 April 1852, L/no. 52/3069, Colonial Secretary Letters Received Main Series: 1852, 4/3075, SRNSW.

53 See Tom Petrie's testimony at Mickaloe's committal hearing, *MBC*, 16 August 1851, p. 3.
54 *MBC*, 10 January 1852, p. 2.
55 *MBC*, 19 June 1852, p. 2. 'Make-i-light' was one of the settler renditions of Mickaloe's name.
56 J.J. Knight, *In the Early Days: History and incident of pioneer Queensland*, Brisbane: Sapsford, 1898 [2nd edn], p. 315.
57 'Billy Barlow' was the title of a popular song in 1840s New South Wales. It was based on an East London character who fancied himself 'a great personage' and was consequently used scornfully to denigrate those with leadership pretensions.
58 *MBC*, 17 January 1852, p. 3. The newspaper spelt his name as 'Murkey', Petrie as 'Murki'. Petrie covers Murki's involvement in another revenge attack in *Reminiscences*, p. 224.
59 *MBC*, 7 February 1852, p. 3.
60 Prison no. 407, Prison Register; *MBC*, 5 June 1852, p. 2.
61 *MBC*, 26 June 1852, p. 2.
62 *R v Stinkabed* in Supreme Court Criminal Jurisdiction: Clerk of the Peace, Brisbane, 1853, 9/6378, SRNSW; *MBC*, 26 June 1852, p. 2; *MBC*, 3 July 1852, p. 3.
63 Cash witness statement in *R v Stinkabed*, 9/6378, SRNSW.
64 *MBC*, 3 July 1852, p. 3.
65 Gaiarbau's story, p. 46.
66 *MBC*, 26 June 1852, p. 2; *MBC*, 3 July 1852, p. 3; Prison no. 464 Perriha & Prison no. 465 Durruguree, Prison Register: 1852; *R v Mickaloe* in Supreme Court, Brisbane, 1853.
67 *MBC*, 11 September 1852, p. 3.
68 There were no facilities for hard labour sentences at Brisbane. Tinkabed was held in the gaol under the name of 'Stinkabed alias Johnny' and tried as Stinkabed. See Prison nos 595 & 657, Prison Register: 1852; Judgment Book, 1852–1853, 4/5745–5753, SRNSW; *R v Stinkabed* in Supreme Court, Brisbane, 1853.
69 Prison no. 635, Prison Register: 1852; Judgment Book, 1852–1853, 4/5745–5753, SRNSW; *R v Mickaloe* in Supreme Court, Brisbane, 1853.
70 The *Courier* spelt his name as 'Mickey', the criminal justice system as 'Mickie'. *MBC*, 27 November 1852, p. 3; Judgment Book, 1852–1853; Prison no. 707, Prison Register: 1852.
71 Prison nos 34, 42 & 44, Prison Register: 1853.
72 *Maitland Mercury & Hunter River General Advertiser*, 20 April 1853, p. 4 [*MM*]; Prison nos 34, 42 & 44, Prison Register: 1853.
73 *MBC*, 21 May 1853, p. 3; Judgment Book, 1852–1853. The paper spelt the defence counsel's name as 'Fawcett'.
74 Death was commuted to seven years' hard labour on the roads or other public works. Justice Therry to Colonial Secretary 11 July 1853, L/no. 53/6065 in bundle beginning 52/3069, CS Letters Received Main Series: 1852, 4/3075,

SRNSW; Prison no. 152, Prison Register: 1853; Judgment Book: Brisbane Circuit Court, 1852–53, SRNSW.
75 *MBC*, 28 May 1853, p. 2.
76 Commandant Native Police to E. Deas Thomson, 11 July 1853, L/no. 53/6063 in bundle beginning 52/3069, CS Letters Received Main Series: 1852, 4/3075, SRNSW [CSLR].
77 Attorney-General to Colonial Secretary 29 July 1853, L/no. 53/6617 in bundle beginning 52/3069, CSLR: 1852, 4/3075, SRNSW.
78 J. Therry to Colonial Secretary 9 August 1853, L/no. 53/6955 in bundle beginning 52/3069, CSLR: 1852, 4/3075, SRNSW.
79 Governor's notings on J. Therry to Colonial Secretary, 9 August 1853, L/no. 53/6955 in bundle beginning 52/3069, CSLR: 1852 4/3075, SRNSW.
80 *MM*, 20 April 1853, p. 4.
81 *MBC*, 31 January 1852, p. 2.
82 If Aboriginal people committed an offence against a European settler or his property, pastoralists were not supposed to take violent action against them. Instead the law required them to make a complaint about the alleged culprit to a magistrate. If the magistrate believed there was sufficient evidence, they then issued a warrant. Copies of warrants could be provided to town police and to individuals who might come across the accused person.
83 On the newspaper debates concerning the force under Walker, see Denis Cryle, *The Press in Colonial Queensland: A social and political history 1845–1875*, St Lucia: UQP, 1989, pp. 7–24.
84 On the early history of the force see L.E. Skinner, *Police of the Pastoral Frontier*, St Lucia: UQP, 1975, pp. 15–66; Connors, Birth of the prison, pp. 205–31.
85 *MBC*, 31 January 1852, p. 2.
86 *MBC*, 27 November 1852, p. 3.
87 *MM*, 20 April 1853, p. 4.
88 Land sales of suburban and coastal allotments at Sandgate and Cleveland were held at the Brisbane Police office 11 a.m. Wednesday 9 and Thursday 10 November 1853. *MBC*, 22 October 1853, p. 2.
89 *MBC*, 24 September 1853, p. 2.
90 Dowse's sons were speared in the leg and hit by a boomerang while an Aboriginal youth was shot. Thomas Dowse, 'Recollections of old times in Moreton Bay', a transcript of the original manuscript, (OM79–68/16) online, JOL, pp. 14–15; *MBC*, 10 December 1853, p. 2.
91 Welsby, *Collected Works*, p. 383.
92 Keen, *Aboriginal Economy*, p. 265.
93 Petrie, *Reminiscences*, p. 56.
94 For Moppy see John Campbell, 'The early settlement of Queensland' and other articles with which is also printed 'The raid of the Aborigines', Ipswich, Qld: Ipswich Observer, 1875, p. 10. For Ubie Ubie see entry for 1 January 1844, p. 22 of Ludwig Leichhardt, *Leichhardt Diary No 4: 23 November 1843–March 1844*, translated by Thomas Darragh, Brisbane:

Queensland Museum, 2013, p. 20. For Mulrobbin see *MBC*, 12 June 1852, p. 3. Daki Yakka, Deciby and Yanmonday were possibly still alive.
95 *MBFP*, 27 December 1853 & 10 January 1854; *Illustrated London News* Saturday 17 June 1854, p. 575; Steele, *Aboriginal Pathways*, p. 133.
96 *MBFP*, 27 June 1854; 'The early days: When Creek Street was a creek—pioneer's memories', *Brisbane Courier*, 9 January 1933, p. 10.

7   THE FEUD CONTINUES

1 *Daily Mail*, 21 January 1924, p. 9; Constance Campbell Petrie, *Tom Petrie's Reminiscences of Early Queensland*, Hawthorn, Vic.: Lloyd O'Neil, 1975 [facs of 1904 edn], p. 175; Memories of E.E. Caswell, *Early Brisbane Clippings 1894–1947*, OM91-36, Box 9256, JOL; Letter from R.R.W., *Truth*, 29 March 1908, in F.S. Colliver Papers, Queensland Museum; Prison nos 95, 111, 119, 120, Prison Register: 1854. An early settler named Cecilia Walsh gave the names of different Aboriginal men said to have been involved in Dundalli's arrest but there are a number of errors in these recollections. Cecilia Walsh, Gympie, March 1908 in Colliver Papers. The Aboriginal role in the capture was conveniently overlooked by Baker when he applied for the reward. The official government reward of £25 was eventually paid to William Baker and £3 each to Constables Tredenick and Downs from the Police Rewards Fund. Inspector General of Police to Colonial Secretary, 15 June 1854, L/no. 54/5274 & enclosures and Inspector General of Police to Colonial Secretary, 11 December 1854, L/no. 54/5274 in CS In Letters: 1854, 4/3256, SRNSW.
2 *R v Dundalli Assault and Robbery*, 2 June 1854, Court of Petty Sessions, Brisbane—Depositions and Minutes Book, 07/12/1850–30/12/1854, Series 753, QSA.
3 Barry Bridges, 'The Aborigines and the law: New South Wales 1788–1855', *Teaching History*, vol. 4, part 3, 1970, pp. 62–3.
4 Ground plan of Brisbane Gaol 1853 (drawn by gaoler) in CS Special Bundles: Returns of the State of the Gaols, 4/7341, SRNSW.
5 Sippy was admitted to the gaol from the southern Darling Downs on 1 October 1853. He could not be tried in November owing to the non-appearance of witnesses and escaped 10 January 1854 but was retaken in time for the May circuit when the non-appearance of witnesses again made it impossible to proceed with the murder charge against him. He was then tried for the theft of two horses by which he had made his way back to the Darling Downs and sentenced to three years' hard labour in Darlinghurst Gaol. He was transferred to Sydney on 22 May 1854. Judgment Book, 1853–1854, 4/5745–5753, SRNSW; Prison nos 209 & 277 for 1853 and 97 for 1854, Brisbane Gaol, Prison Register: 1853–54, PRI 1/25, QSA.
6 His second admittance to the gaol was under the name of Billy but he was entered as Billy Dorobbery in the Judgment Book. Judgment Book, 1853–1854, 4/5745–5753, SRNSW; Prison nos 214 & 251 for 1853, Prison Register: 1853.

7   Davy was a young man who had not struck any of the blows that killed Trevethan but had been part of the party that launched the attack and so was deemed guilty of murder. Judgment Book, 1854, 4/5745–5753, SRNSW; Prison nos 178 for 1853 and 96 for 1854, Prison Register: 1853–54; *Moreton Bay Courier*, 26 August 1854, p. 2 [*MBC*].
8   *MBC*, 10 June 1854, p. 2; *Maitland Mercury & Hunter River General Advertiser*, 21 June 1854, p. 4 [*MM*].
9   None of the reports for May to December 1854, Dundalli's time of incarceration, have survived, but there is a reasonable spread of other months to indicate the state of discipline. L/no. 52/1798, Monthly Report of the Visiting Justice of Her Majesty's Gaol Brisbane in CS Special Bundles: Monthly reports of visiting magistrates: Brisbane Gaol, 1850–1858, 4/7192, SRNSW.
10 Petrie, *Reminiscences*, pp. 40–1.
11 *MBC*, 26 August 1854, p. 2.
12 Queen Victoria signed Letters Patent to form the separate colony of Queensland on 6 June 1859, but it didn't formally separate from New South Wales until the arrival of its first governor, Sir George Bowen, on 10 December 1859. Museum of Australian Democracy, Documenting a Democracy, available at <www.foundingdocs.gov.au>.
13 Milford to Colonial Secretary, 13 June 1858, Letter no. 58/1966, Clerk of Works, Moreton Bay, Correspondence: 1856–59, WOK/1, QSA.
14 Judgment Book, 1851 & 1854, 4/5745–5753, SRNSW.
15 In 1857 a resident judge was appointed so it was no longer necessary for the Supreme Court judges to make the journey. Therry retired in 1859 and was knighted in 1869 to become Sir Roger Therry. C.H. Currey, 'Sir Roger Therry (1800–1874)', *Australian Dictionary of Biography*, vol. 2, 1967, pp. 512–13.
16 Inquest papers in *R v Mickie* in Supreme Court, Criminal Jurisdiction: Clerk of the Peace, Brisbane, 1854, 9/6378, SRNSW.
17 *MBC*, 25 November 1854, p. 2.
18 *Moreton Bay Free Press*, 28 November 1854, p. 2 [*MBFP*].
19 See *MBFP*, 28 November 1854 & *MBC*, 25 November 1854, p. 2.
20 *MBC*, 25 November 1854, p. 2.
21 *MBFP*, 28 November 1854, p. 2.
22 *MBC*, 25 November 1854, p. 2.
23 *MBC*, 25 November 1854, p. 2.
24 *Queen v Dundalli*, 2 June 1854, Court of Petty Sessions, Brisbane—Depositions and Minutes Book, 07/12/1850—30/12/1854, Series 753, QSA.
25 Both press reports agreed on the very short deliberation of the jury in the Gregor case. *MBC*, 25 November 1854, p. 2; *MBFP*, 28 November 1854, p. 2.
26 *MBFP*, 28 November 1854, p. 2.
27 Libby Connors, 'Sentencing on a colonial frontier: Judge Therry's decisions at Moreton Bay', *Legal History*, vol. 12, no. 1, 2008, pp. 88–9.
28 *Illustrated Sydney News*, 16 December 1854, p. 440.

29 Roger Therry, *Reminiscences of Thirty Years Residence in New South Wales*, Sydney: Sydney University Press for Royal Australian Historical Society, 1974 [facs edn of 1863], pp. 287–8.
30 Therry, *Reminiscences*, pp. 288–9.
31 Attorney General Plunkett tried repeatedly in the 1840s to convince the New South Wales Legislative Council and the British Parliament to allow Aboriginal witnesses to give evidence in the law courts. Queensland did not allow Aboriginal witnesses in qualified circumstances until 1876 when the Oaths Act Amendment Bill was passed. *Brisbane Courier*, 16 November 1876, p. 3.
32 As a young man, Therry had been private secretary to Prime Minister George Canning. See Connors, 'Sentencing', p. 86.
33 Therry, *Reminiscences*, p. 287.
34 *MBC*, 6 January 1855, p. 2, & 13 January 1855, p. 2.
35 Enclosure in Sheriff Brenan to Colonial Secretary, 14 December 1854, l/no. 54/10807, CS In Letters: 1854, 4/3256, SRNSW.
36 *MBC*, 13 January 1855, p. 2.
37 *MBC*, 6 January 1855, p. 2; Petrie, *Reminiscences*, p. 175; J.J. Knight, *In the Early Days: History and incident of pioneer Queensland*, Brisbane: Sapsford, 1898 [2nd edn], pp. 336–7.
38 *Brisbane Courier*, 20 October 1923, p. 18.
39 Robert Lane's recollections, *Brisbane Courier*, 18 January 1919, in *Early Brisbane Clippings, 1894–1947*, OM91–36, Box 9256, JOL.
40 *MBC*, 6 January 1855, p. 2. See also the account in *MBFP*, 9 January 1855, p. 2.
41 *MBC*, 13 January 1855, p. 2.
42 *MBC*, 6 January 1855, p. 2; Petrie, *Reminiscences*, p. 175; Knight, *Early Days*, p. 337.
43 *MBC*, 26 August 1854, p. 2.
44 *Sydney Morning Herald*, 3 October 1854, p. 5 [*SMH*].
45 Libby Connors, The 'birth of the prison' and the death of convictism: The operation of the law in pre-separation Queensland 1839 to 1859, PhD (History) thesis, University of Queensland, 1990, p. 154.
46 Entries for 9 & 10 March 1855, Rev. William Ridley, 'Narrative of labour among the Aborigines of Australia', 1853, Missions Queensland, MS Q165, CY3386, ML. Ridley only arrived in Brisbane 28 January, 23 days after Dundalli's execution. He immediately commenced learning the local language and by February had established a Moreton Bay Aborigines Protection Society.
47 *Brisbane Courier* clipping, 25 August 1923, p. 19, in Box No. 9, F.S. Colliver Papers, Queensland Museum.
48 *MBC*, 28 October 1854, p. 2; *MBC*, 13 February 1855, p. 2.
49 On Aboriginal thefts and surveillance of Bidwell and Halloran see CCL Wide Bay to Chief Commissioner, 17 January 1850, 14 October 1852 & 22 November 1853, l/nos 50/2648, 52/9967 & 53/4188 in CS Special Bundles: Wide Bay, 1849–57, 4/7173, SRNSW.

50 Walker's emphasis. Commandant Native Police to Colonial Secretary, Traylan, 1 January 1853, l/no. 53/1380 in CS Special Bundles: Wide Bay, 1849–57, 4/7173, SRNSW.
51 Commissioner Halloran to the Chief Commissioner of Crown Lands, 7 February 1854, l/no. 54/5192 in CS Special Bundles: Wide Bay, 1849–57, 4/7173, SRNSW.
52 *MBC*, 29 September 1855, p. 2.
53 *MBC*, 7 June 1856, p. 2.
54 Skinner, *Police of the Pastoral Frontier*, pp. 188–9; pp. 376–7.
55 *MBC*, 29 September 1855, p. 2.
56 They included the McConnel brothers, Police Magistrate and Sheriff William Brown, former missionary Leopold Zillmann and Thomas Dowse. *MBC*, 12 November 1853, p. 2, 11 March 1854, p. 2, 13 May 1854, p. 2.
57 *MBC*, 5 April 1856, p. 1.
58 *MBC*, 26 April 1856, p. 2.
59 *MBC*, 31 May 1856, p. 3.
60 Skinner, *Police of the Pastoral Frontier*, pp. 374–7.
61 *MBC*, 31 May 1856, p. 3.
62 'Recollections of my early life', John W Zillmann, Upper Caboolture, 19 July 1926, in Walker Papers, OM64–9/123, JOL.
63 *MBC*, 20 September 1856, p. 3
64 *MBC*, 11 October 1856, p. 3.
65 *MBC*, 31 October 1857, p. 2. See also lobbying by Jordan and Zillmann for protection at Caboolture in this same period, Skinner, *Police of the Pastoral Frontier*, pp. 264–5.
66 *MBC*, 21 November 1857, p. 2. The German missionaries had also reported the use of smoke as warning signals during their expeditions in the Blackall Range in 1842. See Karl W. Schmidt, Report of an expedition to the Bunya Mountains in search of a suitable site for a mission station, translated by Dr L. Grope and edited and notated by P.D. Wilson, F.S. Colliver & F.P. Woolston, Acc. 3522/1 & 3522/2, Box 7072, JOL, p. 10.
67 *MBC*, 21 November 1857, p. 2.
68 *MBC*, 27 January 1855, p. 2, 30 July 1855, p. 1, 11 September 1858, p. 2, 27 October 1858, p. 3.
69 *MBC*, 1 August 1857, p. 1.
70 *MBC*, 31 October 1857, p. 2.
71 Colonial Secretary to Government Resident, Brisbane, 26 August 1856, enclosing extract from a letter from Henry Buckley MLA to Colonial Secretary, in Government Resident Moreton Bay, IL: 1856, Res/A7, QSA.
72 Drawn from Government Resident at Moreton Bay to Colonial Secretary, 21 April 1858, l/no. 58/1492 & enclosure in CS Letters Received re Moreton Bay: 1858, A2/39 QSA, & *MBC*, 24 April 1858, p. 2.
73 Drawn from Government Resident at Moreton Bay to Colonial Secretary, 21 April 1858, l/no. 58/1492 & enclosure in Colonial Secretary, Letters received re Moreton Bay, 1858, A2/39, QSA.

74 MBC, 24 April 1858, p. 2.
75 Petrie, *Reminiscences*, p. 180.
76 Francis had gone into debt in 1847 and his parents had taken over the station. When George died it became his widow Jane's property.
77 Petrie, *Reminiscences*, pp. 178–87; see also Alex Bond, *The Statesman, the Warrior and the Songman*, Nambour, Qld: Interactive Community Planning Australia, 2009, p. 6.
78 Recollections of A.J. McConnel, 1856–1937, Box 3, Item 206, McConnel Family Papers, UQFL89, Fryer Library.
79 MBC, 3 December 1859, p. 2.
80 MBC, 27 April 1859, p. 2.
81 MBC, 14 May 1859, p. 1.
82 Petrie, *Reminiscences*, p. 8; A.J. McConnel, Diary [transcription by Margaret Chittick] OM79–13/18/2, p. 4.
83 Jonathan Richards, 'Frederick Wheeler and the Sandgate Native Police Camp', *Journal of the Royal Historical Society of Queensland*, vol. 20, no. 3, 2007, p. 115.
84 Richards, 'Frederick Wheeler', p. 116.
85 Richards, 'Frederick Wheeler', pp. 117–18.
86 MBC, 29 January 1859, p. 2.
87 MBC, 7 May 1859, p. 2; 2 March 1859, p. 2; 29 January 1859, p. 2; Petrie, *Reminiscences*, pp. 8–10.
88 MBC, 2 March 1859, p. 2.
89 MBC, 5 March 1859, p. 2.

EPILOGUE

1 C.E.W. Bean, 1948, on home page of Australian War Memorial website, available at <www.awm.gov.au>. Thanks to Henry Reynolds for recalling this quote from Bean. Henry Reynolds, *The Forgotten War*, Sydney: New South, 2013, pp. 41, 240.
2 *Brisbane Courier*, 18 January 1919, p. 12.
3 John Campbell, 'The early settlement of Queensland' and other articles with which is also printed 'The raid of the Aborigines', Ipswich, Qld: Ipswich Observer, 1875, p. 18.
4 Campbell, 'Early settlement', p. 22.
5 Ludwig Leichhardt to David Archer, Hughes & Isaacs Station, 19 November 1846, Archer Family: General & Business Correspondence, A3882, CY3690, ML.
6 *Moreton Bay Courier*, 20 May 1850, p. 1.
7 *Moreton Bay Courier*, 20 May 1850, p. 1.
8 Commissioner Halloran to the Chief Commissioner of Crown Lands, 7 February 1854, l/no. 54/5192 in CS Special Bundles: Wide Bay, 1849–1857, 4/7173, SRNSW.

INDEX

50-mile [80-kilometre] exclusion zone 32, 45, 89

A

Aboriginal camps and villages, permanent
   Bribie Island 79
   Sandstone Point 73
   York's Hollow 28, 119, 120, 121, 122, 123, 125, 127, 129, 133, 134, 143, 147, 167, 198
Aboriginal name exchange 36–8, 65, 96, 153
Aboriginal women 6–9, 11–12, 24, 61–2, 100, 134–40, 148
   childcare 9
   disciplining children 8
   dispute settlement 14
   food preparation 2
   funeral rites 116
   giving birth 5–6
   intimidation by convicts 53
   marriage 25–6, 52, 110
   medicine women 50
   moiety 25
   naming children 7
   preparation of Toors 64
   station work 84
   treatment of wounds 204
Aboriginal–European economy 94, 153, 210
Aborigines Protection Society 127
Albany Creek 170
Amity Point 4, 30, 31, 141
Anbaybury 26, 27, 38–9, 41–2, 43, 48, 56, 65
Anderson, Thomas 197
Angee 163
Anglicanism *see* Church of England
Apsley mission 125
Archer brothers 8, 43–5, 48–51, 55, 57–9, 61, 64, 75–8, 88, 89, 90, 99, 103, 108, 207–8
   education 90
Archer, Charles 8, 15, 44, 45, 48, 50
Archer, David 8, 44–6, 50, 65, 66, 76, 77, 107, 108, 112, 129, 207, 213
Archer, Jack (John) 44, 45, 46, 47
Archer, Tom 44, 45, 46, 47, 49, 50, 59, 61, 76, 77, 78, 79, 90, 92, 94, 102, 108, 110
Australasian Chronicle 121
Australian 126

B

Backhouse, James 28
Badtjala 5, 23, 199
Baker, William 182, 183, 194
Balfour, John 58, 59–60, 70, 178
Balfour, Robert 58
Ballow, Dr 146–7
Barlow, Billy 101, 151, 168, 171, 172, 176, 178, 185, 193, 196
Baroon Pocket 4
Barrow, Ralph
   christened by Bishop Broughton 91
   confusion at Dundalli's trial 186–9, 192
   court witness 107, 157–8, 162, 173
   death of John Gregor 157
   educated at Narellan 91
   gaoled for prevarication 158–60
   living with Andrew Gregor 90, 93
   living with John Gregor 107
   moves to Nundah 157
   sent to Brisbane 91–2
   Wiradjuri background 91, 125
   witnesses Forgie station attack 99–100, 104, 106, 172
bauple nuts 23
beheadings
   Aboriginal men, by Europeans 30, 69, 116
Berlin Missionary Society 33
Bianco 38
Bickerton, Richard 115, 137
Bidwell, John (commissioner of crown lands, Wide Bay) 164, 199
Bigge brothers 45, 58, 59, 68, 83, 166
Binjy 74–5
Biralli 37, 52, 55
Blackall Range 1, 4, 32, 164
Blamire, Lieutenant Charles 122
blood brother *see* Aboriginal name exchange
Boddin, William 152–3
Bora council 10, 12, 14, 23, 24, 25, 26, 36, 53, 56, 57, 74, 96, 150, 168, 171
Bora ring 49, 170–1, 208
Boralee 37
Border Police 117, 177
Borthwick, John 59

Bracewell, David 62, 64, 67
Bribé 17, 18, 21
Bribie Island 5, 19, 20, 21, 39, 52, 65, 71, 76, 78, 79, 80, 82, 85, 88, 89, 94, 135, 140, 149, 151–4, 155, 165, 168, 171, 178, 179, 181, 184, 195, 197
Brisbane Courier 212
Brisbane Gaol x, xi, 143, 156, 159, 160, 161, 162, 166, 167, 168, 169, 171, 172–3, 183–5, 186, 192, 195
Brisbane Hospital 60, 116, 134, 139, 165
Brisbane locations
  Albion 28
  Bald Hills 204
  Breakfast Creek 28, 51, 115, 131, 143, 165, 169, 171, 198
  Bridgeman Downs 202
  Bulimba and Bulimba Creek 115, 119, 137, 140
  Cornwall Street 179
  Eagle Farm 31, 198
  Eagle Street 212
  Exhibition Grounds 28
  Fortitude Valley 182, 198
  Indooroopilly 180
  Juliette Street 179
  Kangaroo Point vi, 135, 142
  Leichhardt Street 128
  Luggage Point 178, 209
  Lytton 21, 115
  Mt Coot-tha 17
  Murrarie 115
  Normanby Fiveways 28
  Nundah 27, 31, 32, 61, 74, 85, 107, 157, 198
  Queen Street xi, 128, 134, 143, 156, 159, 185
  Roma Street Parklands 128
  Sandgate 178, 197–8, 200–2, 205, 206, 208–9
  Sandgate Road 32
  South East Freeway 179
  Spring Hill 128, 196
  Spring Hollow 127–8, 198
  Stones Corner 179
  Taringa 180
  Wickham Street 182
  Wickham Terrace 128
Brisbane Valley 43, 44, 45, 58–9, 82, 83, 87, 93, 94–5, 166, 172, 176, 177
British regiments, detachments at Moreton Bay 28, 145
  11th Regiment of Foot 143, 146, 151, 213
  99th Regiment of Foot 83, 96
Broughton, Bishop William Grant 91–2
Brown, William 200, 205
Bruce Highway 85
Buaraba station 59
Buckley, Henry 205
bullanbullan *see* pullen pullen
Bundamba 114, 116, 130
Bundjalung people 63

Bunya Bunya people (Bonyi, Bonyer people) 19, 39, 116; *see also* Dalla people
Bunya gatherings, summits or Toors xi, 4, 9, 13, 63
  December 1841–January 1842 60
  December 1842–January 1843 72, 74–5, 95, 130
  December 1843–January 1844 148
  December 1846–January 1847 176
  December 1852–January 1853 176, 177–8
  December 1858–January 1859 210
Bunya Mountains National Park 4
bunya nut 4
Bunya pine 68
Burnett River and district xi, 43, 60, 67, 102, 108, 163, 164, 177, 184
  South Burnett 2, 4, 45
Burpengary 84–5, 106
Burra 164–5, 166, 167, 168
Burumballi 22, 66

C
Caboolture 112, 196, 202, 204, 209
Caboolture River 89, 90
Cambayo
  arrest 77
  attack at Durundur Station 76, 78
  Gregor attack, aftermath 112
  training of Dundalli 71, 78
  sentence 77–8, 148
  trial 77
Cameron, Lieutenant George 143, 146, 147
Campbell, John 97, 102, 212
  name exchange with Multuggerah 96
Canary 122, 134, 135, 136, 137
Cash's Crossing 170
Cash, James 169, 170, 171, 177, 198, 202, 203
Cash, Mary 169–70, 172, 173
Castlereagh River 49, 59, 79
Catholic Church 33, 121, 123, 134, 136
  Passionist priests 136
  Sisters of Charity 136
  Stradbroke mission 136–7
children
  Aboriginal 8–10, 18, 20, 30, 41, 47, 51, 54, 60, 62, 64, 84, 99, 100, 103, 106, 116, 120, 131, 135–6, 169, 206, 210, 211
  birth 6
  discipline 8
  naming 7
  European xi, 8, 99, 100, 101, 103, 106, 116, 131, 157, 160, 195
Church Missionary Society 33, 125
Church of England 33, 90, 91, 99, 157
Clarence pastoral district 177, 202
Cockatoo Island 78, 112
Coley, Richard J. 201
Colinton Station 26, 58, 59–60, 70

INDEX

Collins, Bob 209–10
Colonial Observer 34
Colonial Office (London) 120, 143, 177, 191, 202
colonial self-government 92, 147, 201
colonial violence 53, 214
  sexual assault 53, 75, 135-6, 210
Commandant 57, 62, 64, 65, 68–71
commissioner of crown lands 64, 66, 69, 93, 95, 123, 164, 199
committal hearings
  Cambayo 77
  Constable 99, 104, 113
  Dundalli 183
  Mickaloe 156, 163, 186
Congregationalists 45
Constable 99, 100, 101, 102, 113
convict barracks 28, 156, 183, 185
convict buildings 28, 107, 109
convicts, including ticket-of-leave men x, 28, 30, 31, 48, 53, 61, 62, 64, 66, 67, 80, 109, 112, 113–14, 115–18, 119, 126, 127, 129, 130, 132, 135, 141, 156, 160, 161, 162, 184, 186, 193
  Norfolk Island 114, 172
Cooloola Coast 1, 67, 101, 164, 168
Cotton, Major (commandant, penal station) 31, 32
Coutts, Donald 95–6, 97
Cowper, Charles (premier of New South Wales) 147
Cressbrook Station 58, 60, 68–9
Crosby Hall 127
'Cry for the Dead' 16, 73
customs department 120, 122, 136, 152, 161

D

D'Aguilar Range vii, 1, 2, 57, 58, 59, 70, 87, 89, 93
Dabianco (Dabionionne) 38, 52, 54, 65, 73, 131
Daki Yakka 5, 17, 21, 27, 28, 29, 31, 52, 119, 120, 122, 132, 134, 135, 147, 148
Dalaipi 94, 97, 104–5, 207
Dalla people 2, 4, 58, 59, 70, 76, 79, 99, 107, 134, 140, 204, 207, 209
  Bora rings 23, 49–50
  childhood 7–11
  courtship and marriage 25–6, 52
  entertainment 11–12
  fertility sites 50
  healing places 50
  hosts of bunya meetings 4, 13, 60, 74
  language 2
  neighbours 5, 51–2, 65, 88, 89, 94
  response to Europeans 27, 39–42, 46–7, 48–9, 50–1, 58–61, 87
    reassessment of European presence 57, 64, 65, 83, 101, 130, 139
  response to Kilcoy poisonings 65, 78
  sacred sites 50
  settling of disputes 13–22
  sporting contests 9, 11, 14
  Toors 64–6, 74
  totem system 7
  trade 22–3
  tribal scars vi, 23
  women 141
Dal-ngang 207
Darling Downs vi, 44, 82, 95, 96, 107, 144, 160, 177, 184, 212
Darlinghurst Gaol 169, 184
Darryguree 170–1, 184, 199
Darumbal people 63
Davis, James *see* Duramboi
Davy xi, 184, 192
Dawson pastoral district 202
Deciby 33, 37, 38, 40, 41, 43, 52, 165
  authority 52, 56, 88, 130–1
  protection of mission 48, 52, 54–5, 57, 61
  withdrawal of protection 71–3, 83
Demerara, uprising in 44
Diamond 178, 180
Dick Ben 98, 100–2, 104, 105, 113
Dickinson, Judge John 171
Dillon, John Moore (criminal crown solicitor) 163, 186
Dingy, Billy 210
Dorsey, Dr William 114
Doucette, Eugene (Lucette) 127–8, 141–2
Dowse, Thomas 95, 152, 154, 178, 205
Doyle, Daniel 117–18, 122
Dulingbara people 164, 166
Duncan, William (sub-collector of customs, Moreton Bay) 120–3, 125–6, 132, 133, 134, 135, 136, 137, 139, 147, 154, 156–8, 160, 161, 192
Dundalli
  acts as envoy to German mission 27, 41–3, 48, 56
  arrest 182–3, 199
  attacks on
    Durundur Station 76, 78
    Forgie Station 97–101, 102–4, 106, 108, 130, 212
    mission outstation 85–6, 106
    Whiteside Station 137–40, 162, 210
  battle leader and lawman 106, 140, 149, 168, 208, 211, 214
  birth 5–6
  childhood 1–5, 7–11, 28
  committal hearing 183
  defusing conflict 150–1, 152–4, 155, 179–81
  gallows speech 193–7, 214
  imposes limits on violence 170–1
  incarceration 183–5, 192–3
  initiation 23–4, 26, 30
  killing of his brother 127–9, 140–2
  kooringal 150
  marriage 25–6, 193

Dundalli *continued*
  moves to Bribie Island 78–82, 88
  name exchange 153, 183
  naming 7
  protégé of young men 151, 152–4, 156
  reputation vi–ix, xi–xii, 88, 97, 109, 140, 149, 150, 152, 154, 155, 182
  takes work in Brisbane 179, 182
  trial vii, 121, 185–92
  tribal cuts 23
  warrior training 16–22, 57, 70–1, 112
Dungidau people 49
Dunkely 38
Dunwich 30, 136–7
Duramboi (James Davis) 48, 62, 64, 66–8, 75, 156, 160–1, 163
Durundur Station 26, 43–51, 61, 64–7, 74–5, 76–7, 78, 79, 82, 83, 87, 88, 90, 92, 98–9, 101, 104, 106, 107, 108, 116, 127, 130, 131, 175, 196, 197, 203, 207–9

E
Eales' station 68, 75, 164
Eipper, Reverend Christopher 10, 32, 33, 34, 38, 39, 51, 53, 65, 66, 71, 75, 76, 77, 84
Eskdale Station 58
Eton Vale Station 59
Eulopé 17–19, 21, 30
evangelism 27, 33, 45, 73, 147
Executive Council 166–7, 174, 192–3

F
Fairnie Lawn Station 87
Faucett, Peter 163, 173–4, 186–9
Ferriter, J.S. 87, 156–8, 160, 161
Finnegan, John 15, 16
Fitzpatrick, William (chief constable, Brisbane Police) 91, 146
FitzRoy, Sir Charles (governor of New South Wales) 111, 129, 177
Forgie Station 90, 93–4, 97, 104, 108; *see also* Gregor, Andrew
  attack on 97–8, 102–7
  Aboriginal men and women accused of participation in 99–102
Franz 38
Franz, Charles 38, 61
Fraser Island 2, 5, 124, 199
Fyans, Foster (commandant, penal station) 4, 29

G
Gaiarbau 52
Gairwar (rainbow snake) 50
Garumngar 59
Gatton-Tenthill area 17, 20, 21
Gavanmary 37, 38, 52, 65; *see also* Nicker
German Mission 8, 10, 13, 14, 26, 27, 49, 51, 57, 75, 80, 83–4, 105, 107, 157, 187

Aboriginal garden 37, 55–6; *see also* Girkum
  cottages for Aboriginal men and their families 37
  dissolution of Sydney support committee 84
  establishment of 31–3
  expeditions 34–6, 40–3, 53–4, 55, 61, 69, 71, 72–4
  founded by J.D. Lang 31, 91
  new outstation at Burpengary 43, 75, 84–6, 106, 150, 186
Gipps, Sir George (governor of New South Wales) 31, 45, 68, 120, 121
Girkum 37, 38, 51, 52, 53, 54, 60, 72
  destruction by Gubbi Gubbi people 55–6
Glass House Mountains 1, 2, 90
Glynn, Peter 135
Goenpul people 5, 15, 21, 28, 30
Goold, Joseph 197
Gorman, Owen (commandant, penal station) 53, 59, 60
Gorowamba 17, 18, 19, 21
Gossner, Reverend 33
Government Gazette 115
Government Stock and Agricultural Establishments 114, 116, 117, 118
Graham, John 30
Gray, Charles 152–4
Great Dividing Range 96
Green, Alexander x, 194
Gregor, Andrew 90, 93, 94, 97–8, 99
  attack on his station 100–4, 106, 107, 108, 116, 117, 121, 122, 127, 129, 155, 156, 157, 161, 162, 167, 172, 173, 175, 176, 178, 186, 188, 189, 192, 212
Gregor, Reverend John 99, 122, 124
  conservatism 92
  conversion to Anglicanism 91
  falling out with Lang 91
  guardian of Ralph Barrow 91–2, 107, 157
  moves to Nundah 157
  recruitment 91
  response to death of his brother 111–13, 115
Griffin, Captain Francis 92, 94, 98, 103
Griffin, Captain George 92, 93, 126, 129, 137–8, 139
Griffin, Jane 92, 200, 205, 206–7
Griffin, John 92, 137, 138, 206–7
Griffin, William 92
Gubbi Gubbi people 5, 7, 21, 22, 23, 36, 56, 68, 75, 101, 102, 150, 155, 163, 164, 165, 167, 168, 169, 170–1, 172, 184, 187, 193, 199, 207
  attack on Whiteside Station 139
  language 2, 34, 194
  response to Kilcoy poisoning 62, 66, 83
Günther, Reverend James 123, 124, 125
Gympie 75

H
Halloran, Arthur (commissioner of crown lands, Wide Bay) 199, 213

INDEX

Halloran, Michael 171, 172
Haly, William O'Grady 98
Hanly, Father 134, 136, 192
Hartenstein, William 14, 38, 40–1, 43, 85
Hausmann, Johan (John) 38, 54, 61, 70, 71, 196
    speared at Nonga Creek 85–6, 106, 186–7
head man 2, 12, 14, 15, 48, 99, 150;
    see also komaron
Helidon 83, 96, 123
Helidon Station 75
Hodgson, Pemberton 59
Horse Jemmy see Waakoon
Huxley, Thomas 80

I

initiation 7, 10, 23, 24, 30, 67; see also kippers
inquests
    Aboriginal 63, 105, 142
    British 96, 98, 99, 104, 107, 113, 117, 120, 122, 128, 129, 152, 154, 156, 158, 173, 187, 188
Inquiry into Affray with Aborigines 122, 125–6
Inskip Point 36, 165
interpreters 77, 160, 163
Ipswich 20, 21, 22, 86, 95, 109, 113, 114, 116–18, 130, 132, 134

J

Jackey 101, 119–20, 133, 134
Jackey Jackey 113, 119–20, 122, 128, 133, 134, 135, 137, 140, 168, 169, 176
    wife of 133, 134
Jacky 101, 113
Jagera people 20, 21, 23, 37, 64, 86, 109, 117, 130, 133
Jarbu people 57, 65, 66
Jimna Range 2, 11
jindig see sacred stones
Joliffe, Captain 68
Joondaburri people 5, 17, 21, 38, 39, 65, 76, 78, 79, 85, 88, 133, 139, 150, 152, 154, 168, 176, 178, 179–80, 193, 195, 197, 204, 209, 210, 211
    architecture 81–2
    change in politics 81–2
    hospitality 80
Joyner, William 88, 93, 95

K

Kamilaroi people 63
Kent, John 114, 116, 118
Kent, William 38
Kilcoy 22, 66
Kilcoy Station 26, 45, 50, 58, 59, 196
    mass poisoning 56, 61–2, 66, 70, 73–4, 75, 78, 105, 130
    shepherds killed or speared 56, 60, 62, 65, 70, 75
King Billy 21, 62, 64, 65, 68–9

kippers 7, 18, 20, 24, 148, 154, 161, 170
kipper-making 156, 170–1, 184, 191;
    see also initiation
Kitty 122, 134, 135
Knight, J.J. 168, 195
komaron 9, 10, 12, 13, 16, 23, 26, 49

L

Lady Blackwood 164
Lake Baroon Dam 4
Lang, Reverend John Dunmore 31, 33, 34, 37, 62, 91
law, Aboriginal vii–xii, 26, 36, 50, 68, 70, 71, 87, 102, 104–5, 106, 108–10, 125, 136, 137, 141, 143, 148, 149, 150–1, 153, 154, 180, 195, 197, 210, 214
    decision-making 64, 167, 196
    hand-to-hand combat 155
    lawman and lawmen xi–xii, 106, 112, 134, 140, 149, 150, 170, 190, 208, 211
    moiety and skin system 6, 10–11, 24
    payback 63–4, 78, 88, 97, 102, 105, 133, 138, 140, 168, 193
    revenge party 64, 165, 196
law, British viii, 45, 70, 77–8, 102, 105, 108–9, 110–14, 128–9, 136, 141, 144–8, 151, 155–6, 163, 173–7, 180, 185–95, 207, 210, 211
Leichhardt, Ludwig 11, 69, 83, 107, 108, 148, 149, 212
Leslie brothers 44
Liddiard, Joseph 115
Limestone 113, 134, 135
Lindon, John 117–19, 122
Little, Robert 174
Lockyer Creek and Valley 83, 96, 97
Logan River district 2, 95, 168, 180, 205
Logan River people 128, 179, 205;
    see also Yugambeh
Loudon 205

M

McAllister, James 120, 122, 125
McConnel, Arthur 51, 208, 209
McConnel, David 43, 51, 58, 60, 62, 69, 70, 87, 135, 207
McConnel, Frederic 96
McConnel, John 43, 51, 135, 207, 208
McConnel, Mary 162
McConnel, William 87
MacGillivray, John 80
McGrath, Darby 171, 177, 198
Mackenzie, Colin 58
Mackenzie, Sir Evan 43, 45, 48, 50, 55, 56, 58, 61, 76
makaratta 179
Manumbar 11
martial law 111, 122

Mary River 1, 5, 22, 66, 88, 164, 208
Maryborough 156, 163, 164, 172, 173, 199
Mason, William 88, 93, 95, 106
Masters and Servants Act 160
Mayhall, John 118, 119
Meston, Archibald vii–viii, 194, 196
Mianjin people 5, 21, 28, 29, 31, 35, 38, 49, 52, 56, 86, 109, 117, 119, 120, 132, 133, 134, 135, 137, 143, 146–8, 149, 167, 168, 169, 171, 176, 178, 180, 182, 213
    women 134, 147
Mickaloe (Moggy Moggy) 151, 160, 168–9, 174, 176, 179, 191, 192
    attacks at
        Cash's station 169–70, 172, 173
        Forgie Station 100–2, 104, 105, 113, 155, 157–8, 167, 186
        Whiteside Station 139, 161–2
        The Gap 171
    brother of Burra 164–5, 166, 168
    multiple names and pseudonyms 105, 139–40, 156, 158, 161, 163, 167
Mickey 168
Mickey Mickey 78
Mickie 172, 173–5, 176, 178, 188, 191
military barracks 143
military sorties 30
mingom *see* sacred stones
Moggy Moggy *see* Mickaloe
moiety system 6–7, 14, 25, 36, 37, 67
Monday 62, 64, 68, 69
Mooky (Murki)
    attacked by Billy Barlow 168
    part in police attack on Jackey Jackey 119, 133
Moongalba 30
Moppy 17, 19, 21, 57, 59
    death 82, 83, 87, 130, 179
    sons 95, 96
Moreton Bay Courier 95, 99, 110, 112, 115, 116, 118, 121, 123, 124, 125, 126, 127, 131, 132, 139, 141, 144, 146, 152, 154, 155, 156, 158, 161, 162, 167, 168, 170, 173, 174, 176, 177, 180, 185, 192, 194, 195, 197, 200, 201, 202, 204, 210
Moreton Bay Penal Establishment 27, 34, 67
Moreton Island 5, 30, 79; *see also* Ngugi people, Quandamooka people
Morning Chronicle 120
Morrisset, Lieutenant Edric (commandant, Native Police) 202
Mort, Henry 68, 69, 87
Mount Archer 11, 50
Mount Beerwah 77, 79
Mount Brisbane Station 58, 68, 70
Mount Coolum 165
Mount Coot-tha 17
Mount Esk Station 58
Mount Mee 89, 90, 97

Mount Nebo 89
Mulrobbin 17, 19–20, 21, 64, 116, 117, 132, 179
Multuggerah (Jemmy Cambell, Cambela, Black Campbell) 21, 95–7, 130, 212
    death 96
    name exchange with John Campbell 96
muningburum *see* komaron
Murrumba Downs 207, 208, 209
Murray, Hon Mr 59
Mwoirnewar 5, 65

N

Naimany 21, 39, 52
Native Police Force x, xi, 100, 155, 163, 169, 172, 175, 177, 178, 179, 198, 199, 200, 202, 204, 205, 206, 208, 209, 211, 213
New England Tableland 5
Newcastle Gaol 77
Ngugi people 5, 15, 30
Nicker 37, 38, 76, 101; *see also* Gavanmary
Ningy Ningy people 5, 32, 34, 35, 36, 38, 39, 42, 43, 49, 52, 55, 56, 61, 64, 71, 73, 74, 83, 85, 86, 94, 100, 101, 117, 138, 168, 176, 178, 179, 180, 193, 195, 204, 209
Niqué, Peter 14, 37, 38, 40, 41, 43, 55, 56, 61
Noosa 1, 19, 22, 164
Noosa lakes 164
Noosa River 165
North, Major 87, 95, 117, 118, 122
Nundah 27, 31, 32, 61, 74, 80, 83, 85, 86, 107, 157, 198; *see also* Zion's Hill
Nunukul people 5, 15, 21, 28, 30, 130, 136, 137, 141, 143, 149
    women 136, 138, 140

O

Orphan School 107, 160
Oumulli (Marmoulli) 7
    accused of involvement in Gregor station attack 102, 104, 106, 127
    killed at Spring Hollow 127–9
    part in internal politics 140, 141–2, 143, 176
Oxley, John 79, 80

P

Paddy 49, 50, 64, 78, 106, 116, 127, 131
    head man, Durundur Station 48, 49, 66, 98, 99, 102, 104, 105, 207
    protection of the Archers 50, 57, 61, 65, 88
Pamphlett, Thomas 15, 80
Pamby Pamby 62, 66, 67
Papooniya (Parpunyi) 21
Parry 37, 52, 55, 65
Parsons, Richard 15
Pastoralists' Association 120
Paul Paul 119, 133, 134
Peak Mountain people 17, 18
Pearce, John Canning 75

INDEX

Peattie, David 135, 160
Peattie, Mrs 160
Perika 170, 171
Perowa, Jemmy 98, 99, 102, 104, 106
Petrie, Andrew 68, 79, 147, 159
Petrie, Constance 63, 80, 105, 115, 142, 195
Petrie, John 161
Petrie, Tom viii, 13, 16, 20, 21, 22, 24, 48, 52, 85, 104, 116, 126, 128, 131, 133, 148, 153, 160, 179, 183, 206, 207, 209, 210
pilot station 30, 114
Pine River and valley 54, 61, 88, 89, 95, 112, 138, 142, 152, 161, 162, 169, 177, 178, 179, 195, 196, 198, 200, 202, 203, 204, 206, 210
Pine River people 5, 19, 20, 38, 63, 94, 101, 112, 139, 171, 172, 176, 197, 200, 202, 204, 207, 209
'Ploughed Station' *see* Government Stock and Agricultural Establishments
Plunkett, John (attorney-general, New South Wales) 163, 186
   1st assize Brisbane 144–5, 146–7
   prosecution of Myall Creek trials 121, 146–7
   publicly attacked over Aboriginal cases 173–5
   refuses reward for Oumulli's death 129
Polding, Bishop John 123, 136
Port Phillip 177
Power, Edward 171, 172
Presbyterianism 31, 45, 91
pullen pullen 13, 86, 116, 130, 136, 137–8, 179, 181
Purefoy, William 163, 186, 189

Q

Quaker missionaries 28–9
Quandamooka people xi, 5, 17, 21, 30, 31, 35, 52, 122, 133, 134, 141, 148, 153, 168, 176, 178, 179, 180; *see also* Goenpul people, Ngugi people, Nunukul people
Quart Pot, Billy 101, 172, 176, 178

R

Redbank 117
Redcliffe 28, 35, 55–6, 61, 64, 69, 71, 73, 89, 196, 213; *see also* 'Umpie Bong'
rewards 132, 182
   government 111–2, 113, 115, 116, 117, 120, 127, 129, 178
   private 113, 114, 115, 116, 117
Reynolds, John 117–19, 122
Ridley, Reverend William 196
Rockhampton 5, 63
Rodé, August 38, 53, 55, 56, 61, 72, 73
Rosewood 57, 83, 95, 96, 117–18, 125, 130, 132
Rosewood Station 95
Russell, Henry Stuart 36–7, 68

S

sacred stones 50
St Helena Island 209
Samsonvale Station 93, 94, 106, 200, 203
Sandstone Point 39, 40, 72, 165
Schmidt, Reverend Karl 4, 38, 62, 72, 73
Scott brothers 58–9
Select Committee on the Condition of the Aborigines, 1845 123, 124, 125
Shannon, Eliza 94, 107
Shannon, Margaret 94, 98, 99, 100, 103, 105, 107, 160, 186
Shannon, Mary 94, 97, 98, 99, 100, 104, 106, 160
Shannon, Mary Ann 94, 107, 113, 117, 118, 129, 130, 133, 158, 167, 173, 175, 186
Shannon, Thomas 94, 97, 98, 99, 106, 107
Simpson, Dr Stephen (commissioner of crown lands, Moreton Bay) 69, 75, 79, 80, 82, 83, 86, 87, 90, 93, 94, 95, 96, 97, 98, 99, 116, 122, 139, 154
Sippy 184
slavery, abolition of 44
Smith, James
   attack at Whiteside 137, 138, 139, 156, 161, 162, 163, 186, 187, 193, 210
   confusion with Dick Smith accused of abducting Stradbroke Island women 122, 137, 139
   killing of Yilbung 115, 140
Sneyd, Samuel (chief constable, Brisbane Police) 171, 182, 196, 204
Stanley River 1, 23, 43, 50
Stephen, Judge Alfred 77
Strange, Frederick 154, 155
Supreme Court of New South Wales 163, 183, 191
   Brisbane, on circuit
      conditions 162–3, 185
      assize of May 1850 144, 151
      assize of November 1851 156, 163
      assize of May 1852 169
      assize of November 1852 172
      assize of May 1853 172–4
      assize of May 1854 182
      assize of November 1854 vii, 186–91
   Maitland, on circuit 77
Sydney Chronicle 119, 121, 123, 125

T

Tarampa Station 83
Taribelang people 67
Tenthill Station 78, 83
Tenthill Valley 17, 21
The Gap station 171, 172, 198
Therry, Judge Roger xi, 144, 145, 162, 163, 173, 186, 187–8
   attitude to Dundalli 189–90, 192–3
   background 121, 191
   reprieves
      Mickaloe 166, 191
      Mickie 174, 191
   reprimands Frederick Walker 174–6

Thomas King 164, 167, 172
Thomson (convict overseer) 118
Thomson, Sir Edward Deas (colonial secretary, New South Wales) 111, 115, 122, 175
Tiaro 66, 67, 164
ticket-of-leave men 31, 114, 117, 141
Tingalpa 11, 130
Toorbul 13, 24, 26, 43, 55, 61, 72, 85, 89, 130
Toorbul people 48, 167
totem system 7, 10, 24, 67, 104
town police x, 54, 91, 113, 114, 119, 130–1, 132, 133, 137, 139, 140, 141, 142, 144, 146, 151, 161, 172, 176, 177, 178, 180, 193, 196, 199, 200, 204, 205
    capture and trial of Dundalli 182, 183, 186, 190
    Constable Connor 120
    Constable Conroy 147, 213
    Constable Murphy 120
    Constable Ramsay 128
    Constable Scanlan 132
    night raids 119–20, 127–8, 129, 133, 134, 168, 171
trade 4, 5, 22–3, 29, 50, 81
Trimberri 85–6
Tweed Heads 137

U

Ubie Ubie people 22, 56, 59, 60, 64, 66, 88, 179
Ugarapul people 21, 96, 117, 118, 132, 135
Uhr, Edmund 87, 157, 172, 173
Uhr, John 87, 93, 94–5, 113, 116, 117, 118, 119, 121, 129
'Umpie Bong' 35; *see also* Redcliffe
Undambi people 5, 22, 24, 29, 40, 88, 101, 154, 178; *see also* Ningy Ningy people, Joondaburri people
Uniacke, John 79, 80

V

Vaccari, Father Raymund 136
Vagrants Act 125
Vant, William 76–7, 78, 112, 148, 150

W

Waakoon (Horse Jemmy) 118, 121, 122, 123, 127, 131, 132, 133, 137, 140
Wagner, Gottfried 38, 39
Wakka Wakka people xi, 4, 5, 23, 26, 164, 184
Walker, Captain James 164, 165, 166, 167
Walker, Edward 46
Walker, Frederick (commandant, Native Police) 99, 175, 176, 177, 178, 192, 198, 199
Walker, George (missionary) 28
Wamgul 147, 148
Watson, William (missionary) 91, 125

Wellington Valley 91, 125
Westaway 203
Wheeler, Lietuenant Frederick 208–9
Whiteside Station 92, 93, 98, 200, 203
    attack on Native Police patrol 205–6
    attack on station sawyers, 1847 137–40, 187
    poisoning of Aboriginal men 126
    sale of coastal portions, 1859 206–7
Williams, Lieutenant Evan 205–6
Wilson, William, name exchange with Dundalli 153, 183
Winter, Bobby ('Bobbiwinta') 128, 141, 142
Wiradjuri people 91; *see also* Barrow, Ralph
Wivenhoe Station 87, 157, 172
Wogan (Worgan, Woorgan) 21, 38
    Girkum cottage 37
    Girkum garden 55
    second to Yilbung in fight with Deciby 54
Woodford 43, 207
Woogaroo 86
Worumillo 75
Wumbungur (Woomboonggoroo) 182, 183, 193, 194, 195, 196, 197
Wunkermany (Uncle Marney, Uncle Mainey)
    arrest 117, 132
    Girkum cottage 37
    Girkum garden, anger over its destruction 55
Wynyard, Major-General (commander, British regiments in New South Wales) 145–6

Y

Yaggera language group 5, 21, 34, 57, 58, 59, 60, 61, 70, 75, 78, 82, 83, 87, 95, 96, 116, 212
Yanmonday (Yunmonday, Eumundi) 22, 40, 41, 48, 52, 65
Yarun 21, 39, 79, 80; *see also* Bribie Island
Yilbung (Millbong Jemmy, Ilboo)
    accused of involvement in attack on Gregor's station 101, 131
    belated invitation to Bunya summit, January 1843 74, 75
    entrapment 115–16, 118, 119, 121, 137
    fight with Deciby over the mission 54–5, 130
    opposition to British presence 130–1
    opposition to mission 53–6, 72, 73
    payback for his killing 132, 137, 138, 139, 140
    upholding of Aboriginal values 131
York's Hollow inquiry *see* Inquiry into Affray with Aborigines
Young, Mr 203
Yugambeh people (Logan River people) 37, 84

Z

Zillmann, Johann 54, 61, 85, 203
Zion's Hill 31, 36, 39; *see also* Nundah, German Mission